THE NEGRO RACES

A Sociological Study

VOLUME II

BY

JEROME DOWD

ISBN: 978-1-63923-751-7

Printed: February 2023

Published and Distributed By:
Lushena Books
607 Country Club Drive, Unit E
Bensenville, IL 60106
www.lushenabks.com

ISBN: 978-1-63923-751-7

PREFACE

The author presents herewith the second volume of his proposed series of sociological studies of mankind from the standpoint of race.

The division of Africa into separate economic zones is not susceptible of exact demarcation for the same reason that it would be impossible to draw a precise dividing line in Asia between the agricultural and pastoral regions, or in North America between the cotton and wheat belts. Nevertheless these different areas, when looked at broadly, reveal very distinct characteristics and exercise a profound and determining influence upon the social and psychological life of the people.

JEROME DOWD.

Norman, Okla., June 12, 1913.

TABLE OF CONTENTS

PART I

THE GALLAS

TABLE OF CONTENTS

PART II

THE BANTUS

PART I

THE GALLAS

THE NEGRO RACES

CHAPTER I

THE NUBIANS OF THE GOAT ZONE

General Character of the Zone.—This zone comprises the country known as Nubia, lying between the Nile and the Red Sea, and extending from Assuan near the first cataract to Khartum at the conflux of the White and Blue Niles. It is mainly arid wastes, rocky in the east and sandy in the west, relieved here and there by grassy steppelands and small oases. Inland and parallel to the Red Sea and the Nile are moderately elevated hills, separated from the Abyssinian plateau by deep depressions and dried river beds, called wadys. Some of the elevations skirting the Red Sea near Cape Elba rise to the height of 6,900 feet [1] and other peaks in the northern districts range from 4,000 to 6,000 feet. These mountains run transversely either from the east to the west or from the northeast to the southwest.[2] They are broken by low passes and sandy plains. On the western slope, leading towards the Nile, are numerous wadys, occasionally flushed

1 Standford, I, p. 547. 2 Reclus, I, p. 285.

by sudden freshets from the uplands, retaining some moisture in the deeper depressions. "This moisture supports a scanty vegetation of coarse grasses and thorny scrubs, some of which afford excellent fodder for camels, sheep and goats."[3]

In the south is a region, Taka, of considerable fertility, being well watered by streams from Abyssinia. It contains tropical forests, extensive pastures and arable tracts. Besides Taka the only fertile and permanently habitable region is the valley of the Nile itself, which is narrow and often hemmed in between granite and sandstone hills.

"The greater part of the land lies almost within the rainless zone, for the tropical rains are now arrested about the latitude of Khartum."[4] The climate is dry and hot, the temperature varying from 44° to 104° Fahrenheit.[5] Except in Taka the natural flora is very poor, and consists chiefly of the date palm, doom palm, lentils, senna, and several varieties of gum trees. Wild animals are rare except in the south where the elephant, lion, panther, rhinoceros, giraff, hyena and wild boar are met. The crocodile and hippopotamus infest the upper streams, and the leopard and antelope are found in the mimosa forests on the banks of the White Nile.[6] Among the birds are the stork, goose, partridge, ibis and ostrich.[7]

3 Stanford, I, p. 551.
4 Encyclopædia Britannica, XVII, p. 611. Old Edition.
5 Stanford, I, p. 520.
6 Reclus, I, p. 292.
7 *Ibid.*, I, p. 292.

The Inhabitants.—In a great part of Central, Eastern and Northern Africa are groups of Negroes of a lighter color and more Caucasian physiognomy than those of the other sections of the continent, and, for lack of a better ethnological term to characterize them, they will be referred to in this book as the Gallas, for the reason that the country known as Galla was probably the door of entrance of this type into Africa.

The northernmost branch of this type are the Nubians, also called Nubas, Ethiopians, Kushito-Hamites, including the Bejas, and Ababdehs, Hamans, Hadendowas, etc.

The first historic inhabitants south of Egypt appear to have been the Uaua whose name occurs in an inscription on a tomb at Memphis of the VI Dynasty about 2,500 B. C. Throughout the historical period, down to the arrival of the Romans, the Nile above Egypt was occupied by a Negro people. In the third century the domain of these people began to be encroached upon by the Hamitic tribes from the east, known as the Blemmyes or Bejas. The raids of these tribes caused Diocletian to withdraw the garrisons above the cataracts. Some Negro tribes originally from Kordofan known as the Nebatae were called in to protect the frontier from the attacks of the Blemmyes. These Nebatae passed into the Nile valley, absorbed the other kindred Uaua stock and came to terms with the Blemmyes. The two races intermingled, and, making common cause against the Romans, were defeated by Maximinus in 451. Thus the Nubians were first affected by the Hamitic elements.

This new negroid race was now, 545 A. D., converted to Christianity and welded into a great political power under the leadership of Silko. The remnant of Blemmyes in the population, remaining pagan, were driven back eastward among their kindred Hamites who from time immemorial had held the steppe region between the Nile and the Red Sea. Here they became known as the Bejas.

Soon after overrunning Egypt, 639, the Arabs penetrated into Lower Nubia and amalgamated with the natives. In the fourteenth century they overthrew the Christian Dongola kingdom, aided by a detachment of Bosnians, sent from Turkey, who settled in the country and intermarried with the Arabs and Nubians, their descendants still holding lands between Assuan and Derr. Hence it is that the Nubians of this district, fairest of all the race, still claim Arab and Bosnian descent. Thus were the Nubians affected in the second instance by the Semitic and European elements. Nevertheless, they remain essentially Negro.

They are marked by very dolichocephalic head, long sinuous limbs, rather long frizzy hair, intermediate between the curly hair of the Arab and the woolly hair of the Negro. They have an oval face, dark mahogany or bronze skin, tumid lips, thick but not snoutlike, large black eyes, and prominent narrow nose.[8] Race intermixture counts for most,

[8] Stanford, I, pp. 589, 591; Ratzel, III, p. 192; Deniker, p. 439; Combes, I, p. 244; Hahn, p. 539.

perhaps, in the present type, but unquestionably climatic influences have been important factors.

Economic Life.—Except along the Nile valley and in a few districts in Taka, the Nubians are a pastoral people. The Bejas of the middle desert region, and the Ababdeh and Bisharin of the southern steppe are typical nomad pastors.[9]

The domestic animals are the horse, camel, sheep, goat, ox and buffalo,[10] but the chief of these is the goat, since it has been the most important factor in determining the life and institutions of the people. It was probably the first animal domesticated in Africa.[11] The horse and camel are comparatively recent importations.[12] The horse and cow do not thrive in the desert owing to the rareness of graminaceous vegetation. A plant called "Faleslez" is poison to the horse and ass.[13] The goat satisfies three prime needs of the people: nourishment, clothing, and lodgment, the tents being made of its hide. The goat's milk nourishes the tribes during a great part of the year, but in the winter months of January and February the winds from the north wither and dry up the leaves and small branches of plants, and they fall to the ground as if burnt by fire. The goat and camel then suffer from hunger and difficulty in breathing.

9 Hahn, p. 115.

10 Ratzel, History of Mankind, III, p. 187.

11 Hahn says that the earliest known goats were those from Teneriffa of the Nile Valley. "Die Haustiere," p. 142.

12 Reclus, I, p. 292.

13 Préville, p. 42.

To compensate for the scant supply of animal food nature furnishes a nourishing product from a gum tree, *acacia mimosa,* which grows throughout the country. The dry air cracks the bark from which oozes a sap, forming transparent globules which adhere to the trunk. This gum is easily collected. It is eaten by itself or mixed with milk. The date is another supplementary source of food-supply. A small bag of dates suffices for a journey of several days.[14]

Agriculture in northern Nubia is adapted to the cereals, and here the horse abounds, but the cultivated area is small, and the limitation of resources forces a part of the population to migrate to Egypt. The date palm is one of the chief products of this district. The narrow valleys along the Nile are here and there inhabited by sedentary people who cultivate the soil by irrigation. The products are durra *(sorghum vulgare)*, beans, lupins, cotton, tobacco, and some maize, wheat and barley. The grain crops are preserved in cylinders of clay placed upon tall stones. Oranges and citrons are cultivated in some of the gardens.[15] In the valleys of the Atbara and the Mareb rivers the agricultural areas are larger and more fertile. In this district, on account of the insects, the domestic animals are kept in barns during the day and let out to graze at night.[16] The area suitable for cultivation in the whole of Nubia

14 Irby, p. 114.

15 Ratzel, III, p. 210; Reclus, I, p. 292.

16 Reclus, I, p. 221.

is so circumscribed that there is a tendency to over-population and emigration. Some of the surplus population find employment in various menial capacities in the trade towns, some have founded settlements in Kordofan, the cradle of the race, while others have enlisted as mercenaries with the Arab traders and slavers.[17]

Cotton is manufactured into coarse cloth, and various garments are made from the wool of the sheep and goat. There is some manufacture of pottery, and articles of gold, silver and iron. The practical arts failed to reach Nubia from the Lower Nile on account of the intervening desert.[18]

The chief trade of Nubia has followed almost entirely the course of the Nile, but there has been a limited commerce between the interior and the Red Sea. One of the routes is between the Red Sea and Kaasala, along the bed of the Baraka river, which is dry for a considerable portion of the year. It connects the coast with the fertile districts of Taka.[19] The most frequented route from the Nile to the Red Sea is that extending from Berber to Suakin, now traversed by railroad. Formerly 20,000 camels laden with gum annually passed across from Berber.[20] The trade in ivory, gold and slaves used to be extensive between Nubia and Egypt,[21] but the ex-

17 Stanford, I, p. 590.

18 Frobenius, "The Origin of African Civilizations," Annual Report Smithsonian Institute, 1898.

19 Stanford, I, p. 568.

20 Reclus, I, p. 253.

21 Reclus, I, p. 284.

haustion of these articles of commerce caused the natives in their distress to wage war upon each other to obtain a livelihood. The settlements were turned into garrisons, fortified by hedges or stockades, as a basis for raids. The settlements on the Upper Nile are now partly trade depots, partly arsenals and partly plantations.[22] There are a number of trade centers and caravan stations along the Nubian Nile. A large traffic passes through Nubia by boat and caravan between the Sudan and Egypt. Since the suppression of the slave trade the exports have been limited chiefly to senna, grain, leeches, musk and honey.

Although the slave trade is now quite extinct in Nubia, domestic slavery is still common. Along the Nile valley the slaves are used for agriculture, and among the nomad tribes of the interior they are used for tending the herds and as porters. Pastoral people generally have little need for slaves.[23] The primary cause of slavery is found in the disagreeableness of the labor and the effort to shift the burden. But, as pointed out by Cooley, the shifting of the burden upon others is due to lack of fellowship. Among civilized people where good fellowship obtains, the most drudging work will not be shirked but borne with patience and even with pleasure. For example, members of a camping party do not object to cutting wood, drawing water or washing

22 Ratzel, III, p. 214.

23 Dowd, "The Negro Races," I, pp. 122, 128.

dishes.[24] On account of the good fellowship which usually prevails in small groups or tribes, the first slaves were probably introduced from outside. According to Sumner, slavery is "due to ill feeling towards members of an outer-group, to desire to get something for nothing, to love of dominion which belongs to vanity, and to hatred of labor."[25] The last fact named is the primary one.

Family Life.—The Nubians generally obtain their wives by purchase, but in some districts capture of women is still in vogue.[26] The marriage ceremony recalls the practice of wife-capture[27] which at a former time was more prevalent. The natives of Nubia are probably immigrants from the Galla country where hunting and wife-capture were once universal. The ruling class form a strict caste, and do not allow common men to marry into it.[28] Though polygamy is permitted, monogamy is the prevailing practice. Young girls are valuable to their parents as economic factors, and they command a good price. Owing to the difficulties of existence few men are able to afford a plurality of wives. Marriage is an affair of the girl's parents.[29] Chastity before marriage is esteemed by the men, but neither married nor single women are adverse to intrigues. The Barea tribes make no discrimination against illegitimate children.[30] The necessary

24 "Social Organization," p. 245.
25 Folkways, p. 261.
26 Ratzel, III, p. 187.
27 *Ibid.*, p. 219.
28 Reclus, I, p. 238.
29 Combes, I, p. 14.
30 Reclus, I, p. 231.

commingling of men and women in a pastoral group exposes both sexes to temptation.

The houses of the settled tribes are made of clay tiles with wooden framework, or of straw and reeds, or of palm leaves. The herdsmen live in shokabs, huts which can be struck like tents and loaded onto camels. The walls consist of thin rods interlaced like mats and capable of being rolled up. "The roof is made of black goat's hair. In the south the huts are made of the leaves of the doom palm."[31] The furniture of the homes consists chiefly of a framework, with leather straps, which serves as a bed, sofa or table.[32]

The support of the family among the sedentary groups falls upon the women almost exclusively. The men help in a precarious way by hunting, fishing and raiding. In the nomad groups the men give more substantial and regular assistance by protecting the group and tending the herds. Women occupy relatively a high position.[33] If a man insults or speaks rudely to a woman he is driven from the tent and can gain readmittance only by presenting to her a cow and camel.[34] It is said that a married woman in some tribes reserves every fourth day to do as she pleases. Nomadism everywhere seems to give to women a certain independence.[35] This is because they have to work semi-publicly. They, as the men,

[31] Reclus, III, p. 207.

[32] Johnston, Lydekker, et al., p. 460.

[33] Reclus, I, pp. 223, 237.

[34] *Ibid.*, p. 238.

[35] Huntington, p. 129.

must meet and mingle with strangers, and they thus acquire a certain boldness.[36] They often have to take the initiative, and this develops in them a power of self-command which causes them to be respected.[37] The employment of slaves, and the use of the horse, camel and ox as beasts of burden, here as elsewhere, have tended to alleviate the status of the free women by relieving them of the task of porterage. The first emancipator of the free women was the slave. Higher up in civilization the position of women has been elevated by the harnessing of the wind, water, steam and electricity to perform the heavy tasks.[38] Economic, rather than moral, forces everywhere explain the improvement in the status of women.

The Nubians generally trace descent in the female line.[39]

36 Huntington, p. 129.

37 *Ibid.*, p. 132.

38 Sumner, p. 266.

39 Ratzel, III, p. 187.

CHAPTER II

THE NUBIANS OF THE GOAT ZONE (*continued*)

Political Life.—The Nubian environment modifies the political life in several particulars. In the first place the country being relatively healthful, the population has a tendency, common among all pastoral people, to increase beyond the means of subsistence. The area available for cultivation or for pastures is absolutely limited, and the surplus population in each group, not being able to find new land, is tempted to rob and raid the neighboring group. Hence the life of the people is organized on a military basis for defense and attack. A separate warrior caste of unmarried men is set apart for executing raids, —a caste such as is found, for similar reasons, throughout the pastoral regions of East Africa.[1]

In the elevated districts of this zone the army consists only of infantry, owing to the poisonous vegetation which is fatal to the horse and ass. In the low plains it is composed of men mounted upon the vigorous and rapid Arab ass.[2]

The scant and scattered nature of the resources does not permit the massing of a large fighting force, and hence there is a lack of political unity.[3] The

[1] Ratzel, II, p. 408. [2] Préville, p. 42. [3] Reclus, I, p. 234.

military operations are mostly expeditions of plunder. For this purpose the mounted men are well equipped. They can strike at a considerate distance and escape the disaster of defeat by rapid flight. Raiding is so common that every man carries at all times his dagger and sword.[4] "Marauding tendencies," says Semple, "are ingrained in all dwellers of the deserts and steppes."[5]

Each community is governed by an hereditary Mohammedan chief. The diffusion of property among pastoral people generates a spirit of independence which is opposed to the absolute form of government, but the military organization, necessitated by the conditions in Africa, often leads to personal despotism. A despotism, however, among pastoral people does not imply that degree of abjectness of the subjects which characterizes societies where property and property-rights are less developed. Among the Nubians rulership must be firm, since otherwise peace could not be maintained among the individual families which would wrangle over the herds and the collection of gum.[6] An objectionable chief, however, is sometimes deposed or hanged.[7] As for the relation of one group to another all is anarchy and independence, due to the remoteness of the populations from any accessible central power.[8] The internal government of the tribes is in most cases left to the law of retaliation, but

[4] Irby, p. 115.

[5] Page 490.

[6] Préville, p. 45.

[7] Reclus, I, p. 225.

[8] Préville, p. 45; Reclus, I, p. 231.

among the Barea there is an assembly to settle all disputes.[9] The Nubians are protected in their territory by the nature of their country. Invaders from the north would have to depend on the horse for transportation, and this animal would perish in the desert. Invaders from the Abyssinian plateau of the south would be arrested by the scarcity of water and the inadaptability of the people to a mephitic atmosphere.

Religious Life.—The greater part of the Nubians have long been zealous Mohammedans, governed, as the Arab nomads, by hereditary sheikhs. But they are by no means fanatical.[10] Some of the more isolated tribes, however, have not advanced beyond the stage of animism.[11] They venerate the partridge and the serpent.[12]

The severe struggle against nature for existence develops a degree of courage and intelligence that renders the mind inhospitable to the grosser forms of superstition. The phenomena of nature are uniform and mild, and on that account the people are not so terror-stricken as the natives of other parts of Africa. There is, however, little in the environment that the people can change, and consequently they have a disposition, common among desert people, to submit stoically to its decrees. The magic doctor, human sacrifices, and idol worship, so characteristic of Central Africa, are scarcely found among the Nubians. Their superstitions are mani-

9 Reclus, I, p. 231.
10 Stanford, I, pp. 590, 592.
11 Reclus, I, p. 225.
12 *Ibid.*, p. 297.

fested mostly by the wearing of charms to keep off the evil eye, etc.[13]

Information on the subject of ancestor worship is lacking, but inferring from a general principle, it should not be highly developed. "Restless nomads," says Frobenius, "are seldom reminded of their past: hence the tendency towards worship of the manes and of ancestors is slight among them. On the other hand, turn in whatever direction they will, island races encounter traces of their former life. The natives of Oceania know some tale to tell of every locality: likewise the mythology connected with manes flourishes in West Africa."[14]

Ceremonious Life.—Aside from the marriage ceremony, which in some cases simulates wife-capture, and some formalities of greeting and parting, ceremony does not seem to have much place among the Nubians. Strangers coming into the tribe are required to undergo the ceremony of blood-brotherhood. "A sheep or goat is killed and the blood received in a calabash in which all the assistants dip their hands, and then embrace. Henceforth the stranger is safe from all attack."[15]

Aesthetic Life.—The Nubians show the Negro love of personal decoration. The men tattoo their faces as a mark of success in war. The women also in some tribes tattoo their faces, forming "little pustules like those of smallpox." The ear lobes and septum

13 Irby, p. 113.
14 "The Origin of African Civilizations," p. 647.
15 Reclus, I, p. 225.

of the nose are bored for the insertion of rings.[16] In some tribes the warriors paint their bodies red. The women generally wear bracelets and anklets of beads and shells, silver finger rings set with cornelians, strings of the same stone round the waist, and necklaces of glass and even of amber.[17] The Nubian women wear their hair in plaited ringlets or in the form of a bushy mop.[18]

The dress of the men consists of a loose white shirt and a turban. In a few tribes the men are uncovered except for a cloth round the waist.[19] The young girls wear loin strips ornamented with cowry shells and beads.[20] The women wear a brown garment reaching to their knees.[21]

The same causes that limit the industrial life also limit the development of art. Since the plastic arts, or arts of rest, cannot be fostered under nomadism, being too inconvenient to transport, the arts of motion receive an accentuation. Dancing is universal: among the nomad groups it is individualistic and solitary, while among the sedentary groups it is *en masse* or social. Vocal music is highly developed, and most tribes are acquainted with rude poetry. It would be surprising if the Nubians had not been influenced by the Arab talent for poetry and song expressing the sentiments of love and re-

16 Reclus, I, p. 224: Johnston, Lydekker, et al, p. 440.
17 Ratzel, III, p. 204; Irby, p. 116.
18 Johnston, Lydekker, et al, p. 434.
19 Irby, p. 113.
20 Irby, 116.
21 Irby, p. 116.

ligion. Judging from the general desolation of the environment and the isolation of the groups the music should be of a melancholy strain.

Psychological Life.—No reliable data are available concerning the cranial capacity of the Nubians, but it is a fair inference from the admixture of Hamitic and Semitic blood that it is above the average of the African Negro. In general intelligence, however, the Nubians exhibit no marked superiority. Dunn thinks that pastoral people are stationary and do not develop brain power.[22] Such mental characteristics as the Nubians possess are amply accounted for by environment.

The isolation of the nomad groups develops suspicion, and also would produce cowardice, as among the isolated Asiatics,[23] but for the frequent occasions of war which stimulate their pugnacity. Their wild life and self-reliance give them a common love of freedom.[24] They have a strong attachment to their group, and a spirit of mutual helpfulness growing out of their hardships and dependence upon each other. They are proud, obstinate and domineering,[25] and belong to what Giddings calls the dogmatic-emotional type of mind,[26] or what Ribot calls the mediocre active.[27] Their vigor of body and resolute mind give them a predominant feeling of force-

22 Irby, 17.

23 Huntington, p. 24.

24 Stanford, I, p. 592; Reclus, I, pp. 239, 297.

25 Semple, pp. 497, 510.

26 "Inductive Sociology," p. 87.

27 Page 396.

fulness.[28] Perhaps the electrical atmosphere characteristic of arid plains imparts a degree of nervous energy.[29] "The dry, pure air stimulates the faculties of the desert-dweller," says Ellen Semple, "but the featureless, monotonous surroundings furnish them with little to work upon. The mind, finding scant material for sustained logical deduction, falls back upon contemplation. Intellectual activity is therefore restricted, narrow, unproductive; while the imagination is unfettered but also unfed."[30] The nomad Nubians are wary and keen witted. Hard natural conditions and adverse social environment are apt to compel alertness. The Jew, for example, owes his shrewdness to social opposition and deprivations,[31] and the Nubians have to thank nature for a shrewdness uncommon among the Negroes. The sedentary Nubians have the submissive traits common to slaves.[32] They are also given more to laziness, frivolity, vice, and are less honest and dependable.[33] A similar contrast is found in Asia between the nomad and sedentary peoples.[34] Of the latter peoples of Asia

[28] Williams classifies the moods of men into three kinds corresponding to conditions of life awakening certain predominant feelings. First, the forceful mood, characterized by vigor, strength, resolution and conviction. Second, the expansive, characterized by contentment, restfulness, cheerfulness, good will. Third, the agitative, characterized by weariness, despondency, anxiety, etc., p. 741.

[29] Dexter, p. 39.

[30] Page 512.

[31] Williams, p. 760.

[32] Combes, I, p. 242.

[33] Reclus, I, p. 298.

[34] Huntington, pp. 132, 361.

Huntington remarks, "Laziness leads to dishonesty and both tend to insolence and vulgarity."[35]

The nomadic Nubians have little sense of nationality, because of the isolation of the groups. A similar lack of national feeling is found among the sedentary people of Asia for the same reason.[36] The Nubians, especially the nomad groups, are extremely conservative, and bound by tradition. Their tradition is of that low order which contains no record of reasoned or speculatively acquired knowledge.[37] All pastoral people are notoriously conservative because the simplicity of their life affords little food for thought. Their traditions, therefore, are based upon impression and belief rather than upon critically established knowledge which makes for innovation.[38]

All of the Nubians are characterized as thievish, treacherous, malicious, "base and full of wickedness and lechery."[39] There is, however, reason to doubt the justice of this characterization. Indeed, the psychological characteristics of the African Negro have never yet been correctly reported or understood. The reason is that civilized people fail to measure the Negro by a rational standard. The author of this volume frankly admits his failure, in his first volume,

35 Page 127.

36 Huntington, p. 138.

37 Giddings distinguishes two kinds of tradition of which the higher is that of "conceptual thought" as opposed to "mere impression and belief." Elements of Sociology, p. 151.

38 Giddings, "Inductive Sociology," p. 207.

39 Stanford, I, p. 590; Irby, p. 113.

to interpret correctly these characteristics. The most essential starting point is the recognition of the difference in the size of the civilized and the primitive cultural group. A civilized cultural group embraces sometimes several nations, because the life of the people is so interrelated that common characteristics belong to the whole population. In Africa the cultural groups are small. They are sometimes limited to a single family, again to a small tribe, or at most to a small confederacy. Now, the point is, that if we compare the traits manifested within a civilized group with the traits of Africans manifested between opposing groups, the result is, of course, unfavorable to the latter; but that is the usual way of making comparisons. If we reverse this point of view, and compare the traits of Africans manifested towards each other within the small group with the traits of Europeans as manifested towards members outside of their group, the result is highly favorable to the Africans, and the civilized people take rank with the barbarian and the savage. In support of this statement it is only necessary to recall the treatment of the native Australian by the English, of the Congo Negro by the Belgians, of the frontier Indians by the people of the United States, of the Tripolitans by the Italians, or the attitude of the ancient Egyptians, Babylonians, Assyrians, Hebrews and classic nations towards all strangers. If we compare the characteristics of civilized and uncivilized people as manifested within their respective groups we shall discover a wonderful likeness of fundamental traits. For instance, if we compare the characteristics of different peoples, as manifested in their respective family group, we shall find everywhere a common moral unity,—sympathy, kindness, truthfulness, and readiness to make mutual sacrifices. In the larger group of the tribe there is a common good will, hospitality, a willingness to fight and defend, a resentment towards outside oppression, and a distinct respect for custom and justice, just as in the still larger civilized group. In respect to the quality of kindness "the main difference between civilization and savagery," says Cooley, is that "under the former the group tends to enlarge. One reason for the restriction is that kindness is aroused by sympathy and can have little life except as our imaginations are opened to the lives of others and they are made part of ourselves."[40] The failure of the Negro to extend these primary feelings is due to the difficulty of forming and maintaining confederated groups, resulting from a lack of communication "to give that promptness in the give-and-take of suggestions upon which moral unity depends."[41] Hence, in this volume a distinction will be drawn between the characteristics which each group manifests among themselves and those manifested towards foreigners. Towards alien groups the Nubians, as to a less extent the English, French

[40] "Social Organization," p. 42. [41] *Ibid.*, p. 54.

and Germans, are hostile, treacherous and cruel. Their pugnacious instinct has its outlet in petty wars, since there is no inviting field for it in commercial competition, and social and scientific rivalry.

CHAPTER III

THE GALLAS, SOMALIS, ETC., OF THE NORTHERN CATTLE ZONE

General Character of the Zone.—From the southern Nubian frontier to the Zambesi basin there is a continuous plateau, varying greatly in width, with precipitous escarpments on its east side, but sloping rather gently towards the west. Abyssinia, the northern extension of this plateau, forms a vast table-land whose eastern approaches rise sharply from the low-lying coastlands. Northward it falls in broad terraces towards the plains of Nubia, and westward slopes continuously to the valley of the Blue Nile, and southward merges into the less elevated plateau of Gallaland. The mean altitude of the country is about 9,000 feet. Its surface is rugged and presents "the aspect of a storm-tossed sea suddenly solidified." "The eye sweeps over a boundless vista of hilly plains, rugged plateaux, and deep upland valleys, dominated here and there by precipitons mountain masses, towering 6,000 or 7,000 feet above the normal level."[1] Some of the peaks run up to 15,000 feet and are snow-clad for a great part of the year.[2]

[1] Stanford, I, p. 450.

[2] Goodrich, p. 151.

Gallaland is a southern extension of the Abyssinian plateau, and resembles it in general relief and altitude, but is less rugged. It also has precipitous escarpments on its east side and gentle slopes towards the Nile Valley.[3] Many of the isolated peaks are separated by crevasses or canyons, like those of Colorado or Mexico, sometimes 5,000 feet deep and scarcely 700 feet wide.

Somaliland, the triangular projection of the continent, or "Eastern Horn" of Africa, is still less elevated, and takes the character of a plain, varying in its northern section from 4,000 to 5,000 feet, in its southern section from 2,000 to 3,000 feet, and falling below the altitude of 500 feet near the coast.[4]

Masailand is a still more southern continuation of the Abyssinian plateau, but much narrowed and much less rugged in general aspect. The altitude in the northern division is from 5,000 to 9,000 feet. Through the line of highest elevation runs a trough which encloses a chain of lakes.[5] "A more charming region," says Thomson, "is probably not to be found in all Africa. The country extends in billowy, swelling reaches and is characterized by everything that makes a pleasing landscape. Here are patches of flowering shrubs—there noble forests. Now you traverse a parklike country intervened by groups of game; anon great herds of cattle or flocks of sheep and goats are seen wandering knee-deep in the splendid pasture."[6] The southern division of

[3] Stanford, I, p. 455.

[4] *Ibid.*, p. 459.

[5] Thomson, p. 407.

[6] *Ibid.*, p. 408.

this narrow strip ranges from 3,000 to 4,000 feet in height. It is rather sterile and unproductive, due to scant rainfall, and it produces only scattered tufts of grass.[7]

A spur of this great Abyssinian plateau branches off from southern Gallaland and makes a half circle on the west side of Lake Victoria.

The entire plateau is well watered and penetrated by copious rivers, except in the southern limits of Masailand. The climate and the biological conditions depend more upon altitude than distance from the equator. The lower slopes of the plateau, ranging from 5,000 to 6,000 feet elevation, have a temperature varying from 70° to 100° F., and a luxuriant vegetation with large areas of forest. At this elevation cotton, indigo, gum-yielding acacias, ebony, boababs, bananas, sugar-cane, coffee and the date-palm flourish; and here also the animal kingdom is represented by the lion, elephant, panther, zebra, giraff, gazelle, huge snakes and deadly scorpions.[8] The higher or middle region, ranging from 8,000 to 9,000 feet elevation, has a temperature like that of Spain or Italy, varying from 60° to 70° F. European grasses, cereals, and shell-fruits are here indigenous. The orange, citron, peach, apricot, and other fruit grow plentifully, and in the depressions are extensive areas of forest. Everywhere the soil affords rich pasture, and all of the European domesticated animals thrive there except the pig.[9]

7 Thomson, p. 405; Hahn, p. 270. 9 *Ibid.*, p. 471.
8 Stanford, I, p. 470.

Upon the higher region the temperature frequently falls to the freezing point. The large timber is scarce, yielding to a herbaceous or scrubby vegetation. Forage, however, can be found for the cattle, goats and sheep in the highest altitude. Gallaland, being near the equator, receives a greater rainfall and has a more exuberant and diversified flora than Abyssinia, while Masailand merges into desert. The narrow little spur west of Lake Victoria is cool and covered by a short, coarse grass.

The Inhabitants.—A type of Negro, similar in color and other features to the Nubians, is found in the grass regions of the table-lands above described.

The substratum of the Abyssinian population is the Agaw, or Ethiopian. The ruling classes are strongly affected with Semitic blood.[10] The Galla population represents the purest Ethiopian type,[11] which may be explained by the relative inaccessibility of the country, and its greater freedom from immigration. The type is characterized by a lighter color, and even Galla slaves in Abyssinia are lighter than the native rulers. Some writers put the Gallas above the Arabs in lightness of color.[12] The population of Somaliland is considerably mixed with the Arabs, who for several centuries have overrun the country, entering it from the eastern coast where its exposure tempts invasion from Arabia. The negroid element, however, is more marked among

10 Wylde, p. 16.
11 Deniker, p. 438.
12 Ratzel, II, p. 485.

the Somali than among the Galla. The Masai population is unmixed with the Arab, and while not so light in color as the Galla, it is in some respects a finer type.[13] According to Thomson, the Masai are in no sense negroes. . . . In their cranial development, as in their language, they are widely different from the natives of Central and South Africa, occupying in the former respect a far higher position in the scale of humanity." [14] The aristocratic class have a less depressed nose, thinner lips, and, but for prominence of cheek-bones and Mongolian eye, chocolate skin and frizzy hair, might pass for Europeans.[15] Their eyes are bright and the sclerotic coat whiter than is common in the African. They average about six feet in height; they are spare in figure and recall the "Apollo Type." The young women are especially pleasing in their physiognomy.[16] The Wahuma, or Bahima, who occupy the plateau west of Lake Victoria, are a tall, and finely formed race, of nutty-brown color, with almost European features.[17] They have oval faces, thin lips and straight noses. The girls are often beautiful, but inclined to be too corpulent. Their movements are languid and graceful.[18]

13 Johnston, "The Uganda Protectorate," p. 803.

14 Page 411.

15 *Ibid.*, p. 413; Kallenberg, p. 92.

16 Thomson, p. 428.

17 Ratzel, III, p. 1.

18 Cunningham, p. 21; Junker, III, p. 550; Johnston, "The Uganda Protectorate," p. 616; Stanley, "In Darkest Africa," II, p. 386. The ethnologist Keane classes the Galla, Somali and Wahuma with the Caucasian race. Ethnology, p. 380.

Economic Life.—The people throughout this great table-land are for the most part pastoral, although in the valleys and lowlands may be found sedentary groups devoted to agriculture.[19] The domesticated animals are abundant. Abyssinia is estimated to have twenty million head of sheep and goats besides great herds of cattle. A Somali family has about 200 to 300 goats or sheep, 10 to 40 camels, and 10 to 20 cows.[20] The Galla, Masai, Bahima, Somali and a large portion of the Abyssinians live chiefly upon animal food, particularly the flesh and milk of the cow. The Abyssinians often eat raw beef, and, on feast days especially, drink the warm blood drawn from the living cow, sometimes mixing it with milk.[21] The Bahima eat the flesh of cattle, sheep and goats, and also drink blood and milk.[22] The scant supply of salt probably led to the fondness for blood.[23] The drinking of blood from the living animal has been common among pastoral people over a great part of the world. The Scythians, for instance, used to drink the blood of the horse. The Bahima drink milk only in the fresh state, and sometimes cleanse the pots with cow urine. All wealthy people have meat for the evening meal. The Masai eat any bullock that has died a natural death.[24] The Abyssin-

19 Johnston, "British Central Africa," p. 431; Hahn, p. 115.
20 Paulitschki, p. 323.
21 Bruce, p. 231.
22 Johnston, "British Central Africa," p. 818; *Ibid.*, "Uganda Protectorate," p. 620.
23 Thomson, p. 430.
24 Hollis, p. 318.

ians do not use butter except in districts verging on Nubia where they have learned its use from the Arabs.[25] They use the root of the herb "mocmoco" to prevent it from melting.[26] The Masai tribes prefer their milk flavored with urine.[27]

Wild game is a food resource in many localities, but it is often supplied by a subject population inhabiting the forest. The Masai soldiers disdain hunting as unworthy of their dignity. In some districts dried fish is much eaten; also jerked meat which is cured by hanging it in the huts of the people, exposed to the smoke and fire.[28] The animal food is supplemented to a varying extent by fruits, grain and vegetables. Agriculture is carried on mostly by slaves or a subject class.[29] The products in Abyssynia are the sweet potato, yam, pumpkin, coffee, maize, wheat, sugar-cane and cotton.[30] Somali produces corn, beans and pumpkins.[31] Cotton is grown in Abyssinia and Somali, and in the latter country great quantities of myrrh, frankincense and balsam, which require no cultivation.[32] The Gallas cultivate their fields with a hoe, and a wooden plow drawn by oxen.[33] They store their grain in circular granaries supported on stilts.[34]

Handicrafts are little developed. Beyond a certain skill in making weapons the industrial life is

25 Ratzel, II, p. 488; Thomson, p. 430.
26 Bruce, p. 314.
27 Thomson, p. 480.
28 French-Sheldon, p. 370.
29 Johnston, "Uganda Protectorate," p. 620; Ratzel, II, p. 494.
30 Wylde, p. 277.
31 Stanford, I, p. 476.
32 *Ibid*, p. 476.
33 Koettlitz, p. 51.
34 *Ibid.*, p. 53.

exceedingly simple. There is some clothing made from cotton and skins, and some wood-carving, and weaving of water flasks. The shields and spears are often bought or stolen from the people below the plateau. In many cases the weapons and tents are made by subject people living in nearby villages.[35]

The ivory and slave trade, formerly very great, is now reduced to small proportions. There is some trade in cotton and cotton-cloth, and salt. The latter article is handled in the shape of bricks, and in Abyssinia has long passed as money. The chief exports of Abyssinia at present are live-stock, hides, skins, gum, feathers and coffee.[36] The Masai, neighbors to the Wandorobbo hunters and traders, steal ivory and sell it to the latter, or exchange cattle for game and other merchandise.[37] In Somali trade is largely in the hands of the Arabs. Abyssinia is the only state on the plateau that has a system of coined money and a national bank.

Among the northern Gallas, transportation is chiefly by means of the horse,[38] among the Abyssinians, the horse and ass, and one railroad 180 miles long connecting Dawa with the coast,[39] and among the Masai, the donkey and woman.[40] An extensive

[35] Bruce, p. 342; Thomson, p. 425; Préville, p. 75; Koettlitz, p. 52; Ratzel, II, p. 487.

[36] Goodrich, p. 152.

[37] Bruce, pp. 314, 342; Préville, p. 74; Thomson, pp. 166, 308; Koettlitz, p. 54; Ratzel, II, p. 529.

[38] Ratzel II, p. 488.

[39] Goodrich, p. 152.

[40] Thomson, p. 422.

caravan trade is carried on between the Galla, Abyssinian and Somali countries and the coast. The ports connect by steamers with Aden, the great distributing point for all East Africa.[41] A considerable trade from Abyssinia follows the tributaries of the White Nile. Caravans going eastward comprise great herds of cattle and thousands of people.[42] An elephant tooth costs in the interior $45, paid for in powder, and sells at the coast for $120. The trip from the interior to the coast and back often requires five or six months.[43] The telephone and telegraph have scarcely penetrated the plateau except in Abyssinia.

The population of the Masai is divided into three groups: First, the sedentary group of married men who occupy the central portions of the plateau. Second, the young boys and girls, assisted by slaves, who follow the cattle over the hills in the humid season and down into the valleys in the dry season. Third, the military group made up of the strong young men, and girls who assist in preparing food.[44] The women in many tribes milk the cows and prepare the food, bring water and shave their husbands, but their labor is light, and after marriage they generally become very corpulent.[45] The married men of the sedentary group have scarcely anything to do except to take snuff and drink. Parents are largely free from the care of children who are either in the

[41] Goodrich, p. 152.

[42] Schweinitz, pp. 200, 201.

[43] *Ibid.*, p. 196.

[44] Merker, p. 82.

[45] Hollis, p. 318.

military group or following the cattle. Among the Bahima the men alone enter the cattle kraal, milk and feed the herds. In Abyssinia the tending of cattle is also the work of the men. The grinding of grain and baking of bread is the work of women. Smith-work is done by a subject class of men, while pottery and builders' work fall to the Jews.[46] The Bahima men build the houses, and provide clothing for both sexes. The women generally cultivate the field, where there is any agriculture, and carry loads to market.[46a]

Slavery exists throughout the plateau, but the pastoral life, especially where it is nomadic, requires few slaves,[47] and these are used mostly for domestic work and for carriers.[48] The subject populations are held as serfs rather than slaves. They pay tribute instead of personal service.[49]

The wealth of all of these people of the plateau consists mostly of movable capital, i. e., cattle. Land is generally common property except in Abyssinia. The habit of conservation of resources is a marked characteristic of pastoral people.

46 Ratzel, II, p. 415; III, pp. 228, 229, 231; Wylde, p. 278; Hollis, p. 330.

46a Stanley, "In Darkest Africa," II, p. 396; Sheldon, p. 359.

47 Dowd, "The Negro Races," I, pp. 122, 128.

48 Ratzel, II, p. 488.

49 Stanley, "In Darkest Africa," II, p. 387.

CHAPTER IV

THE GALLAS, SOMALIS, ETC. OF THE NORTHERN CATTLE ZONE (*continued*)

Family Life.—Wives are purchased from parents and paid for in bullocks, money or other goods.[1] Wife-capture, once common, is still practiced in some districts.[2] The Bahima women are not consulted in regard to marriage, and the suitor does not often see the bride before the union.[3] He gives a few head of cattle to the girl's father, and several head to the girl.[4] The bride's father gives to his daughter a dowry of six good cows. The Masai suitor makes love while the girl is quite young. He offers presents of honey and tobacco to her father and later gives her a dowry in cattle.[5] When a Galla marries, his wife receives a dowry from her father, and in case of divorce the dowry is taken by the husband. But this is contrary to the usual practice among the Negroes.[6] In Abyssinia girls

1 Thomson, p. 441; Burton, II, p. 182; Johnston, "British Central Africa," p. 632; Wylde, p. 182.

2 Paulitschki, p. 198; Kallenberg, p. 127.

3 Cunningham, p. 6.

4 *Ibid.*, p. 7.

5 Hollis, p. 302; Merker, p. 45.

6 Ratzel, II, p. 493.

marry between eleven and fifteen years, and close the child-bearing period at thirty.[7] The subject tribes on the plains and in the forests are of a darker and more negroid type. They are despised by their conquerors, and racial antipathy excludes social intermingling and intermarriage. Smiths are an ostracized class, and no freeman will enter their house or even shake hands with them.[8]

Polygamy is common except among the Abyssinians and Gallas. The conditions favoring it are the ample resources in food, and the wars which deplete the male population and render the women relatively superfluous and cheap.[9] In Bahimaland, where the pastoral resources are very limited, a form of polyandry exists where two men sometimes combine to buy a wife.

Ideas about chastity vary greatly in the different parts of this zone. "Should a (Bahima) girl go wrong before marriage she is degraded and cast out of her clan." She lives in close retirement and is always veiled.[10] While the Masai consider it wrong for a girl to conceive before marriage,[11] in regard to a large part of the population, public sentiment tolerates very loose sexual relations. The population is divided into three groups, one military, one pastoral, and one sedentary, composed of married people. The first comprises the unmarried men and unmarried girls, both living apart from their par-

7 Bruce, p. 314; Wylde, p. 253.

8 Ratzel, II, p. 494.

9 Thomson, p. 419.

10 Cunningham, p. 6.

11 Hollis, p. 311.

ents and the girls offering themselves freely to the men.[12] Each young warrior selects one or more girls, from eight to thirteen years old, to serve as his mistress until he is ready to marry. He gives presents to their mothers in payment.[13] Thomson remarks of a warrior group he visited, that "the sweetheart system was largely in vogue, though no one confined his or her attentions to one only. Each girl, in fact, had several sweethearts, and, what is still stranger, this seemed to give rise to no jealousies." It was common for "a young girl to wander about the camp with her arm around the waist of a stalwart warrior."[14] When a warrior's father dies, his son quits the camp, returns home, buys a wife, and raises "a brood of cattle-lifters."[15] Married women do not hesitate to intrigue with strangers when the opportunity offers.[16] It is a common practice for a husband to tender his wife to a stranger.[17] Free love exists among the Suk, who are neighbors of the Bahima.[18] In the Galla country, says Wylde, all the family huddle under one cover, and the morals are vile.[19] In Abyssinia marriages often take place after a couple have lived together for some time, and "generally prove

12 Préville, p. 71; Kallenberg, p. 94.
13 Johnston, "Uganda Protectorate," pp. 824, 825.
14 Page 431.
15 *Ibid.*, p. 442.
16 *Ibid.*, p. 446.
17 Hollis, p. 288.
18 Dundas, p. 60.
19 Page 238.

happy."[20] Pastoral life is essentially one of leisure. Time hangs heavily upon the people, and this is not conducive to sexual morality. Seclusion of young girls from the company of men is found only in communities influenced by Mohammedanism and Christianity.[21]

The habitations of the people of this zone vary from tents and frail structures of bough and thatch to substantial houses of stone. The huts of the Abyssinians are mostly built of stone, and the majority of them are round in form, having "originated from the circular stick and straw hut of the more savage Africa, copied in stone on an enlarged scale."[22] Then there is a rectangular hut, mostly in the north, which includes a court for cattle, surrounded in the interior by a colonnade, within which are chambers for human occupancy.[23] Great lords often sleep in the same chamber with horses and mules.[24] The windows of the house are small and without glass. The furniture consists of chests for storing, cushioned seats, often covered with bright silk; wooden stools, a table on which meals are served, and cow-horns fixed in the walls as pegs to hang swords, spears, shields and gun. Persian rugs sometimes cover the floor. The courtyard is usually dirty, the atmosphere of the house offensive, and the whole interior infested with insects and vermin.[25] The Bahima hut is made

20 Dundas, p. 161.
21 Ratzel, II, p. 493.
22 Wylde, p. 226.
23 Wylde, p. 226.
24 Ratzel, III, p. 225.
25 Wylde, pp. 229, 230, 239.

of sticks and wattle, round in form, and protected by an outer fence, the inner side of which is strengthened by a bank of cow-dung five feet high.[26] The homes of the sedentary groups of Masai are conical huts of reeds and thatch, while the homes of the nomad groups consist of structures of boughs bent over and interwoven, forming flat-roofed buildings with rounded corners. They are often joined together, forming a continuous, long, narrow house. To keep out the wind a composition of cow-dung is liberally plastered over the boughs. In the rainy season hides are spread over the roof. The huts of a community are arranged in a circle enclosing an area where cattle are kept at night. Outside the circle of huts is a fence of thorns.[27] The Galla huts, nearly all circular, are sometimes made of boughs, and sometimes of stone.[28]

Married men lead a leisurely life, the task of protecting the home and village devolving upon the warrior group.[29] The unmarried men tend the herds. All of the other work falls pretty much to the slave women. They build the hut, milk the cows, go on journeys to buy grain; they trade, bring wood and water, and do almost all the work of supplying food and raiment.[30] The field work is left to the women of the serf class.[31]

26 Johnston, "Uganda Protectorate," p. 626; Ratzel, III, p. 5.
27 Thomson, p. 419; Johnston, Lydekker, et al., p. 459.
28 Wylde, p. 238.
29 Wylde, p. 13.
30 Thomson, pp. 422, 446; Wylde, p. 253.
31 Cunningham, p. 6.

A common interest binds the husband and wife together, and, if they show no marked affection for each other, they do not often separate. Women occupy a high position and do not abase themselves by crouching in the presence of their husbands as is the practice among women in other parts of Africa.[32] Husband and wife associate in a spirit of freedom; they sit and eat together[33] and no taboo separates them when the wife is pregnant.[34] Among the Suk the husband remains apart from his wife till the child is weaned.[35]

The children in most tribes are separated early from parental oversight, and this necessarily lessens the regard of children for parents. Upon the death of a father, among the Masai, the son returns from the camp, picks up the corpse and throws it outside the kraal. The next morning he kicks aside the bones left by the hyena, while the vultures flap their wings grossly overhead.[36] The fact that the sons cannot own cattle of their own capture until the death of the father is not calculated to induce deep grief over a father's demise. Poor boys, among the Bahima, leave their parents at the age of seven or eight years and live with the chief.[37] Among the Galla, Somali and Abyssinian, the family is better united, and respect for old age is sometimes

32 Paulitschki, p. 202.
33 French-Sheldon, p. 385.
34 Joyce, p. 106.
35 Dundas, p. 60.
36 Thomson, p. 440.
37 Johnston, "Uganda Protectorate," p. 626.

marked.[38] The adoption of children is not uncommon.

Generally in this zone inheritance is patrilineal, i. e., in the male line. In Masailand, during the father's life he claims all of the cattle captured by his sons in the war group. When he dies all of the cattle is inherited by the oldest son.[39] The other sons may now, however, claim as their own any cattle that they may capture. Women have no inheritance. A widow goes to the eldest brother of the deceased husband;[40] so also among the Bahima, where the eldest son receives the largest share of the inheritance.[41]

Political Life.—The pasturage limitations do not permit the existence of many large groups. As the groups are small and scattered it is necessary for them to coöperate for defense. But the combination has little stability, as the people here, as everywhere in grass-lands, are exceedingly mobile.[42] The frequent exhaustion of the grass, and the also frequent epidemics of disease among the cattle, compel the groups to seek new pastures and new supplies of cattle. This precipitates a general scramble, resulting in the displacement of the weaker tribes.[43] As the stronger and more numerous tribes are in the north the concussion forces a general movement southward into the narrow extremity of the plateau, and there the vanquished have no alternative but

38 Paulitschki, p. 205.
39 Hollis, p. 309.
40 Merker, p. 49.
41 Joyce, p. 103; Dundas, p. 60.
42 Semple, p. 82.
43 Thomson, p. 414.

to descend and force themselves upon the sedentary populations of the plains. The plateau being a coveted region, gained and held by the strongest tribes, has come to hold the élite of the African race. Besides the defensive coöperation there is a union of tribes for wholesale stealing from neighbors. The scattered groups, therefore, confederate under an elective chief who rules over a large area somewhat after the manner of a mediæval lord.[44] "The nomad," says Semple, "is economically a herdsman, politically a conqueror, and chronically a fighter. . . . The nation is a quiescent army, the army a mobilized nation."[45] The Masai are divided into about twelve clans or sub-tribes with numerous small divisions.[46] They live by robbery.[47]

The political expansion of the groups is hindered by the ruggedness of the country, the frequency of rivers, mountains and canyons intervening between the habitable areas. Hence a great political empire has never been developed on this plateau as in the more open pasture regions of Asia and Western Sudan. While the military life tends to develop men of genius, the geographical conditions fail to afford them a theater for large action. Abyssinia, being a large and more agricultural region and the theater of conflict with the strongest invaders, is an exception to the rule of small, scattered confederations. Here the concussion of strife has welded a

44 Ratzel, II, p. 490.
45 Page 493.
46 Thomson, p. 412.
47 Kallenberg, p. 89.

large empire.[48] The military organizations of the plateau are effective for defense and pillage, but are very capricious, and in only rare cases fitted to conquer and hold foreign territory. The Bahima in their narrow strip of plateau have subjected many of the surrounding populations, and have been aptly called the Normans of Central Africa.[49] The troops and leaders generally upon the plateau are young bachelors; and it is a sociological law that the leadership of youth is despotic and inefficient. Fortunately, where despotism exists it is local in its extent. Among the Masai each military district elects its own chief. He directs the fighting from the rear, but if necessary advances with the body-guard. If he fails to give satisfaction he is summarily dismissed.[50] As individuals the soldiers are good fighters. Each has a sword attached to his side, and through his belt is pressed a knobkerry or skull smasher. He carries a shield in his left hand and a great spear in his right. He is strategic, skillful and courageous.[51] The Abyssinian soldiers are more up-to-date in their equipment. They are armed with every description of old rifle.[52] The Galla also have more up-to-date armament, and add much to the effectiveness of their raids by attacking on horseback.[53] The absence of the bow and arrow is no-

[48] Ratzel, III, p. 235.
[49] Johnston, "The Uganda Protectorate," p. 680.
[50] Thomson, p. 432.
[51] Thomson, pp. 435, 439.
[52] Wylde, p. 202.
[53] Wylde, p. 274.

ticeable among all the pastoral people from Nubia to South Africa.

The neighboring states offer little resistance to invasion so far as fighting ability is concerned, but they are protected by forest and absence of grass which mark the limit of the pastoral empire.

The Galla, Masai, and in some measure the Somali, approximate in their organization somewhat to the republican form of government.[54] The states could not be greatly centralized on account of the natural geographical barriers separating them. A Bahima king owns, at least theoretically, all of the cattle, and exercises absolute authority, except that the district chiefs act with a large measure of independence.[55] The Abyssinian government is rather centralized and absolute, but the emperor is elected within the limits of a certain hereditary ruling family.[56] The government is a feudality with endless ties, rights and duties establishing reciprocal responsibility. The pastoral life does not admit among freemen great inequalities in the possession of cattle,[57] and this puts a check to a too unequal distribution of political power, and keeps alive a spirit of independence. The incessant wars, however, would suppress the independent spirit and tend towards a central despotic régime but for the difficulty of massing great military forces at strategic points, and of controlling military groups scattered over a wide territory.

54 Ratzel, II, p. 489.

55 Joyce, p. 98.

56 Bruce, pp. 231, 237.

57 Ratzel, III, p. 238.

The caste system exists to only a limited extent because the pastoral life is unfavorable to the incorporation of a large subject class. There would be no work for them. The few slaves that exist in the population, however, are socially separated from the free class.[58] Instead of the formation of castes, a sort of feudalism exists in that the pastoral people subject the hunters and agricultural tribes of the border, and force them to pay tribute.

Legislation among the Masai is in the hands of a council of tribesmen. It elects a leader who is rather a guide to the debaters than a ruler.[59] He must be a man of courage, eloquence, and skilled in magic.[60] In Abyssinia lawmaking is mostly an affair of the emperor. Under the wise administration of Menelek II a cabinet has been formed along European lines and a council composed of the princes of the provinces. None of the other plateau states has an extensive executive system. Usually the chief directs the military operations in time of war, and conducts all foreign trade in time of peace.[61] The governments have little to do with the maintenance of internal order. An injured person in most cases redresses his wrongs by revenge. Abyssinia is an exception to this rule. Here each aggrieved person appeals directly to the local chief or to the emperor. Instead of employing a lawyer, the petitioner hires a lamentator who cries and moans at the door of the

58 Paulitschki, p. 240.

59 Préville, p. 70; Thomson, p. 432.

60 Ratzel, II, p. 489.

61 Ratzel, II, p. 490.

palace.[62] Crimes are punished by flaying alive, crucifixion, stoning to death, plucking out the eyes, etc.[63] The Bahima punish murder by death and impose fines for theft.[64] In case of murder among the Masai blood-money is demanded, and obtained by a raid upon the cattle of the offender's family. The elders of the group, however, sometimes intervene to restore peace.[65] Theft is settled by fines.

The revenue of the governments is mostly in the form of tribute, and is paid in kind, such as gold dust, cattle, slaves, ivory, grain, game, honey, butter, etc.[66] In Abyssinia a tithe of the produce is levied, and besides this there are revenues from imports and royalties on concessions.[67]

The several states of this zone have a greater degree of permanence than those of other parts of Africa. The generally prevalent patriarchal régime, with its succession in the male line, favors the development of a governing tradition. Then the uniformity of the economic life, the kinship of language, race, and religion over wide areas, make for cohesion. The independence of all the political groups of this zone is now largely destroyed by European encroachments. Abyssinia is the only country in Africa that retains its native control.[68]

[62] Bruce, p. 235.
[63] Bruce, p. 240.
[64] Cunningham, p. 17.
[65] Hollis, p. 311.
[66] Koettlitz, p. 51; Bruce, p. 315.
[67] Ratzel, III, p. 237.
[68] Morocco is now practically French territory, and the Liberian Republic has never been governed by natives.

CHAPTER V

THE GALLAS, SOMALIS, ETC. OF THE NORTHERN CATTLE ZONE (*continued*)

Religious Life.—The religion of this zone represents every gradation of development from fetichism to monotheism. The Abyssinians are largely Judaized or Christianized, and this has largely suppressed the native tendency to fetichism, witchcraft, and sacrificial rites. They practice, however, circumcision, and keep up the Judaic distinction between the clean and the unclean.[1] In the north and east part of the country Christianity blends with, or gives place to, Mohammedanism, which has made its way through inroads of the Arabs. The geographical barriers have prevented the monotheistic religions of the north from penetrating uniformly towards the south. Hence many tribes upon the plateau remain fetich, while others have a mixture of fetichism, polytheism and monotheism. The Masai are mostly polytheistic. They have several great gods who are supposed to interfere in a beneficent or malignant way in all the happenings of life. The supreme being is Mbaratien. When bands of cattle-lifters start on a raid they pray to Mbaratien, or rather howl at him, for

1 Ratzel, III, p. 234; Bruce, p. 249.

help; and they also at the same time send to a magic man for advice as to the best time to start, and for medicine to make them successful.[2] A very important deity is Neiterhob, an earth spirit; Ngai is a god who is a sort of personification of everything strange.[3] The Bahima have a supreme deity of the sky, a god of war, gods of rain, thunder and the nether world, and a multitude of clan deities.[4] They also worship the spirits of their ancestors,[5] and believe in certain demons of disease.[6] Priests are common among the polytheistic groups. In Abyssinia there exists an hereditary priesthood, and a superfluity of monks who practice open simony and polygamy.[7] On entering a church, says Bruce, you take off your shoes, "but you must leave a servant there with them, else they will be stolen, if good for anything, by the priests and monks before you come out of the church." The priests are very superstitious, and claim to see spirits.[8]

Human sacrifices are rare in this zone but offerings of cattle and other things are common. The Agaw sacrifice cattle and eat the flesh raw.[9] In connection with the ancestor worship of the Suk, offerings are made of meat, honey, tobacco, etc.[10]

2 Thomson, p. 434.
3 *Ibid.*, p. 445.
4 Joyce, p. 110; Dundas, pp. 60, 61.
5 Johnston, "Uganda Protectorate," p. 631.
6 *Ibid.*, p. 632.
7 Ratzel, III, p. 234.
8 Pages 242, 312.
9 Bruce, p. 312.
10 Dundas, p. 59.

The witch-doctor is found everywhere outside of the monotheistic religions, but his functions are not so great as among the Negroes of Central or West Africa. He is less important because the people rely less upon supernatural agencies. The fact that nature is not here over-antagonistic and terrifying, and that the people have to cope with her and lead a somewhat strenuous life, has a tendency to develop reason and to curb the imagination.[11] Hence the fear element does not enter so grossly into the native superstitions. The medicine man makes rain, divines the future, and cures disease, but is not called upon to discover witches and human agencies of death, with the resulting poison ordeals, as is common in other parts of Africa. Sickness and death are not so generally ascribed to mischievous agencies.[12] The medicine man employs some magic, but also makes use of natural remedies. The belief in prayer, common in many districts, has a tendency to diminish the importance of the medicine man. Demons and roving spirits are not altogether terrible. The Bahima have a monthly Sunday or day of rest and festival, with a view of appeasing demons, but these are not held in great dread. The most they will do is to take a man by the arm and shake him roughly.[13] If a patient is delirious the medicine man will make smoke to drive out the ghost.[14] Among the Masai the power of the witch doctor does not lie in himself but in his power of

11 Buckle, I, ch. 2.
12 Joyce, p. 103; Cunningham, p. 12.
13 Cunningham, p. 12.
14 Joyce, p. 103.

intercession with Ngai.[15] When Thomson was exploring Masailand a native married couple came to him and asked for some medicine to procure for them a white boy.[16] The Masai believe very little in ghosts,[17] and this fact limits the activities of the witch-doctor. When they call in the doctor he divines by examining the entrails of a goat, by getting drunk, or by his dreams. The sounds of birds are good and bad omens.[18]

There seems to be observable in this zone a transition in religion from a stage in which fear is the conspicuous motive to that in which the elements of adoration and gratitude enter. The gods seem to be in a measure benevolent and to inspire confidence. Hence the use of prayer in many cases.[19] This transition is dependent, partly upon the friendly aspect of nature, and partly upon the success of the groups in their struggle with foreigners which inspires confidence in their gods. "Thus the early Romans," says McDougall, "as they emerged triumphant from successive wars with their neighboring cities and grew in power and wealth, naturally and inevitably acquired some confidence in the beneficence of their gods; they began to fear them less and to feel some gratitude towards them."[20]

The non-monotheistic groups have a variety of

15 Thomson, p. 445.
16 *Ibid.*, p. 288.
17 *Ibid.*, p. 444.
18 Hollis, pp. 324, 325.
19 Thomson, p. 434; Dundas, p. 61; Hollis, p. 349.
20 Page 311.

notions of the future life. No conception of another life seemed to be discoverable among the Masai visited by Thomson.[21] According to the observations of Hollis, the soul does not come to life again unless it be the soul of a rich citizen or medicine man, and in either case it turns to smoke.[22] There is scarcely any conception of future punishment, except among the Christians and Mohammedans. After death all of the Bahima, good and bad, go to a place of rest.[23] This equality after death may be accounted for by the general lack of governmental machinery and laws requiring public punishment, and holding the individual, and not the community, responsible for crime. The notion of punishment after death, according to McDougall, develops only after private revenge has given way to social punishment of wrong-doers. "Hence we find that while societies are small and compact, communal responsibility for wrong-doing is the rule, and the idea of punishment after death is hardly entertained; but that, with the growth in size and complexity of a society and with the improvement of its moral ideas, belief in communal responsibility declines, and belief in punishment of wrong-doing after death arises to take its place as the effective sanction of custom and law." [24]

Ceremonial Life.—Ceremonies do not develop to an elaborate extent among pastoral people, who generally are little inspired by the desire to impress the

[21] Thomson, p. 444.
[22] Page 307.
[23] Cunningham, p. 23.
[24] Page 312.

crowd. A dense population is one of the prerequisites to a high degree of ceremony. Another fact unfavorable to ceremonial is the absence of great inequalities in the possession of wealth, since one of the chief motives of ceremony is to maintain social rank and subordination.

Marriages require very little formality. A suitor in Ankole, for example, takes to the father of the girl a pot of beer and a cow and calf. "If the suit is entertained the father drinks the amarwe (beer), and the young man milks the cow and presents a bowl of milk to the girl. When she has drunk the milk, the betrothal is complete."[25] Circumcision is widely practiced.[26] An Abyssinian boy on reaching the age of puberty goes to the house of his maternal uncle who shaves the boy's forelocks and bestows upon him a spear and heifer. The event is also celebrated by a festival.[27] Among the Masai a child-birth is celebrated by slaughtering a bullock, the meat being divided between the men and women.[28] The birth of twins is a little suspicious. It is not exactly unlucky but the pair are tolerated only after a ceremony of propitiation.[29]

Some of the ceremonies of civility are rather curious. For instance, the custom among the Masai of spitting on each other. Says Thomson, it "expresses the greatest good-will and the best wishes. It takes the place of the compliments of

25 Cunningham, p. 7.
26 Merker, p. 60; Dundas, p. 60.
27 Ratzel, III, p. 240.
28 Hollis, p. 293.
29 Dundas, p. 60.

the season, and you had better spit upon a damsel than kiss her. You spit when you meet, and do the same on leaving."[30] Spitting on anything also expresses astonishment, or contempt, or good luck.[31] In addition to this ceremony it is customary to shake hands and ask, How do you do?[32] The northern Abyssinians are said to be very polite. They "dismount from animals and make a bow whenever one passes."[33] Generally Abyssinians will not eat or drink with a stranger, and a vessel used by a stranger must be broken or purified.[34]

Burial ceremonies are generally simple. "At the funeral," among the Suk, "a black or red goat is killed and eaten at the grave, and the bones and contents of the stomach are placed upon the mound." A man's milk-gourd, tobacco, etc., as well as the good of which Marc Antony spoke, are oft interred with his bones.[35] Among the Masai the body of a dead child, warrior or woman is thrown away, and the name of the deceased never again mentioned.[36] In many localities it is considered the highest honor for the body of a cattle owner to be buried in a dunghill.[37]

Æsthetic Life.—The Masai give very much atten-

30 Page 290.
31 Hollis, p. 315; Johnston, "Uganda Protectorate," pp. 383, 833.
32 Merker, p. 103.
33 Wylde, p. 241.
34 Bruce, p. 230.
35 Dundas, p. 59.
36 Hollis, p. 305.
37 Cunningham, p. 32.

tion to personal decorations. A young dandy cultivates, not a mustache, but his ear-lobes. These are bored and stretched until he can thrust his fist through them. A piece of ivory six inches long is often inserted. His teeth are beautified by knocking out his two lower middle incisors.[38] He is tattooed by five or six marks on his thigh.[39] His hair is done up into a mop of strings. He wears a necklace of coiled wire, a bead-mitten on his wrists, and a strip of monkey hair round his ankles. He throws over his shoulder a decorated garment of kid skin.[40] The Masai women also pierce their ear-lobes and wear in them heavy coils of pendants.[41] The Bahima also tattoo, and adorn themselves with metallic rings, bracelets, etc.[42] The young belle of Masailand wears telegraph wire coiled from ankle to knee, and also above and below the elbow.[43] An iron wire with ornamental curls is worn round the neck, also beads and iron chains. Ear pendants are worn in profusion. The weight of these articles of jewelry varies according to the rank and wealth of the girl, and amounts often to fifty pounds.[44] The Gallas, and Somalis wear similar decorations, but the metal used is often silver.

The Masai have no musical instruments, and no

[38] Ratzel, II, p. 504; Thomson, pp. 421, 428.
[39] Johnston, "Uganda Protectorate," p. 804.
[40] Merker, p. 131.
[41] Kallenberg, p. 126.
[42] Johnston, "Uganda Protectorate," p. 804.
[43] Thomson, p. 429.
[44] *Ibid.*, p. 429.

songs, except those sung in celebration of a successful raid, or as invocations to deity. Their pleasures seem to be of a gross and somber nature. They have no rollicking fun, and no moonlight dances so common among other Negroes.[45] The Abyssinians have a great variety of string, wind and percussion instruments, while the Bahima seem to have only the flute, lyre, and drum.[46]

The æsthetic talent of the people is shown largely in their dress. The Abyssinians wear garments made mostly of cotton, but the Agaw element of the population dress in hides.[47] The costume of the men for grand occasions is a long undershirt reaching to the knees, made of home-grown cotton, a pair of trousers tight-fitting, embroidered at the bottom, the outer seam of each leg having a strip of embroidery two or three inches broad. Around the waist is a silk cord with silver tassels. Over all is a cotton smock of crimson, dark-blue, or black reaching a little below the knee, richly decorated round the collar, shoulders, waist and back.[48] The women wear on their head a black silk or particolored handkerchief and gold and silver hair-pins. They wear a silver bungler and silver bracelets on their wrists, ankles and legs, a blue silk cord around the neck to which is attached a crucifix of silver and a few charms; they wear also silver and gold necklaces, silver

[45] Thomson, p. 432.
[46] Johnston, "Uganda Protectorate," p. 630.
[47] Ratzel, III, p. 231; Bruce, p. 315.
[48] Wylde, p. 246.

rings on fingers and sometimes on their toes.[49] The women at market may be seen in native cotton shammas with a red stripe down the center, worn like a toga, gracefully draped, leaving one shoulder bare. The men of the peasantry put on a cap of sheep or goat skin. The original dress of the Galla was a leather loin-cloth with often a shoulder covering. The Masai women formerly wore dressed skins hanging from the neck to the knee. The Bahima men of rank strut proudly in leopard skins while the common men go almost nude.[50] The women dress profusely in cow hides that cover the head and shoulders and extend to the feet.[51] Cotton garments are now fast superseding the leather. The use of shoes or stockings is yet very rare. Sandals are sometimes worn for traveling.

Decorations of every kind among the people of the plateau are mostly conventional and do not represent nature.[52]

Dancing is less in vogue than elsewhere in Africa. Such dances as the people have often verge upon the drama. For instance, the Suk dances, of which there are a great variety, are usually in mimicry of hunting or other contests between man and animals. One very remarkable dance imitates the water spirit seizing a drowning man.[53]

[49] Wylde, p. 246.
[50] Stanley, "In Darkest Africa," II, p. 396.
[51] Joyce, p. 94; Schweinitz, p. 143.
[52] Ratzel, III, p. 231.
[53] Dundas, p. 61.

CHAPTER VI

THE GALLAS, SOMALIS, ETC. OF THE NORTHERN CATTLE ZONE (*continued*)

Psychological Characteristics.—There is no satisfactory information in regard to the cranial capacity of the people of this zone, but the presumption is that it is greater than that of the average Negro. The cranial forms characteristic of some of the tribes correspond to those of the Caucasian peoples inhabiting the shores of the Mediterranean.[1] The relation of brain weight to intelligence has not yet been scientifically established, but, if there is such a relation, the brain capacity of the Negro of this zone ought to be relatively high, corresponding to his superior intelligence. There seems to be a correspondence in all the African zones between the size and form of the brain and its activity.[2] Prof. David Hausemann in his article "Ueber das Gehirn von Hermann von Helmholtz," in "Zeitschrift für Psychologie und Physiologie der Sinnesorgane," Band XX, takes the position that there is no connection between brain weight and mental capacity; and several other eminent scholars are of the same opinion. It

1 Sergi, Chs. II to IX inclusive.

2 Dowd, "The Negro Races," I, Pt. 2, Chs. XXXIV, XXXIX.

seems to me, however, quite possible that some great men may have small brains and some mediocre men large brains without discrediting the theory that a race of men having large brains will have an advantage over a race having small ones. A boy with short legs may happen to be the fastest runner in a student-body, whereas upon the whole the long-legged boys will outrun the short. The superior brain of any zone must be accounted for, not by assuming that increased functions enlarge the brain and that this enlarged brain is transmitted by inheritance, but by assuming that natural selection causes those types to survive that fit the more strenuous environment. According to Woodruff, in a tropical country, where existence is easy, a large brain could not evolve.[3] "The general trend of increase of brain is away from the tropics."[4] "The colder and more forbidding and unfriendly the country the larger are the brains of the natives."[5] The brain of man, he goes on to say, reached its maximum of development before the dawn of civilization. It was determined by a process of selection under conditions that called for the employment of all the faculties. It ceased to grow as soon as the division of labor arose by which each man came to exercise but one faculty.[6] The maximum of growth was reached, just after the glacial epoch in Europe, about 40,000 years ago. Some of the Europeans after this epoch migrated southward too soon, and "did not

[3] Page 32.

[4] Page 9.

[5] *Ibid.*, p. 9.

[6] *Ibid.*, p. 34.

stay long enough to develop the necessary brain."[7] For illustration, the Greeks and Romans were superior to the Assyrians and Babylonians; and the modern Europeans, who overran the classic world, were superior to the latter, because they remained longer in the barbaric state, under strenuous conditions that employed all of their faculties.

Without passing judgment upon this theory, it is sufficient to say that in Africa the process of natural selection ought to adjust the brain capacity to the conditions, and there is evidence that it does so, and the process is rapid. For example, when the pygmies get out of their environment, and attempt to live on the plateau, they "droop and die" from cold and exposure, not having the aptitude to protect themselves.[8] Stanley and other explorers have often commented upon the inability of the Negroes of one zone to survive in another. In changing from an easy to a hard environment the dying out of the unfit would lead to a rapid selection of a superior type.

The superiority of the Negroes of this zone is shown in the first place by their less violent sense of fear. Instead of manifesting the self-abasement of the Central African, they are self-assertive, proud and domineering.[9] This characteristic is due to their successful warfare, and to the milder manifestations of nature which appeal less to their emo-

7 Woodruff, p. 22.

8 Stanley, "In Darkest Africa," II. p. 385.

9 Johnston, "Uganda Protectorate," p. 630.

tions and more to their reason. They possess what Williams calls the forceful mood.[10]

They show a high degree of the pugnacious instinct, cultivated under conditions that provoke warfare. "The situation that more particularly excites this instinct," says McDougall, "is the presence of spectators to whom one feels oneself for any reason, or in any way, superior; and this is perhaps true in a modified sense of the animals; the "dignified" behavior of a big dog in the presence of small ones, the stately strutting of a hen among her chicks, seem to be instances in point."[11] Among civilized people this instinct finds play in the economic, political and other spheres, and has a tendency to merge into friendly rivalry and emulation.[12] "Vigorous motor reactions," says Patten, "can always be put to some good use, and once acquired, they are never lost by a progressive race."[13] Existence among the Masai of this zone calls for some courage and mental effort, and hence their feelings do not predominate over their reason to the extent common to the average Negro. They are not strikingly superstitious.[14] In their treatment of the sick they use less jugglery and more knowledge of medicine and surgery. They know how to use many roots and herbs, and how to set or amputate

10 Page 744.
11 Page 64.
12 *Ibid.*, p. 89.
13 "The Development of English Thought," N. Y., 1899, p. 18.
14 Stanley, "In Darkest Africa," II, p. 400.

limbs.[15] Abyssinia has had a system of compulsory education since 1907. Formerly only well-to-do Abyssinians could read and write, having been taught by the priests.[16] The Galla have mathematical terms expressing units up to one thousand, the Tigré up to ten thousand, and the Amharri up to one million.[17]

The frequent disputes over cattle and territory, and the problems of war, furnish themes for animated discussion in the council house. The leaders in this assembly are ready-witted and remarkable for order and decorum in debate.[18]

The people of this plateau have a degree of foresight much above that of pastoral groups generally, and this is accounted for by the greater difficulties of existence. Their defensive organization, involving the division of the population into three groups, and their sparing use of cattle as food, indicate an intelligent interest in conservation.

Their temper is not so rollicking and explosive as that of the Central African, although they often have in them a "spirit of fun lurking, ready to burst out into shouts of ringing laughter."[19] They commonly show a certain reserve and dignity, and do not give way to excitement.[20] This is because their life

15 French-Sheldon, p. 383; Hollis, pp. 343, 335; Cunningham, p. 10.

16 Wylde, p. 245.

17 Crawford, "Numerals as Evidence of the Progress of Civilization," Trans. Ethnological Society, N. S., II, p. 89.

18 Thomson, p. 433.

19 French-Sheldon, p. 360.

20 Thomson, p. 304; Cunningham, p. 21.

is relatively hard, and full of bitter struggle. They lead a "serious life."[21] Much smiling is not adapted to faces that must often assume a fiendish aspect.[22] The mountain people of Asia, living under peaceful conditions, and protected by natural barriers, are noted for their good humor, which Huntington attributes partly to the invigorating air.[23] But, in the heights of Eastern Africa, the military spirit gives the tempter a harder quality. The character here is more forceful and austere, and may be classed as the dogmatic-emotional type, according to the terminology of Giddings.[24]

Within their respective groups the people of this zone display some of the primary virtues of civilized people, i. e., kindness, truthfulness, justice to each other, and a common aspiration and resentment. When a Masai meets with misfortune the others of the group help him by supplying him with cattle, and restoring him to a good condition.[25] The Suk, says Dundas, "are exceptionally truthful and honest."[26] Some of the Masai are said to be "singularly honest and reliable."[27] Johnston says that the Bahima are usually very honest and faithful.[28] According to Stanley they are not easily provoked to anger.[29] "Serious falsehood among friends," says Cooley, "is, I believe, universally abhorred by savages and children as well as by civilized

21 Thomson, p. 432.
22 *Ibid.*, p. 440.
23 Page 60.
24 "Inductive Sociology," p. 87.
25 Merker, p. 117.
26 Page 61.
27 Thomson, p. 453.
28 "Uganda Protectorate," p. 630.
29 "In Darkest Africa," II, p. 403.

adults."[30] According to his view there are three elementary groups in which are developed certain universal feelings. These are the family, the play-group of children, and the neighborhood group of elders;[31] and within these are fostered love, resentment, ambition, vanity, hero-worship, and the sense of social right and wrong.[32] These characteristics, varying in intensity, are found in all groups, savage or civilized, the chief difference being in the area of their expansion, due to circumstances of environment. The virtue of honesty is enhanced anywhere by the development of property. Pastoral people, possessing much property, i. e., cattle, are obliged to respect property rights and to value truthful statement, at least within the kinship group.

The family affections, in most of the groups of the plateau, are weak, on account of the early separation of children from parents, and the chilling effects of the military life. The sexual morality of pastoral people is everywhere low, because of the great amount of idle time which falls to both sexes. Faithlessness is a common characteristic.[33]

Towards individuals outside their particular group, the natives of this zone, as those of civilized countries, are hostile, treacherous, and more or less unsympathetic. The pastoral people are "cattle-lifters," and "inclined to treachery in dealing with

30 "Human Nature and the Social Order," p. 182.

31 *Ibid.*, p. 24.

32 *Ibid.*, p. 28.

33 Ratzel, III, p. 233.

their enemies."[34] The Masai steal their weapons and implements, or force their subject tribes to make them.

The pastoral people, however, are not lacking in humanitarian sentiment. They are neither very cruel to their enemies, nor to beasts, and they are capable of disinterested kindness. They have been known to protect strayed porters, and to send out a caravan to seek porters who had lost their way.[35]

Vanity is not conspicuously developed in this zone. It is an art of deception, and in small groups, where all members are intimately acquainted, the incentive to deceive is not very strong. Vanity requires a large audience to excite its full vigor.

Except for their lack of respect for the home, we might apply to the pastoral people of Africa what Huntington says of the Himalayans: "Their characteristic traits of comparative honesty, courage in spite of superstition, industry, intense love of home, and cheerfulness under difficulty, are those which, all over the world, seem to make mountaineers of whatever race, better men than the inhabitants of the plains, where life is easy."[36]

[34] Dundas, p. 61. [35] Thomson, p. 443. [36] Page 65.

CHAPTER VII

THE ANDOROBO AND OTHER MIXED TRIBES OF THE FOREST ZONE

The conflict for pasture grounds among the Galla peoples of the plateau induces or forces the weaker tribes to descend into the regions where the forest becomes so dense as to render the pastoral life impossible. Here the vanquished tribes disband and scatter. Each family finds an isolated home in the recesses of the forest, retaining a single cow, perhaps, as a reminiscence of their former pastoral life. They take up hunting as the chief means of existence, but, while the men are so engaged, the women remain at home and cultivate in a small clearing a few vegetables, such as maize, sweet potato, yam, etc. Each home is protected, not by armed sentinels, as on the plateau, but by a thicket-fence and ditch. This forest region extends around the flanks of Mount Kenia, Mt. Kilema Njaro and extends on either side of the plateau almost to the Zambezi river.[1]

In all probability the Bantus have occupied this territory from time immemorial, but the tribes of Gallas expelled from the plateau have intermixed

[1] Préville, p. 90.

with the natives of the forest, producing varying degrees of mixture of blood and dialect.[2]

In this forest, hunting must be done in groups, as the game, such as the antelope and monkey, is found in large herds, or such as the elephant or buffalo, is redoubtable. Men, and boys of mature age, join the bands of hunters, and follow the migrations of the animals, often being absent from home many days. This leads to a curious form of polygamy. Instead of having several wives living in separate huts in one place, as among the West Africans, each man has several wives located in different cantons of the forest.[3] The feebleness of the parental tie is here pronounced, especially the tie between the father and the young children whom he seldom sees and does nothing to support.[4]

The loss of foresight, due mainly to the leadership of youth, tends to an unbridled exploitation of the game, and this necessitates among the forest people a constant struggle for new territory. The superior types of mixed peoples in the eastern part of the forest, near the plateau, following the line of least resistance, press against the less spirited and darker people of the West, and thus fight their way by degrees all the way across the forest of Africa, even to the shores of the Atlantic.[5]

[2] Deniker, p. 464; Johnston, Lydekker, et al., pp. 388, 390.
[3] Préville, p. 92.
[4] Préville, p. 92.
[5] Préville, p. 93.

CHAPTER VIII

THE NIAM-NIAM OF THE ELEUSINE ZONE

General Character of the Zone.—This zone is situated in the very heart of Africa, comprising a region west of the Bahr el Jebel, and extending more than halfway across the continent, and from the Bongo country on the north to the Welle river on the south. It is on the dividing line of a network of rivers that flow respectively into the White Nile and the Congo Basins. Its elevation varies from 2,000 to 4,000 feet. Its southern border is about five degrees above the equator. It receives a great rainfall and is a land of luxuriant vegetation and vast forests. Owing to its elevation the climate is less oppressive than that of other parts of Central Africa. Here the banana ceases to grow and also the oil-palm. It is a country infested with the tsetse fly, whose bite is fatal to cattle and horses, but not to the big game of the forest. By thus keeping out the domesticated animals it preserves the territory for the great and small beasts that find in the low and high lands their favorite ranges. In the lowlands where the forest is thick are chiefly the monkeys, leopards and other of the smaller game, while on the plains at certain seasons are troops of elephants, buffaloes and antelopes.[1]

The Inhabitants.—The inhabitants of this zone are a branch of the light-colored Negroes already described as occupying the cattle regions of East Africa. They are known as the Zandeh or Niam-Niam and they number about two million. While they resemble the Galla type, they show strains of the darker Nilotic Negro blood.[2] Schweinfurth says they are "capable of being identified at the first glance amidst the whole series of African races."[3] They have "round, broad heads," covered with thick frizzy hair of extraordinary length, and arranged in long plaits and tufts. "Their eyes, almond-shaped and somewhat sloping, are shaded with thick, sharply defined brows, and are of remarkable size and fullness, the wide space between them testifies to the unusual width of the skull, and constitutes a mingled expression of animal ferocity, warlike resolution and ingenuous candor. A flat, square nose, a mouth about the same width as the nose, with very thick lips, a round chin, and full plump cheeks, complete the countenance in its general countour."[4] The skin has a "dull hue of a cake of chocolate." Some of the women show various shades of copper color, but the general tint is always the same—an earthly red in contrast to the bronze tint of the true Ethiopian races of Nubia.[5]

1 Schweinfurth, I, p. 457.
2 Deniker, p. 442.
3 I, p. 4.
4 II, p. 5.
5 II, p. 6.

Economic Life.—The men devote most of their time to hunting. The elephants are chased during the season when they are upon the plateau. The grass is then burnt, and while the great beasts are blinded by the smoke and fire they are surrounded and killed with spears. In the dry season they take to the forests. Then the hunting season is over for the reason that the natives cannot keep up with the elephants in the forest, nor pursue the smaller game which is frightened away by the snorting and wallowing of the elephants in the pools and swamps, the shaking of the trees, and the breaking-off of twigs. The flesh of wild animals is now scarce so that the people have to fall back upon the domestic dog, and a scant supply of poultry,[6] supplemented by rats, worms, ants and caterpillars.[7] Fish relieves the situation somewhat, being dried, rolled into balls and given a "haut goût" by the heat of the climate. As a final resort the people take to eating each other. This is a land of cannibalism.[8] The name Niam-Niam, in the Dinka dialect, means "eaters," manifestly having reference to the cannibal propensities of the population.[9] The appetite for human butcher-meat is at the bottom of most of the Niam-Niam wars. "Meat! Meat! is the watchword that resounds in all their campaigns." [10] "In times of war," says

6 Schweinfurth, II, p. 16; Long, p. 274.
7 Préville, p. 233.
8 Préville, p. 234.
9 Schweinfurth, II, p. 3.
10 *Ibid.*, p. 17.

Schweinfurth, "people of all ages, it is reported, are eaten up, more especially the aged, as forming by their helplessness an easier prey to the rapacity of a conqueror, or at any time should any lone and solitary individual die, uncared for and unheeded by relatives, he would be sure to be devoured in the very district in which he lived."[11] The only salt available is extracted from a certain kind of wood.[12] Some writers believe that cannibalism is induced by the craving for salt.

But the meat diet is not altogether satisfying, and, to obtain a vegetable condiment, it is necessary to cultivate the soil. The short dry season is just sufficient to permit the ripening of grain, and the particular kind of grain that serves as the mainstay of the population is eleusine.[13] There are three granaries to each dwelling; two for the eleusine meal necessary for cooking, and the other for grain to be malted and made into wine.[14] Minor cultivated products are manioc, yams, etc.

The handicrafts include copper and iron-work, the making of hoes, weapons, knives and pottery, wood-carving, basket-work, bark-cloth, copper rings, etc.[15] Smith-work is clever here as among most Negro tribes.

An irregular trade is carried on with the Nubian

11 Schweinfurth, p. 18.
12 *Ibid.*, p. 462.
13 Schweinfurth, II, p. 13; Préville, p. 236.
14 Schweinfurth, II, p. 14.
15 Schweinfurth, II, p. 25; Long, p. 275; Junker, II, p. 246.

traffickers, formerly consisting of ivory and slaves. The medium of exchange is copper and iron.[16]

As for the division of labor, "The men most studiously devote themselves to their hunting and leave the culture of the soil to be carried on exclusively by the women."

Family Life.—Wives are purchased or obtained by the giving of a few knives to the father of the fiancée.[17] The bargaining, however, is not so commercial as among the pastoral people. The women exercise a considerable choice in the selection of their husbands. Polygamy is permissible, but not prevalent among the masses, perhaps because the proportion of the women to the men does not justify it.[18] Race antipathy shows itself in the tendency of the Niam-Niam to eschew marriage with the darker and more negroid populations found on the borders.

The women are chaste and modest to a degree uncommon among African races. They are very reserved and always turn aside with averted face upon meeting strangers.[19] They, however, occupy a less elevated position than the women of the Monbuttu,[20] i. e., they are more under the subjection of the men.

The families live in small groups. "Two, or at most three families," says Schweinfurth, "reside

16 Schweinfurth, I, p. 502.

17 Long, p. 275.

18 Schweinfurth, I, p. 467.

19 Schweinfurth, II, p. 27; *Ibid.*, I, p. 449.

20 Junker, II, p. 154.

close together. Generally from eight to twelve huts are clustered round a common open space, which is kept perfectly clean, and in the center of which is reared a post upon which the trophies of the chase are hung."[21] The nature of the available agricultural ground necessitates these scattered small groups. The huts occupied by each family are made of boughs and thatch; they are circular in form and have conic roofs.[22] They are neatly built, clean inside, and sometimes attain to æsthetic expression. The inhabitants, says Johnston, "trace on their doors and walls pictures of animals and men, and even make attempts at rude sketches of scenery, either with yellow clay or charcoal."[23]

The maintenance of the family devolves chiefly upon the women. Hunting, the occupation of the men, does not yield a regular or sufficient supply of food. "The domestic duties of the housewife," says Schweinfurth, "consist mainly in cultivating the homestead, preparing the daily meals, painting the husband's body, and dressing his hair."[24]

The marriage bond is relatively strong. "It is one of the fine traits of the Niam-Niam," says Schweinfurth, "that they display an affection for their wives which is unparalleled among natives of so low a grade."[25] "A husband will spare no sacrifice to redeem an imprisoned wife, and the Nubians,

21 Junker, I, p. 449.
22 Junker, III, p. 7.
23 "George Grenfell and the Congo," II, p. 758.
24 II, p. 28.
25 I, p. 449.

being acquainted with this, turn it to profitable account in the ivory trade. They are quite aware that whoever possesses a female hostage can obtain almost any compensation from a Niam-Niam."[26]

Children require little care, but they are valuable as field workers, and this brings to them a parental oversight greater than is common to the natives of the banana or cattle zones.

Inheritance is in the male line, the eldest son being the heir to the family property.[27]

Political Life.—It would seem that the people of this zone, on account of their homogeneity, would form themselves into a single nation; but the geographical divisions, made by the innumerable hills, swamps and rivers, oppose the development of large political units. There are only two groups that rise to the magnitude of empires; the rest of the population is divided into small chieftainships. Not being a country rich in nature's bounty, there is little pressure of outside populations into this region. The necessity for consolidation, therefore, is not urgent on political grounds. An internal factor, however, making for unity in any group is the necessity for conservation. Wherever the conditions of existence demand the cultivation of the soil and the storing of food for winter, there is developed in the community a strong impulse operating to arrest the struggle between individuals. The members of the group feel a common interest, and tend to wage war only upon strangers. Thus the area of peace tends to

[26] I, p. 472.

[27] Schweinfurth, II, p. 22.

expand into the whole territory of a people in proportion to the solicitude, conservation, and foresight necessary to support the population.[28] This natural tendency to unite is enhanced by the desire to raid foreign territory for the capture of game and human flesh.

The aggressive movements in this zone do not often result in empire building, on account of the high grass and many rivers that impede the movements of troops, and thus leave the conquered people in isolation.[29] The spirit of isolation is stronger that that of cohesion. The circumstances of warfare here do not favor the rise of great military captains as in the open country of South Africa. As the raiders launch forth in small bands upon their enemy, they are thrown back largely upon individual skill and cunning, and under this discipline each fighter acquires mastery in the art of attack. "With his lance in one hand," says Schweinfurth, "his woven shield and trumbash (a throw-stick with sharp iron edges and prongs) in the other, with his scimiter in his girdle, and his loins encircled by a skin to which are attached the tails of several animals, adorned on his breast and on his forehead by strings of teeth, the trophies of war and of the chase; his long hair floating freely over his neck and shoulders; his large keen eyes gleaming from beneath his heavy brow; his white and pointed teeth shining from between his

[28] Schrader, "Echanges d'activité entre la terre et l'homme." *Revue Mensuelle de l'École d'Anthropologie*, Vol. 6, p. 35.

[29] Junker, II, p. 185.

parted lips, he advances with a firm and defiant bearing, so that the stranger as he gazes upon him may well behold, in this true son of the African wilderness, every attitude of the wildest savagery that may be conjured up by the boldest flight of fancy. Nowhere in any part of Africa, have I ever come across a people that in every attitude and ever motion exhibited so thorough a mastery of all the circumstances of war and of the chase as these Niam-Niam."[30]

The border states would offer no serious obstacles to the expansion of the Niam-Niam if the internal conditions favored a larger and more compact unity.

The individual governments are hereditary monarchies, the eldest son generally being the heir to title and dignity. The other sons command fighting forces in the outlying districts, and have a share of the booty.[31] The rulers of the small groups are scattered, possess little authority, and "few in any way merit the designation of king."[32] The smallness of the groups, and the consequent individuality developed, do not conduce to absolutism. The difficulties of communication would prevent the possibility of an effective central government. Hence the rulers have not the chance to learn and transmit the art of governing.

Beyond a separation maintained between the ruling and the subject classes there is no caste system among the Niam-Niam. Such a system is every-

[30] II, p. 12.

[31] Schweinfurth, II. p. 22.

[32] Schweinfurth, II, p. 22.

where much more likely to develop among agricultural than pastoral people, since the cultivation of the soil offers employment to a large number of hand-workers. Among the Niam-Niam, however, the women do all of the drudgery, and there is nothing to distinguish one man's occupation from another's, all men being hunters and fighters. Moreover, the smallness of the groups is unfavorable to the development of that racial or class consciousness which builds up castes.

Legislative councils do not seem to be very active in this zone. The chief generally decides for himself the question of war or hunting; he calls the men together and assumes the command. Internal government has passed through the stage of private revenge. Each group, through its officers and guided by custom, punishes for injuries to any individual. Mutilation of the nose, ear or finger is a common mode of punishment for theft and seduction.[33] Where the Nubians have penetrated and usurped governments, as they have in many parts, a whip of the hippopotamus hide has come into vigorous use.[34] A Niam-Niam chief is supported mainly from the produce from his farms, but he takes a large share of booty in the form of elephant's flesh, ivory and slaves. In some cases revenue is paid regularly in boys and girls.[35]

All of the governments of this zone are naturally shifting and unstable, chiefly on account of the geo-

33 Junker, II, p. 310.

34 *Ibid.*, p. 257.

35 Schweinfurth, II, p. 21.

graphical factors that hinder integration, but the invasions of the Arab-Nubians from the northeast prior to 1882 and the recent interference of the Congo Free State and the Anglo-Egyptians have hastened the political disintegration.

CHAPTER IX

THE NIAM-NIAM OF THE ELEUSINE ZONE (*continued*)

Religious Life.—The religion of the Niam-Niam is fetich, but in a form in which terror of spirits is not so dominant as in the ordinary fetich beliefs. The phenomena of nature are not such as to excite a great amount of terror, and the struggle for existence gives to the people a sort of mastery over nature which is unfavorable to the development of the grosser forms of superstition, involving idolatry and human sacrifices. Instead of worshipping terrible gods, falling down before idols, and offering propitiatory gifts and sacrifices, the people seek their ends largely by means of magic, i. e., they consult the oracle and use charms.[1] For example, the possession of certain magic roots contributes to the success of the chase or brings rain.[2] Criminals and witches are detected by ordeal, and the fortunes of war revealed by augury. "An oily fluid concocted from a red wood is administered to a hen. If the bird dies there will be misfortune in war and if the bird survives there will be victory."[3] Diseases and deaths are caused

1 Long, I, p. 437.
2 Schweinfurth, I, p. 493.
3 Schweinfurth, II, pp. 33, 34, 119.

by evil spirits and the wizard man is employed to conjure them. He does a general practice, including exorcism, administration of drugs, roots and herbs, the manufacture of charms, and the prophecy of future events. He dances to the drum beat and catches messages from potent underground spirits.[4] His function is similar to that of the soothsayer among the Romans, and probably in some degree he promotes uprightness. The Roman senate in Cicero's time consulted soothsayers to know the meaning of certain strange happenings. The reply would be to the effect that the sacred places were profaned, the public rites neglected and sundry vices committed. In the same way the African magic diviner censures people for their shortcomings and warns them against departure from custom. The religion of the Niam-Niam has been modified and supplemented to a great extent within the last half century by Mohammedanism.

Ceremonial Life.—Ceremony is not elaborate among the Niam-Niam. Their economic life is not encumbered with rites as among the West Africans of the banana zone. Certain customary rules apply to courtship, marriage, and the relations of parents to children. The people have words of greeting and of farewell. When two people meet they join right hands and nod at each other with a strange movement which, to a European, looks like a gesture of repulse.[5] State ceremony is simple. The equality of the people and their small groups do not conduce

4 Junker, II, p. 137.

5 Schweinfurth, II, p. 27.

to forms and ceremonies intended to overawe the populace and keep each class in its proper subordination. The chief "disdains external pomp, and repudiates any ostentatious display."[6] The wizards have set forms for their various manipulations. For example, in connection with the augury they use a small flat-topped stool. "After having wetted the top of the stool with a drop or two of water, they grasp the block and rub its smooth part backwards over the level surface with the same motion as if they were using a plane. If the wood should glide easily along, the conclusion is drawn that the undertaking in question will assuredly prosper."[7]

Æsthetic Life.—The Niam-Niam are greatly absorbed in the æsthetic life, and, as among most Negroes, give much attention to adornment of their bodies. They make various tattoo marks upon their foreheads, temples and cheeks, and sometimes upon their chests and arms.[8] They file their incisors to a point, and follow the custom, prevalent from the Nile to the Kameruns, of plucking out the eyelashes and eyebrows.[9] They have their "skins painted in stripes, like those of the tiger, with the juice of the Blippo."[10] The painting of the body is done by a class of specialists.[11] They dress in cotton garments obtained by barter, in bark-cloth imported from the

6 Schweinfurth, II, p. 21.
7 Schweinfurth, II, p. 32.
8 Schweinfurth, II, p. 7; Johnston, Lydekker, et al., p. 430.
9 Ratzel, III, p. 49.
10 Schweinfurth, I, p. 440.
11 Junker, II, p. 241.

Monbuttu,[12] or in skins of native manufacture "which are fastened to a girdle and form a picturesque drapery about the loins." [13] Their head-dressing is as profuse as their body-dressing is meager. It is difficult to discover any kind of plaits, tufts or top-knots which have not been in vogue.[14] Hats are worn made of straw and fastened on by means of long bodkins of iron or copper, or ivory, monkey or human bones. Only men wear hats with feathers.[15] It is the fashion to wear rings in the nose and ear, and on the arms and legs.[16] "A very favorite decoration is formed of the incisor teeth of a dog, strung together under the hair, and hanging along the forehead like a fringe." [17] Sometimes a necklace is worn made of the teeth of people who have been slain and eaten.[18]

The dress and decorations of the Niam-Niam suggest that the practice of covering the body grew out of coquetry, as Thomas and Sumner assert,[19] and not, as Ratzel claims, from the desire of the husband to diminish the attraction of the wife.[20]

The Niam-Niam show artistic treatment of utensils which are often admirable works of art.[21] They

12 Schweinfurth, I, p. 480.
13 *Ibid.*, II, p. 7.
14 *Ibid.*, II, p. 7; Long, I, p. 435.
15 Schweinfurth, I, p. 44.
16 Long, I, p. 275.
17 Schweinfurth, II, p. 8.
18 *Ibid.*, II, p. 18.
19 Sumner, "Folkways," p. 446.
20 Thomas, "Source Book for Origins," p. 549.
21 Johnston, Lydekker, et al., p. 471; Junker, II, p. 246.

rejoice in music, and use a variety of stringed instruments of which the favorite is a sort of mandolin.[22] A kind of drama or opera is common in which one man is the whole caste. "There is a singular class of professional musicians," says Schweinfurth, "who make their appearance decked out in the most fantastic way with feathers, and covered with a promiscuous array of bits of wood and roots, and all the pretentious emblems of magic art, the feet of earth-pigs, the shells of tortoises, the beaks of eagles, the claws of birds, and teeth in every variety. . . . Whenever one of his fraternity presents himself, he at once begins to recite all the details of his travels and experiences in an emphatic recitative, and never forgets to conclude by an appeal to the liberality of his audience."[23] Junker says that certain troubadours recite to the accompaniment of a musical instrument the deeds of their ancestors.[24] An embryonic drama may be seen in the sham fighting which takes place in the war dance.[25] Spencer's theory that the dramatist arose from the medicine man seems to find no confirmation in the facts stated in this book.

Psychological Characteristics.—The Niam-Niam have a cranial capacity above that of the average Negro. Their skulls are larger than those of the Monbuttu of the banana zone, and more doli-

[22] *Ibid.*, III, p. 14.
[23] Schweinfurth, II, p. 30.
[24] III, p. 21.
[25] *Ibid.*, II, p. 237.

chocephalic in form.[26] Dunn thinks that agricultural people are generally more progressive and develop larger brains than people living upon the bounty of nature.[27] The dolichocephalic type, according to Closson, is everywhere more domineering and ambitious, and is more generally represented among the higher and ruling classes, and more largely represented in cities.[28]

As the groups of Niam-Niam are small and the life uncomplex, the mental development has proceeded along narrow lines. The efforts put forth in hunting and war have developed keenness of perception, cunning and pugnacity. The cultivation of the soil has developed some foresight and thrift. A considerable degree of independence, will-power and pride is manifested, while the feelings and passions of the people do not so completely submerge the whole mind as is the case among other branches of the Negro race. Abstract ideas are few[29] as little opportunity offers for their use in so simple a social life. The Niam-Niam share, with the other members of the Galla stock, in a somewhat forceful and domineering spirit. Family affection and consideration for women are fostered by the isolated life, imposing mutual interdependence in the home, and the exchange of sacrifices and sympathies. A similar isolation of the Europeans in the Middle

26 Shrubsall, "Notes on Crania from the Nile-Welle Watershed," Jour. Anthropological Inst. n. s. 31, p. 2567.

27 Page 17.

28 Pages 93, 94.

29 Schweinfurth, II, p. 31.

Ages, produced, in a still greater degree, the domestic virtues, and the exaltation of women and the home. The instinct of pugnacity here, as also in Europe in the Middle Ages, has played a part in drawing the members of the groups into bonds of common sympathy through the welding of the population into small defensive groups. This instinct here, as everywhere, has been of vast importance in the socialization of humanity. By inciting wars it has forced people to coöperate, pool their interests, and act harmoniously within the coöperative area. War is thus the agent of peace. It is the disciplinary school in which civilization learns its first lesson. Not only does it promote peace within the group, but it promotes industry, science, and all rational forms of progress, since the instinct to fight is carried over into the realm of peaceful activities. Instead of the war of fire and sword, we have the war of tools, machinery, commodities and ideas. The pugnacious instinct is cultivated by every form of combat, and it is stronger in civilized people than in savages, because of the greater multiplicity of activities that excite it. From the games played by children and adults up to the rivalry of nations for intellectual and moral supremacy we see the play of this instinct.[30]

Within each group the Niam-Niam manifest the traits, common to all natural peoples, of kindness, mutual helpfulness and justice. Junker remarks

[30] McDougall, p. 279; Small, Ch. 20.

that they are less prone than civilized people to rancor and sullen anger that result in deeds of violence.[31] Theft is rare even against strangers.[32] In the trial by ordeal the Niam-Niam administer the poison to a fowl and not to the person accused, and this indicates a less cruel disposition than is found in the banana zone.[33] Princes and chiefs, once won, says Junker, are more loyal than those of other black tribes.[34]

Beyond the felicity prevailing in the primary group there is little opportunity for moral progress. The rule of custom and tradition is sufficient to ensure a continuance of the felicity of the individual groups, but lack of communication with outside groups prevents the expansion of sympathy, and lack of interdependence prevents the development of notions of abstract right. Custom alone is right, and this involves no reflection or moral consciousness. The conception of ideal conduct depends upon rational choice and deliberation, and these depend upon the possession of abstract ideas and critically established knowledge which never develop among people who are governed solely by tradition.[35] Everywhere in Negro Africa the man-

31 II, p. 140.

32 *Ibid.*, p. 310.

33 Johnston. "George Grenfell and the Congo," II, p. 692.

34 II, p. 425.

35 Giddings, "Elements of Sociology," p. 154; Marett distinguishes two stages in the development of morality. First, the synnomic, i. e., sharing customs; and second, syntelic, sharing ends or purposes. The one is conduct based upon habit and the other conduct based upon reflection. Page 266.

ner of life is too simple to give rise to much knowledge or deliberation, and hence the highest type of character does not come to fruition. The Negro acts upon suggestions from the mass of men, or from tradition, and not from any ideal. "For the generation of moral character in the fullest sense," says McDougall, "the strong self-regarding sentiment must be combined with one for some ideal conduct, and it must have risen above dependence on the regards of the mass of men; and the motives supplied by this master sentiment in the service of the ideal must attain an habitual predominance."[36]

Idealism can have little effect in a depressing climate, or under any conditions that produce continuous feelings of weariness. In temperate climates the mind is stimulated, and the imagination remains active, fortifying any temporary state of distress by images of future joy and satisfaction. "When the agitative point begins to be reached," says Williams, "the imagination begins to wander in search of forceful or expansive images." For example, an isolated mother escapes from a mood of agitative anxiety over her absent children (who are at school) by imagining that she is preparing them for the Battles of Free Methodism, or that Jesus will take care of them. The blindness and adversities of Milton sent his imagination in search of forceful images and the result was Paradise Lost.[37] In a mind excessively wearied and vexed, however, the imagination is limp and finds no sustaining images or ideals.

[36] Page 261. [37] Williams, p. 754.

CHAPTER X

THE MONBUTTU OF THE BANANA ZONE

General Description of the Country.—The banana zone in Africa occupies a vast region, as may be seen by reference to the map; but that portion of it inhabited by the branch of the Galla race under consideration comprises a section of country south of the Welle River, extending east to the plateau skirting the Bahr el Jebel, and west to about the 25th meridian, and south to the Ituri River. It has an elevation ranging from 2,500 to 3,000 feet, and it is characterized by alternating depressions and gentle slopes. It is almost under the equator and is therefore more densely forested than the country of the Niam-Niam. It is the land of the banana, plantain and oil-palm. "Unnumbered groves of plantains bedeck the gently heaving soil," says Schweinfurth, "oil-palms, incomparable in beauty, and other monarchs of the stately woods, rise up and spread their glory over the favored scene."[1] In the more open and sloping regions abound the big game, while animals of a smaller kind live in the thicknesses of the forest.

The Inhabitants.—The branch of the Galla type of

[1] II, p. 86.

Negro in this region is known as the Monbuttu, also called Mangbattu, who number about one million. These Negroes, like the Niam-Niam, have the general physiognomy of the Galla,[2] but, in color of skin, they are "of a lighter tint than almost all the known natives of Central Africa." Their color is that of ground coffee as compared to the chocolate or ripe olive of the Niam-Niam.[3] Ratzel thinks that their lighter color is due to the greater immigration of people from the eastern mountains.[4] Another explanation, however, may be found in the dense shade of the country which prevents the skin from developing a very thick layer of pigment. In the curve of their nose the Monbuttu recall the Semitic type.[5]

Economic Life.—The food of the people is fundamentally vegetable,[6] consisting chiefly of the plantain, for the cultivation of which many clearances are made.[7] Systematic agriculture is little practiced on account of the rapid growth of weeds. Some sesame is grown, some earth-nuts, sweet-potatoes, sugarcane, manioc and tobacco.[8] There are no domestic animals except the dog and some poultry.[9] The chase furnishes an occasional mess of meat of such animals as the elephant, buffalo, wild boar and ante-

2 Deniker, p. 441.
3 Schweinfurth, II, p. 100.
4 III, p. 54.
5 Schweinfurth, II, p. 107.
6 Halkin, p. 21.
7 *Ibid.*, II, pp. 86, 88.
8 *Ibid.*, I, p. 526; II, p. 87; Halkin, pp. 21, 23.
9 Schweinfurth, II, p. 89; Halkin, p. 69.

lope; while the streams supply a quantity of fish.[10] The meat supply is irregular and sometimes reaches the stage of famine, and this has probably given rise to the practice of cannibalism.[11] "The cannibalism of the Monbuttu," says Schweinfurth, "is the most pronounced of all the known nations of Africa. Surrounded as they are by a number of people who are blacker than themselves, and who, being inferior to them in culture, are consequently held in great contempt, they have just the opportunity which they want for carrying on expeditions of war or plunder, which result in the acquisition of booty, which is especially coveted by them, consisting of human flesh. The carcasses of all who fall in battle are distributed upon the battlefield and are prepared by drying for transportation to the homes of the conquerors." Schweinfurth once came "unexpectedly upon a number of young women who had a supply of boiling water in front of the doorway of a hut, and were engaged in the task of scalding the hair off the lower half of a human body." . . . On another occasion he was in a hut "and observed a human arm hanging over the fire, obviously with the design of being at once dried and smoked."[12] He considers it a fallacy to suppose that cannibalism is due to a scarcity of meat,[13] yet he himself suffered for lack

10 Schweinfurth, II, pp. 89, 90; Halkin, p. 63.
11 Cureau, p. 642; Junker, II, p. 233; Halkin, p. 13.
12 II, p. 93.
13 II, p. 89.

of meat in that country.[14] Stanley in the Upper Congo region also suffered from want of meat.[15]

In the arts and crafts the Monbuttu take a high rank. They make a great variety and quantity of platters, stools, boats, shields, drums, and copper and iron fabrics; they also make excellent pottery and baskets. They do not, however, weave cloth.[16] Trade is carried on at local markets, and transportation is by porters and canoes. Slaves used to be the chief standard of value and medium of exchange.[17]

There is not much division of labor. "Whilst the women attend to the tillage of the soil and gathering of the harvest, the men, except they are absent either for war or hunting, spend the entire day in idleness." [18] The women and children perform the labor of collecting the bananas.[19] While savage men appear to shift too large a burden upon the weaker sex, it is probable that division of labor between men and women is rather well balanced. The men work with irregularity but with greater and more violent expenditure of energy.[20]

Slaves as a class scarcely exist, since there is no agriculture to give them employment. The cap-

14 II, p. 68.
15 "In Darkest Africa," I, p. 152.
16 Schweinfurth, II, pp. 88, 91, 113.
17 Halkin, p. 141.
18 Schweinfurth, II, p. 90.
19 Préville, p. 218.
20 Thomas, "Sex and Society," pp. 123, 146.

tives in war are used for food or for sale to slave traders.

There is almost no capital employed in industry. Even the building of a granary to conserve surplus grain is unknown. When a man dies there is nothing of value to transmit except the plantain grove, and this passes from father to son.[21]

Family Life.—The Monbuttu obtain their wives by capture, or by gifts to parents. The bride-price is paid in knives, dogs, slaves and lances.[22] Polygamy is common, and wives must be obtained from outside the community. This practice (exogamy) wherever it has existed, says Lang, developed under the system of totem superstitions and tabus, but prior to these the tendency may have developed through sexual jealousy and superstition, and indifference to persons familiar from infancy.[23] In contrast to the Niam-Niam the women are immodest and forward, and not a few are openly obscene.[24] All girls lose their virginity before puberty and sometimes by rape.[25] The dwelling houses are generally large and rectangular in form, and display some artistic taste.[26] The round hut with conic roof is also found.[27] The interior is furnished with stools,

21 Halkin, p. 133.
22 Halkin, p. 83.
23 Thomas, "Source Book for Origins," p. 34.
24 Schweinfurth, II, p. 91.
25 Halkin, pp. 81, 83.
26 *Ibid.*, pp. 49, 51; Junker, III, p. 7.
27 Halkin, p. 49; Ratzel, III, p. 56.

benches, mats, platters, etc.[28] The women do most of the work of maintaining the population, and it is partly on this account and on account of the matrilocal marriage (husband living with his wife's people) that they enjoy a degree of independence. They do not abase themselves before their husbands as is common in other parts of Africa. Affection between husband and wife seems to be very marked here, as also among the Niam-Niam, and there seems to be a considerable affection between parents and children. Men will risk their lives to save their wives and sisters, and will even fight against the loss of their children.[29] The Monbuttu, says Junker, take pleasure in their children and fondle them more than other Negroes.[30]

Political Life.—The abundant natural resources attract into this zone, and maintain, a large population; and the pressure from outside compels the grouping into large masses,[31] and the organization of government upon a military basis. Successful defence here, as everywhere among military states, leads to aggression upon neighbors. In the case of the Monbuttu, the craving for human flesh adds a keen zest to the predatory tendency. The homogeneity of the race favors unity, and excludes federation with, or absorption by, the darker peoples of the south. The expansion of the Monbuttu into the north is hindered by the superior Niam-Niam, and by the geographical obstructions already

28 Junker, II, p. 282.

29 Halkin, pp. 27, 91.

30 II, p. 233.

31 Halkin, p. 21.

described. On the south and west they are checked by the still more impenetrable forest, and on the east by the domain of the more aggressive pastoral people. The superiority in numbers would give the Monbuttu a great military advantage but for the difficulties mentioned. The frequency of war and the complex problems due to the dense population would seem to develop superior leadership. The fighting force, however, is relatively inefficient, since the men are enervated by the climate, and have too easy a time with nature to develop spirit and intelligence. They hold their own against their neighbors by superiority of numbers.

The forest of the country is open enough to facilitate communication, and this fact, together with the defensive warfare conduces to centralized authority. The population is divided principally into two large kingdoms; one in the east, and the other in the west,[32] and the form of the governments is that of absolutism modified by a council of elders.[33] The indolence of the people and their low order of intelligence are also factors favorable to absolute rule. Everything touched by the king becomes sacred: no one henceforth is allowed to touch it. The king is a man of large possessions. His provincial governors are chosen from the royal family. His council is composed of a keeper of weapons, master of ceremonies, superintendent of the commissariat, master of the household of royal ladies, and an interpreter for

32 Schweinfurth, II, p. 83.

33 Préville, p. 224; Halkin, p. 159.

strangers.[34] "The sub-chieftains or viceroys," says Schweinfurth, "are distributed over various sections of the country, and they are accustomed to surround themselves with a retinue and state little inferior to those of the kings themselves. The chiefs claim all the ivory of the country and a share of the products of the soil." They also exact tribute in boys and girls whom they sell to slave traders, along with ivory, in exchange for provisions and trinkets. In fact, the subjects live upon the residue of production after the chiefs have taken all that they want. The Monbuttu governing class, however, should not be judged too harshly. It is little different from those who govern elsewhere. "There is no class," says Sumner, "which can be trusted to rule society with due justice to all, not abusing its power for its own sake. . . . The ruling classes in mediæval society were warriors and ecclesiastics and they used all their powers to aggrandize themselves at the expense of the other classes." [35] Something of the same kind might be said of our modern classes.

At the end of each Monbuttu village is a palaver house where the council of elders meets to dispense justice.[36] In the judicial proceedings the chief is the principal judge. "On one occasion," says Junker, "a man brought a complaint against the wooer of his daughter that he had not yet paid over the customary number of spear-heads. . . . In such

[34] Schweinfurth, II, p. 96.
[35] "Folkways," p. 169.
[36] Halkin, p. 57.

contests the contending parties vie with each other in volubility, the man who holds out longest remaining master of the situation, and doubtless usually wins the case. Still the prince has the last say and from his decision there is no appeal."[37]

The Monbuttu have passed the stage of revenge as a process of adjusting wrongs. Offenders are tried in court and the penalty, fixed by custom, is enforced by the government. For adultery the penalty is death, but the accused often settles the case by compensation.[38]

Common race, language and economic life, and the density of population, once gave to the Monbuttu a great degree of stability, but their governments have now been almost completely demolished by the invasion of Arabs.

37 II, p. 243.

38 Halkin, p. 85.

CHAPTER XI

THE MONBUTTU OF THE BANANA ZONE (*continued*)

Religious Life.—The Monbuttu religion does not differ substantially from that of the other inhabitants of the banana zone.[1] It is fundamentally fetichism, with some admixture of polytheism, and a slight coloring of Mohammedanism. The people live in a world of fantastic spirits, and under the dominion of the magic doctor. There are no temples or priests connected with the native religion. The gods roam about and have no settled abode. The temple never develops except among people who live a settled life and in substantially built houses. When man himself occupies a substantial dwelling he presumes that the gods need one, and when a home for the gods is built there must be a keeper of the house, or priest.[2] The element of fear is a prominent factor in all of the Monbuttu superstitions; and while it would seem to evoke only absurdities and degrading abasements, there is reason to believe that it is a necessary and useful factor in the evolution of intellectual or moral culture. Indeed, the value of the fear emotion in

[1] Halkin, pp. 93, 95, 103.

[2] Montesquieu, "Spirit of Laws," II, p. 133.

human nature can scarcely be estimated. Of the primitive man, McDougall remarks, that "This instinct must have kept his thoughts at work upon those objects of his wonder, and especially upon those which excited not only wonder but fear; and the meditation upon these fearful objects led to theories explanatory of them." Hence the beginning of philosophy.[3] Fear is also at the bottom of custom and morals, enforcing obedience to common standards.[4] "In the struggle for existence," says McDougall, "only those societies survived which were able to evolve such a crust of custom, binding men together, assimilating their actions to the accepted standards, compelling control of the purely egoistic impulses, and exterminating the individuals incapable of such control.[5] . . . And this essential step of social evolution was, as we have seen, in the main produced by the coöperation of the instincts of fear, curiosity and subjection."[6]

A fact, however, overlooked by McDougall, and other psychologists, is that the instinct of fear is even stronger among civilized than among primitive people, and that it does not diminish with civilization, as asserted, for instance, by Giddings[7] and Buckle.[8] In the opinion of Giddings fear is opposed to rational deliberation. On the contrary, is

[3] Page 303.
[4] Ross, "Social Psychology," p. 203.
[5] Page 307.
[6] Page 309.
[7] "Elements of Sociology," p. 228.
[8] "History of Civilization in England," I, Ch. II.

not fear one of the chief incentives to deliberation? Among savages the fear instinct is appealed to by so few stimulations that its expression is impulsive and violent, whereas among civilized people it is appealed to by such a variety and multiplicity of stimulations that its expression is controlled and refined. "An enlightened age," says Stückenberg, "moving in a larger mental realm than a primitive one, may have as much feeling, or even more, though mostly different in kind."[9] The civilized man's apprehension about his health, sweetheart, property, social standing, or political fortune, is at the bottom of all of his deliberations. Not only is fear an instinct behind all of our practical thinking, but it is an essential element in the creation and enjoyment of grandeur in all works of art.[10]

Ceremonial Life.—Public and private ceremonies are more elaborate than among the Niam-Niam. This is explained by the more dense population, and the more absolute form of the governments. Fixed forms and ceremonies are prescribed for eating, hunting, cultivating the soil, and manufacturing. There is a ceremony of initiation into manhood, and a ceremonial dance connected with marriage.[11] The ordinary form of salutation, says Schweinfurth, "consists in holding out the right hand and saying, 'Gasseggy,' and at the same time cracking the joints of the middle fingers." Ceremonies of State are

9 "Sociology," I, p. 363.
10 Burke, "Essay on the Sublime and the Beautiful."
11 Halkin, p. 83.

highly developed, and great dances are a popular means of stirring up the war spirit.[12] State dress corresponds in elaboration to State ceremony. King Munza, says Schweinfurth, adorns his "head in a skin of a great black babboon, giving him the appearance of wearing a grenadier's bearskin; the peak of this was dressed up with a plume of waving feathers. Hanging from his arms were the tails of genets, and his wrists were encircled by great bundles of tails of the guinea hog, a thick apron, composed of the tails of a variety of animals, was fastened around his loins, a number of rings rattled upon his naked legs." [13]

The Monbuttu follow the custom, prevalent among the ancient Babylonians, of placing food and drink upon the graves of their dead.[14]

Æsthetic Life.—The artistic faculty of the Monbuttu seems to be of a high order.[15] This is conspicuous in their propensity to decorate and adorn all of their handiwork. They even presume to improve upon their physiognomy by several artful modifications; for instance the common practice of altering the form of their teeth; the boring of the inner muscle of the ear, into which they insert a bar of copper about the size of a cigar; the tattooing of figures upon their breasts, backs and shoulders.[16] They are more successful, however, in beautifying their utensils, weapons, wicker, earthen, and iron-

[12] Halkin, p. 109.
[13] II, p. 75.
[14] Halkin, p. 97.
[15] Junker, II, p. 233.
[16] Schweinfurth, II, pp. 105, 106.

work, all of which strikes the attention of the traveler by the excellence of the designs. They are good sculptors and boat-builders.[17] Both sexes wear their hair in a long cylindrical tuft in a backward slanting direction. On top of this the men wear a straw hat.[18] The clothing of the people consists of bark-cloth made from the fig tree.[19] Women, however, do not wear any dress until married.[20]

Dancing is an accomplishment greatly admired by the commonalty, and even practiced by the king. Schweinfurth who saw king Munza dancing said that his "arms dashed themselves furiously in every direction, though always marking time to the music, whilst his legs exhibited all the contortions of an acrobat's, being at one moment stretched out horizontally to the ground, and at the next pointed upward and elevated in the air."[21]

The people also show great fondness for singing. They have a national war-song and many court ballads.[22] Most of their songs, as those of the Bushmen, have a tinge of melancholy.[23] The chief musical instruments are the drum and trumpet.[24] These instruments seem to predominate everywhere among people who are violently excited by the fear instinct.

17 *Ibid.*, II, p. 233; Ratzel, III, p. 56; Johnston, Lydekker, et al., p. 470.

18 Schweinfurth, II, p. 106.

19 *Ibid.*, II, p. 88.

20 Halkin, p. 45.

21 II, p. 75.

22 Halkin, p. 111; Schweinfurth, II, p. 97.

23 Halkin, p. 111.

24 Schweinfurth, II, pp. 97, 113.

Certainly no other instruments are so well calculated to arouse a disturbing emotion. Stringed instruments, on the other hand, seem to be associated with people who are rather mildly agitated by fear, and live in a continuous mood of expansion and complaisance. The Monbuttu have no stringed instruments.[25] Painting and sculpture seem to be limited to some rude representations of animals upon the walls of the houses, and the carving of wooden utensils, furniture, masks and idols.[26] The wood carving excites the admiration of travelers.

Psychological Characteristics.—The Monbuttu have smaller crania than the Niam-Niam, and less dolichocephaly.[27] They should therefore have less intelligence, according to the theory of Woodruff mentioned in chapter VI.

The Monbuttu are actuated strongly by the instinct of flight. This instinct is usually dominant in an environment that is antagonistic and terrifying. Where nature manifests herself in outbursts of thunder and lightning, floods, devastating winds, and surrounds man with dangerous beasts, poisonous reptiles and insects, and stagnant waters that breed much sickness—man is terrified, cowed and whipped; and instead of seeking to overcome nature he is inclined to flee from it. His predominant emotion is fear, and this excites his imagination and peoples the universe with malignant spirits,

25 Schweinfurth, II, p. 117.

26 Halkin, pp. 53, 117.

27 Shrubsall, "Notes on Crania," pp. 256, 257.

ghosts, demons and gods. Man here becomes engrossed in superstitions, and is under the sway of the magic doctor. An examination of the people and conditions in Africa reveals the fact that the most terrified and superstitious tribes are found in the regions where nature is most violent and antagonistic, and that where nature is manifested in a milder form the people are more self-assertive and less superstitious.

The instinct of self-abasement is very marked among the Monbuttu and also among other tribes of the banana zone, and gradually merges into self-assertion as we go north and south from the equator. This instinct is close kin to that of flight but is a milder manifestation of the impulse to withdraw from danger or things disagreeable. It discourages man and tempts him to crouch rather than flee. It awakens the emotion of humility rather than fear. It results from a comparison of man's self with the forces that surround him in such a way that he himself is made to appear very insignificant. The people of the banana zone, seeing themselves in the midst of powerful and antagonistic forces of nature against which they are unable to cope, feel a deep sense of inferiority, while in the agricultural and cattle zones, where the forces of nature are less violent, man is more inclined to hold up his head, and grapple with opposition. This feeling of self-abasement in proper subordination is a necessary and valuable characteristic of all races, for the reason that it renders them submissive to control, and implants in them a reverence for authority which conduces to a higher development of character, and culminates in that noble sense of humility which is the highest attribute of religion. The humility that the highest type of man feels is the result of comparing himself with some exalted ideal.

The instinct of pugnacity is weak among the Monbuttu as it is directly opposed to the instincts of flight and self-abasement. The instinct of repulsion is, however, strongly marked. It is a greatly inferior instinct to that of pugnacity, as it may exist in an individual who has not the courage to act aggressively. It is characteristic of people who are timid and live in small isolated groups. It is associated with fear,[28] suspicion and distrust, and is manifested in hostility to strangers, or even neighbors,[29] or to any one who may offer an affront. Instead of meeting opposition boldly and openly, the repulsive instinct rather incites indirect methods of attack without the risk of injury to self. For example, the people of the banana zone generally are much given to treachery and the use of poison. The tribes poison their arrows and attack from ambush. They place poisoned instruments in footpaths and in streams of water to catch the foot of the unwary stranger; and the poisoning of one individual of a tribe, or of a family, by another is a common means of squaring a grudge.

The instinct of repulsion may be traced very far

[28] Bain, p. 184. [29] Halkin, p. 27.

back in organic evolution. "The earliest movements of animal life," says Thomas, "involve, in the rejection of stimulations vitally bad, an attribute which is the analogue of prejudice. . . . The micro-organism will approach a particle of food placed in the water and shun a particle of poison."[30] Among men the feeling of repulsion often prompts an impulsive attack upon any object that may happen to offend. Says Montaigne, "Who has not seen peevish gamesters tear the cards with their teeth, swallow the dice in revenge for the loss of their money? Xerxes whipped the sea and wrote a challenge to Mount Athos . . . and Caligula demolished a beautiful palace for the discomfort his mother had once had there." Instincts or motor reactions, such as that of repulsion, are necessary to the preservation of the species, and they survive and sometimes manifest themselves in a most ludicrous fashion. "They are slowly formed," says Patten, "and still more slowly changed. Many of them were created ages ago under conditions unlike those that now exist. Once formed they have continued through a long series of environments, because the new conditions contained nothing to interfere with their activity. They remain unmodified or are modified in ways that make them stand out even more clearly."[31] The repulsive nature of the Monbuttu, as of the Chinese, is heightened by the self-sufficiency of isolation. It might have a valuable so-

[30] "Sex and Society," p. 103.

[31] "The Development of English Thought," New York, 1899, p. 12.

cializing effect if conditions permitted it to be carried over into the social life and to be spent upon whatever is unjust, or harmful to the general good. Properly directed repulsion is a necessary element in aggressive righteousness.[32] "The mass of mankind," says Cooley, "are sluggish and need some resentment as a stimulant. . . . Surround a man with soothing, flattering circumstances, and in nine cases out of ten he will fail to do anything worthy, but will lapse into some form of sensualism or dilettanteism. There is no tonic, to a nature substantial enough to bear it, like chagrin—'erquickender Verdruss,' as Goethe says. Life without opposition is Capua. No matter what the part one is fitted to play in it, he can make progress in his path only by a vigorous assault upon the obstacles, and to be vigorous the assault must be supported by passion of some sort. With most of us the requisite intensity of passion is not forthcoming without an element of resentment; and common sense and careful observation will, I believe, confirm the opinion that few people who amount to much are without a good capacity for hostile feeling, upon which they draw freely when they need it."[33] "How can a man rightly care for anything without in some way resenting attacks upon it?" Thus it is that the basest of savage instincts are transformed into virtues, just as the carrion of which Emerson speaks converts itself into grass

32 Blackmar, F. W., "Elements of Sociology," p. 263.
33 "Human Nature and the Social Order," p. 241.

and flower. Among the Monbuttu, however, the instinct of repulsion is spent blindly and yields nothing valuable.

The Monbuttu are remarkably gregarious. They live in large groups, facilitated by the abundance of vegetable food, and the homogeneity of the population. The gregarious instinct, by the way, like that of repulsion, is one of very great social importance, especially in primitive societies. Of its value McDougall remarks that, "in early times when population was scanty it must have played an important part in social evolution by keeping men together and thereby occasioning the need for social laws and institutions as well as by providing the conditions of aggregation in which alone the higher evolution of the social attributes was possible; but that in highly civilized societies its functions are less important, because the density of population ensures a sufficient aggregation of the people; and that facilities for aggregation being so greatly increased among modern nations, its direct operation is apt to produce anomalous and even injurious social results."[34] This instinct, no doubt, often produces bad results among both savage and civilized people. For example, the Negro has a tendency everywhere to follow the crowd, and in his own land never builds a house on a farm and lives to himself as is common among the farmers of Europe and America. The power of isolation is a late development of evolution and be-

[34] Page 301.

longs only to the most advanced races. Even the Italian and Teutonic races differ much in that respect. There is, however, no reason for supposing that the gregarious instinct has lost its importance for the civilized man. It is shown in the grouping of people into clubs, societies, social sets and schools of thought. Both Giddings and McDougall take the view that the satisfaction of this instinct is in proportion to the degree of resemblance or likeness of the individuals.[35] There are reasons for thinking, on the contrary, that people are attracted to each other rather by unlikeness than likeness. If two people were exactly alike in all particulars they would have absolutely no interest in each other. It is a law of the chemical and biological world that unlikes and contrasts attract. The interest which one individual finds in another is always something in the way of novelty or contrast; a conflict of ideas and emotions, and these act as stimulations.[36] The fact that a too great contrast repels has led to the mistaken supposition that it is likeness that attracts. The so-called gregarious instinct, therefore, may be nothing more than an expression of some other and more fundamental spring of action. Very probably it is a combination of the instinct of curiosity, and the instinct of fear. There can be no doubt that the instinct of fear was a chief motive for the gregarious tendencies in the Middle Ages.[37]

[35] Giddings, "Inductive Sociology," Ch. III; McDougall, pp. 299, 300.

[36] Stückenberg, I, p. 85. [37] Sumner, "Folkways," pp. 214, 215.

The Monbuttu are extremely self-sufficient and conservative, resulting from their isolation. They have nothing within or without to encourage innovations. A similar isolation produces the same characteristic among the inhabitants of the oases of Asia.[38]

The Monbuttu have a strong instinct of curiosity if we may judge from their fondness for hunting. The hunting life seems to have an educative effect upon this instinct, and civilized people have to thank the hunting stage of their ancestry for its cultivation. It may be seen behind every mechanical invention and every discovery in science, art and philosophy. The Aryan peoples, who have gone through a long hunting period, have carried over this instinct into their economic, political and moral realms and built upon it a great and progressive civilization, while the Chinese, who have lacked the hunting stage in their history, have not developed the impulse to investigate, and hence have remained for thousands of years in a condition of stagnation. The superiority of the Japanese over the Chinese is primarily due to their hunting experience in passing through Corea and the island of Nippon. The reason that this instinct has not been of greater advantage to the Negroes of Central Africa is the antagonism of the climate which has discouraged energy and prevented the development of a differentiated social life in which the instinct could be employed along productive lines. In the

[38] Huntington, p. 140.

absence of opportunity to employ it in practical life the people tend to gratify it by artificial stimulation, i. e., by gambling. In seasons when the game is scarce the men spend much time in gambling. This manifests the instinct in its lowest form, for the reason that it furnishes the stimulation of surprise and excitement without the risk of serious discomfort. Gambling and games of chance are most common in regions where the climate or other conditions do not invite man into the fields of industrial activity. The instinct of curiosity then seeks an artificial outlet. In the agricultural and pastoral regions of Africa this instinct has a chance to be carried over somewhat into the industrial and social life and is less expended in gambling. The hunting or other instinct is a safe guide and tends always to promote the interest of the group until reason begins to replace it. Then man is liable to act in a thousand ways injurious to society and is prevented from destroying it only through the development of group sentiment.[39]

The natives of this zone are said to be mentally and physically lazy. For this trait two explanations may be offered. One is the oppressive climate, and the other a lack of stimulating interests.[40] Even tropical people show an astonishing amount of energy when their appetites or passions are strongly appealed to. This is shown in their dances, fighting, hunting, and even in their laborious hair-

[39] Ward, Lester F., p. 133.
[40] Buckle, I, Ch. II.

dressing. "Primitive people," says Sumner, "use great patience and perseverance when they expect to accomplish something of great importance to their interests. The same is true if they expect to gratify their vanity."[41]

The Monbuttu show less self-control, less foresight, and more abandonment to passion and impulse than the Niam-Niam. They approximate closely to the mental type which Giddings calls the idio-emotional.[42] Their predominant mood is that of agitation due to feelings of weariness, anxiety and fear.[43] Nevertheless they are superior to the Negro of West Africa [44] and even excel the Niam-Niam in oratorical powers "which in parliamentary and judicial proceedings are developed to a perfectly amazing degree of fluency."[45] They have a wide acquaintance with nature and human nature, but little knowledge of other kinds. They know nothing of astronomy, and can count only up to fifty using the fingers as a basis.[46]

Among members of the same group of Monbuttus there are not found, to the same extent, those primary virtues of kindness, mutual helpfulness and justice, so characteristic of other groups. A reason, perhaps, is that the aggregation of the peo-

[41] Page 133.
[42] "Inductive Sociology," p. 87.
[43] Williams, p. 744. Their mood might be classified according to Ribot as the humble-sensitive, pp. 388, 394.
[44] Junker, II, p. 233.
[45] *Ibid.*, p. 242.
[46] Halkin, p. 119.

ple has been more the result of the gregarious instinct than of war or coöperation; and hence the socializing effect of acting in concert has been very slight. The attitude of the ruling class towards the subject class is that of extreme coldness. The latter is regarded in the light of strangers. Upon any pretext a subject is liable to be seized, killed and eaten.

Before concluding the study of this last branch of the Galla type of Negro, it may be of interest to quote what Verner says by way of contrasting all of the darker and lighter populations of Africa. "The brighter-colored Africans are also generally more intelligent, and of more sensitive nervous organism, less emotional but more vivacious, and much more apt to cherish resentment. They are quicker in motion, and they seem to have a far livelier sense of humor; they are also more sensitive to pain and less capable of prolonged endurance or privation."[47]

[47] Page 541.

PART II

THE BANTUS

CHAPTER XII

THE BANTUS OF THE EASTERN BANANA ZONE

General Description of the Zone.—In order to comprehend the populations of this zone it is necessary to divide it into an eastern and western partition. The western partition includes the territory of some of the Nigritian peoples discussed in Volume I of this series; and also includes a large group of Bantus living in the relatively low grounds between Central Africa and the Atlantic Ocean. The eastern partition includes, besides the territory of the Monbuttu, described in Chapter X, the regions of the Upper Congo, the western borders of lakes Albert Nyanza, and Victoria, about one-half the western borders of Lake Tanganyika, and the countries intervening.

The Bantus now under consideration are those belonging to this eastern division. The contour of this region is very irregular. Upon the whole it is elevated and characterized by many broad table-lands with interspersed valleys. The rainfall is heavy, the streams copious and numerous, and the forests for the most part extensive, but not dense as in the lower levels. There are frequent and dangerous thunderstorms.[1] The country of Uganda (or Buganda) which is the chief point of interest in this territory, is one of the most beautiful parts of the world. It has mountain peaks forever snow-capped.[2] "Its groves of banana trees, that everywhere abound, adorn the verdant landscape on hill and dale."[3] It consists of "rolling green downs rising in places almost into mountains, and every valley in between is a marsh."[4] The temperature averages about 70° Fr., rising to 97½° in the day and falling to 50° at night.[5]

The banana and plantain grow in great abundance.[6] In Karagwé the plantain is so common that nothing is said if a stranger is seen plucking a bunch from a tree.[7] The rubber tree and fig tree are also common, and of great value to the inhabitants. The country was once well supplied with big game, but this has been in a large measure killed out. There remain, however, the lion, leopard, wild cat, monkey and many species of brilliant colored birds.[8] The python and the deadly puff-adder lurk in the path of the traveler, and mosquitoes pursue you whether you travel or not.[9]

1 Johnston, "Uganda Protectorate," p. 119.
2 Goodrich, p. 154.
3 Long, p. 125.
4 Johnston, "Uganda Protectorate," p. 85.
5 Tucker, I, p. 93; Grant, p. 203.
6 Johnston, "Uganda Protectorate," p. 85; Grant, p. 198.
7 Grant, p. 143.
8 Johnston, "Uganda Protectorate," p. 114.
9 *Ibid.*, pp. 87, 88, 94.

The Inhabitants.—The inhabitants of this part of the banana zone are the Waganda (or Uganda), the Manyuema, Ruandas and the Kinyoro-speaking peoples of Mpororo, Nkole, Karagwé, etc.[10] They belong to the great Bantu race which occupies almost the whole region of Central and Southern Africa. The Bantu represent a great variety of types, due to mixture with the Pygmies, Bushmen and Hottentots of the south and the Galla peoples of the east.[11] Nevertheless, they have common characteristics that clearly distinguish them from the other branches of the Negro stock. They are darker than the Galla, not so tall as the Nigritian, nor so dolichocephalic, prognathous, or flat nosed.[12] The Waganda are lighter in color than the average Bantu on account chiefly of the admixture of Bahima blood.[13] The elevation of the country may have something to do with the lighter color. In Uganda there may be distinguished four different types of Negroes besides the Bantu proper. These are the Pygmies, The Nile Negro, The Masai and the Hamite. The Waganda are taller than their neighbors.[14] Livingstone says that the Manyuema men have a superior shape

10 In the Bantu language *Mu mo m* mean man. Example, Muganda=Ganda man. *Ba wa a ma* mean men. Example, Baganda=Ganda men. *Ki tshi si* mean language. Example, Ki swahili=Swahili language. *Bu U* mean country. Example, Buganda=Ganda country.

11 Ratzel, II, p. 513; Johnston, "George Grenfell and the Congo," II, p. 511.

12 Deniker, p. 458.

13 Tucker, I, p. 93.

14 Johnston, "Uganda Protectorate," p. 473.

of head and physical form, and that many of the women are light colored and pretty.[14a] The Pygmies belong to the Negrito type which has been fully discussed in Volume I of this series.

Economic Life.—The chief food of the people is, of course, the banana and plantain,[15] supplemented by the proceeds of hunting and fishing, and by the cultivation of small patches of ground, yielding pumpkins, tobacco, sweet potatoes, sugar-cane, millet, sesamum, etc., and by keeping a few domestic animals, as the goat, cow, and chicken.[16] The latter species reached Africa first through Egypt at the time of the Persian occupation about 450 B. C.[17] Cattle do not flourish in this zone, and are found only upon the highlands.[18]

The cessation of the slave trade, and abolition of slavery in many districts, have tended to increase the interest in agriculture.[19] "The peasants," says Tucker, "live in the midst of the plantain gardens and have merely a few feet of cleared space in front of their huts."[20] The people seldom eat animal flesh,[21] but human flesh is a coveted article of food

14a Last Journals, I. p. 371.

15 Burton, II, 58; Johnston, "British Central Africa," p. 427; Stanley, "Through the Dark Continent," I, p. 402; Tucker, I, pp. 19, 92; Stuhlmann, p. 180; Long, p. 125; Weiss, p. 325; Livingstone, "Last Journals," II, p. 34.

16 Long, p. 125; Burton, pp. 68, 196.

17 Johnston, "British Central Africa," p. 480.

18 Grant, p. 167.

19 Stanley, "Through the Dark Continent," II, p. 453.

20 I, p. 96.

21 Stanley, "How I Found Livingstone," p. 550.

in many localities.[22] Cannibalism is induced partly by lack of employment for war-captives and partly, as Sumner thinks, by "defects of the food supply." [23] Stanley, Schweinfurth and other explorers have complained of scarcity of meat in Central Africa.[24] Weismann writes that "our people (his porters), since the passage of the Sankuri, therefore for six weeks, have eaten no meat except caterpillars, grasshoppers and similar small creatures." The universal drink is a banana wine which the natives drink out of the corner of their cow-skin coverings.[25] The banana not only serves as the basis of alimentation but also as the material for nearly all industries. It furnishes thatch for the houses, fronds for the vessels, leaves for tablecloths and for wrappers, stems for fences and rollers, fiber for cord, and stalk to make shields for soldiers and sun-hats for fishermen.[26]

Among the articles of manufacture in Uganda are soap, plates, dishes, napkins, bark-cloth, shawls, skin-cloaks, mats, baskets, knives, shields, boats, drums, etc.[27] The natives are fine craftsmen.[28] Local trade is carried on at market places and on

[22] Stuhlmann, p. 181; Stanley, "Through the Dark Continent," II, pp. 156, 241, 338.

[23] "Folkways," p. 329.

[24] Stanley, "In Darkest Africa," I, p. 152.

[25] Grant, p. 234.

[26] Stanley, "Through the Dark Continent," I, p. 414.

[27] Johnston, "Uganda Protectorate," p. 101; Grant, pp. 159, 233; Long, pp. 125, 126.

[28] Stanley, "Through the Dark Continent," I, p. 410; Long, p. 127.

fixed days. Communication and transportation are difficult in many places on account of the high grass which cannot be crossed without the use of a knife.[29] The ordinary money consists of copper, shells and European goods.[30] The foreign trade, i. e., that between Uganda and the East Coast, was formerly carried on by means of porters. "Of the natural products of the equatorial regions," says Grant, "such as slaves, ivory, salt, copper, iron, bark-cloth, coffee and sugar-cane, Karagwé scarcely yields any, but it is a great depot for trade." The Arabs and coast men bring up beads, cloth and brass-wire, and meet people of all the nations around and trade with them for ivory and slaves.[31] In recent years the slave trade has ceased, and the ivory trade almost so, both finding substitutes in rubber, skins and hides. The building of the Uganda railroad to the coast has almost entirely destroyed the old caravan routes. Steamboats on Lake Victoria run in connection with the trains from the coast.[32] Also boats ply on the Victoria Nile and on Lake Albert Nyanza.

The division of labor among the Waganda does not throw so much work upon the women as elsewhere in this zone. The men build and repair the houses, make the bark-cloth, knives, baskets, pottery, shields, and do the tanning.[33]

29 Long, p. 152; Hahn, p. 127.

30 Long, p. 127.

31 Page 158.

32 Goodrich, p. 155.

33 Tucker, I, p. 95.

Family Life.—Wives are obtained usually by purchase, though capture of women is a common accompaniment of war. In the ordinary course, the suitor makes his purchase of a wife in the form of presents to the father, sometimes of considerable value.[34] Stuhlmann says that a lover sends to his sweetheart a load of wood instead of a bouquet. If this is acceptable he later sends to her father a goat, two cows and two chickens.[35] The bride-price in Mpororo is from ten to thirty goats.[36] It used to be common in German East Africa for the white soldiers to buy native girls as temporary wives at each camp.[37] Virginity before marriage is esteemed a virtue but not generally preserved. The women of Uganda are all modest as to dress.[38] In some districts sexual morals are loose, and intercourse before marriage frequent.[39] Polygamy is the prevailing form of the family. This is induced by the frequency of war which kills off the men, and gives to the women a preponderance in numbers.[40] The proportion of the sexes is seven women to one man.[41] The king of Uganda used to have 7,000 wives.[42] The husband, instead of going to live with his bride, takes

[34] Johnston, "Uganda Protectorate," p. 687.
[35] Page 183.
[36] Weiss, p. 328.
[37] Schweinitz, p. 186.
[38] Stanley, "Through the Dark Continent," I, p. 408.
[39] Stuhlmann, p. 183.
[40] Goodrich, p. 224; Stuhlmann, p. 171.
[41] Ratzel, III, p. 257.
[42] *Ibid.*, p. 184.

her to his home which he builds assisted by friends.[43] The house is generally bee-hive shaped, made of timber, reeds and grass.[44] In order to exclude the wind and prying eyes it has no windows.[45] The interior has a partition to give privacy to the occupants of the rear room.[46] The furniture consists of a carved stool, some pots, a few wicker or grass basins. The walls are ornamented with bark-cloth, hoes, pipe-stems, charms, etc.[47] The upper-class houses have highly dressed skins and beautiful mats on the floor.[48] The meals are served in the hut upon banana leaves.[49] After the meal the members of the family wash their hands with the juicy skin of a banana stem.[50] The women, by the way, are said to be excellent cooks.[51]

Here, as elsewhere in Africa, the women are the chief supporters of the family. They gather the fruits, cultivate the fields, and do nearly all of the labor connected with the food-supply. They work in the garden while the men snooze and smoke.[52] Women seem to be less respected here than among the Monbuttu. In most cases they eat apart from

43 *Ibid.*, p. 183.
44 Tucker, I, p. 96.
45 Ferree, p. 149.
46 Stanley, "Through the Dark Continent," I, p. 384.
47 *Ibid.*, p. 384.
48 Tucker, I, p. 97.
49 Stuhlmann, p. 180; Grant, p. 234.
50 Stuhlmann, p. 181.
51 Grant, p. 234.
52 Cunningham, p. 168.

their husbands.[53] Parental affection is strong. Grant remarks, of the death of a three year old Negro boy, that the "father mourned for the child, crying most grievously."[54] Boys are preferred to girls,[55] but the former are sometimes killed if they chance to be sons of a chief. In that case they are killed by their mother to spare her the suspicion of wanting an heir to succeed her husband.[56] Any child is killed if born feet-foremost.[57] The attitude toward "in-laws" is very frank and hostile. "No man may see his mother-in-law or speak to her face to face."[58] Through the influence of the ruling Bahima, and the invading Arab, inheritance has been changed in some of the tribes from the female to the male line.

Political Life.—This zone, by reason of its rich spontaneous products, is a coveted region, and hence its inhabitants are obliged to maintain themselves upon a military footing. The factors that determine the political character of the people are practically the same as those described as existing among the Monbuttu in a similar region of this zone of the banana. The chief difference is a less spirit of independence among the Waganda, due to race inferiority, lower altitude, and more enervating climate. Here the people lend themselves still more readily to the despotic form of government.[59] The political hier-

[53] Stuhlmann, p. 180.
[54] Page 146.
[55] Stuhlmann, p. 185.
[56] Roscoe, p. 120.
[57] *Ibid.*, p. 120.
[58] *Ibid.*, p. 124.
[59] Stuhlmann, p. 189.

archy is maintained by the exploitation of one class by another. As there is no economic interdependence, society can be held together only by coercion. The population of Uganda is estimated at from one half to one million.[60] The mass of the people are ruled ever by a lighter and less negroid type known as the Bahima (or Wahuma),[61] a branch of the Galla race, probably expelled from the eastern plateau. According to Lapouge, the superiority of the lighter colored people is a universal phenomenon.[62] Thus governed the Waganda once formed a powerful State. At the time of Stanley's visit the empire embraced Koki, Usoga, Unyoro, Karagwé, Usui, and other districts covering an area of 70,000 square miles.[63] Up to the recent domination by the British, the Waganda were governed by an emperor who had a well-organized government. His council included a prime minister, several princesses, a chief butler, chief baker, and a commander of the army and navy.[64] There were feudal lords ruling over provinces and owing allegiance to the king.[65] The population was divided into three classes: the feudal gentry, the peasants or serfs, and the slaves. The local chiefs exercised almost autocratic power. It is a sociological law that chiefs have little authority where the tribe is independent, and much au-

60 Long, p. 128; Stuhlmann, p. 171.
61 Grant, I, p. 146; Cunningham, p. 6; Weiss, p. 329.
62 Page 56.
63 "In Darkest Africa," I, p. 306.
64 Tucker, I, p. 95.
65 *Ibid.*, p. 95.

thority where the tribe is a unit in a larger government.[66] The gentry or aristocratic class ruled their subjects with an iron hand and oppressed them sorely. It is difficult to see what function of any value such an aristocracy performed. It must be remembered, however, that Uganda once attained to a considerable advance over the other peoples of Central Africa in the comforts of life, in manners and material culture; and there can be no doubt that this culture owed its introduction to the aristocratic class, through imitation of the foreigners with whom they came in contact. They had borrowed from the Egyptians, Arabs and Europeans. International imitation always spreads from above downward through the social strata. "In earlier ages," says Cooley, "royal courts have served as centers for the reception and diffusion of foreign ideas."[67] "An aristocracy has," according to Ross, "a certain value as an inlet for foreign tastes and ideas. Even though it be not inventive, it can still afford a good launching place for inventions and novelties. . . . The French upper classes catch from the English nobility field sports, tweeds, racing, appreciation of country life, etc. In the sixteenth and seventeenth centuries the English aristocracy formed itself upon Italian models, and thereby incidentally injected some Italian culture into England: later it took on French fashions, fine arts, free thinking. etc."[68] In this light the aristocracy of Uganda may have ren-

[66] Czekanowski, p. 596.
[67] "Social Organization," p. 342.
[68] "Social Psychology," p. 161.

dered some service. The establishment of privilege seems to be necessary to enable one person or group to impress culture upon others. A system of aristocracy, however, like a system of slavery, is beneficial only in certain stages of culture. In modern times the great cities, such as Paris, London, New York, and Berlin, have superseded the aristocracy in the function of receiving and disseminating foreign ideas.[69]

Every young man of Uganda who could carry a shield used to belong to the army.[70] Stanley estimated the fighting force at 25,000 men.[71] When marching the army was accompanied by women and children carrying spears, weapons, provisions and water.[72]

The administration of justice in Uganda, and in some of the other kingdoms of this zone, had evolved beyond the independent tribal state, in which blood revenge ruled, to a state in which the government backed by public sentiment prescribed rights and redressed wrongs. The Uganda penal code was severe. For adultery the penalty was loss of an ear, torture or throat-cut; for theft the offender was placed in the stocks; for striking or assaulting with a stick the fine was two goats, while assaulting with a spear brought confiscation of property, half going to the sultan and half to the injured party;[73]

69 Cooley, "Social Organization," p. 343.
70 Ratzel, III, p. 10; Stuhlmann, p. 191.
71 "Through the Dark Continent," I, p. 306.
72 Burton, p. 189.
73 Grant, p. 181.

for murder all the property of the guilty one was made over to the relatives of the victim, and the eyes of the murderer were gouged out, or he was thrown from a precipice. If a husband came upon an adulterer he was permitted to kill him upon the spot. It is clear from these facts that criminal law was an expression of social anger, and revealed a well-developed social sentiment. Grant thinks that crime among the Waganda was less than among civilized people,[74] an observation that agrees with the theory of Arthur Hall that crime necessarily increases with civilization, due to the progressive raising of the moral standard.[75] The practice of torture in Uganda represented a higher form of justice than the ordeal, because the former is used only when suspicion or facts point to a reasonable probability of guilt.[76]

In former times there was no regular system of taxation. When the king needed anything he commandeered it.[77] Generally the chief of each district claimed a tusk of every elephant found dead or alive.[78] A special levy was sometimes made on persons who had enlarged navels.[79]

The long relatively stable life of the Uganda empire was due in a great measure to its lake frontier

[74] Page 182.
[75] "Crime and Social Progress," Ch. XIV.
[76] Welling, p. 197.
[77] Cunningham, p. 233.
[78] Grant, p. 160; Stuhlmann, p. 181.
[79] Cunningham, p. 234.

which protected its people from invasion and also from emigration.[80]

Succession was generally in the male line. The chief was usually the eldest son of the first wife.[81] If there was no son then the brother or nephew was elected.[82]

80 Semple, p. 374.
81 Hobley, p. 359.
82 Johnston, "Uganda Protectorate," p. 694.

CHAPTER XIII

THE BANTUS OF THE EASTERN BANANA ZONE (*continued*)

Religious Life.—At the time of the invasion of the European the people of Uganda had a well developed polytheism. They had gods of the sky, earthquake, lightning, rain, hurricane, war, etc.[1] But with the polytheism was a large element of fetichism or animism, so that the total number of spirits to be reckoued with ran into the hundreds. Since 1884 their religion has undergone a rapid revolution. Large numbers of people have been converted to Mohammedanism, or to some form of Christianity, mostly Catholic. They seem to have displayed a remarkable capacity, as well as eagerness, to acquire a knowledge of letters, and of religious principles, both in the Protestant and the Catholic communities.[2] At present the followers of Mohammedanism are few. In many of the remoter districts the people remain fetich, and in the daily round of life encounter a multitude of spirits, of which many are the spirits of the dead. These natural people of the Uganda forest agree with Milton that

[1] Johnston, "Uganda Protectorate," p. 678.

[2] Keane, "Man, Past and Present," p. 93.

> "The spirit of man
> Which God inspired, cannot together perish
> With this corporeal clod."

But according to the fetich view, the spirit of man, instead of soaring to some ethereal home, abides here below, haunts the living and causes mischief. This belief in the survival of the body spirit gives rise to a kind of ancestor worship.[3] Within the hedge-enclosed yard of each home is a small, square hut, sacred to the genius of the family, the household *muzimu*. Certain stones stuck in the ground in front of the family hut are supposed to have been placed there by ancestors.[4] Some spirits of the dead, however, are not regarded with favor. If the ghost of an objectionable deceased person is seen in a dream the body is disinterred and burnt to ashes.[5] The body of a thief is always cremated to prevent its ghost from troubling the village by causing sickness.[6] Not only the spirit of man returns after death but that also of animals.[7] Sometimes a human spirit returns in the form of a reptile, and hence some families have reptile ancestors.[8]

These disembodied spirits, being always present in large numbers, get into mischief and cause trouble and expense. If a mother loses a child its spirit may come back and cause the mother to become barren.

[3] Swann, p. 208; Cunningham, p. 138.
[4] Hobley, p. 344.
[5] *Ibid.*, p. 339.
[6] *Ibid.*, p. 340.
[7] *Ibid.*, p. 344.
[8] *Ibid.*, p. 348.

If this happen the bones of the deceased child are dug up and thrown into the bush as a preventive against further annoyance.[9]

Belief in charms and magic is much in vogue. A bit of broken pottery, fixed as a finial on the house top, prevents children from becoming cross-eyed.[10] A sprig of a certain herb worn in the lobe of the ear will avert a long list of evils.[11] Grant observed that the sultan of Karagwé had bunches of charms hung on his arms, around his neck, and below his knees.[12] Various charms are hung up in the houses.[13] The Wanguana march up and down beating tin cooking-pots to frighten off the sun, and prevent it from devouring the moon.[14]

Disease and calamities are the work of evil spirits, and hence the need of the witch-doctor. This all-important magician makes charms for the people, detects thieves, and administers potent medicines, makes songs to the ancestral spirit upon the birth of a child, divines the future, and makes offerings to ancestral ghosts.[15] The sultan of Karagwé "combined the offices of prophet, priest and king." He predicted rain by means of charms.[16] The first step in sickness is to call in the

9 Hobley, p. 340.
10 *Ibid.*, p. 343.
11 *Ibid.*, p. 345.
12 *Ibid.*, p. 146.
13 Stanley, "Through the Dark Continent," I, p. 384.
14 Avebury, p. 245.
15 Johnston, "Uganda Protectorate," pp. 587, 678.
16 Grant, p. 139.

village doctor who decides at once if the patient will die or recover.[17] In cases of stealing a very unique kind of witch-doctor is employed by the king as a ferret. Grant observed "a one-eyed man with a cow's horn in his hand to detect the thief. The horn was capped over with a rag of bark and had an iron bell tinkling from its top." This was carried through the village and shaken in the face of the suspected.[18] In the vicinity of Ujiji, where canoes are hewn from logs and brought down the mountain to the water, "the village medicine man, for a fee, performs an elaborate ceremony on the newly born infant, as he calls it." [19]

The witch-doctor is the center of interest in this zone. His physiognomy, dress, manners and arts are of the most unusual kind. He is the people's ideal—their hero. The secret of his power lies in the strangeness and mystery that envelop him and his work. And, by the way, it may be said that love of the mysterious is just as marked a characteristic of civilized as of savage people; and is one of the greatest factors of human progress. Our civilized hero owes a large part of his power to his abuormalities, physical and psychological, which excite our imagination. Says Cooley, "a strange and somewhat impassive physiognomy is often, perhaps, an advantage to an orator, or leader of any sort, because it helps to fix the eye and fascinate the

[17] Cunningham, p. 36.
[18] Page 197.
[19] Swann, p. 77.

mind."[20] The savage witch-doctor, therefore, gives the people a slight training in hero worship.

Sacrifices of various kinds are common, including sometimes human beings. Upon the death of a chief some of his household or followers must accompany him into the other world.[21] In Uganda when the health of the king was in danger cattle were sacrificed,[22] and at the command of the witch-doctor people were driven into Lake Victoria to relieve the toothache of the queen-mother.[23] An island in this lake was supposed to be inhabited by invisible spirits that invaded the surrounding country, causing sickness and death. If things went wrong, if children died or became sick, etc., offerings of goats, beer and other things were despatched to the island to propitiate the spirits.[24]

Idolatry is almost universal. Referring to the people about Lake Tanganyika, Swann says, that "close by, in a grove of banana trees, I saw a group of images placed in a circle. They were beautiful specimens of carving but represented most hideous faces of men and beasts."[25] Avebury thinks that idolatry represents a higher form of religion than fetichism, and agrees with Spencer that it is connected with ancestor worship.[26]

20 "Human Nature and the Social Order," p. 314.

21 Johnston, "Uganda Protectorate," p. 716.

22 Cunningham, p. 146.

23 *Ibid.*, p. 146.

24 Hobley, p. 341.

25 Page 208.

26 Avebury, p. 361; Spencer, "Principles of Sociology," I, p. 447, Appleton ed., 1884.

The superstitious practices above named do not now obtain in the neighborhood of the missions and trade centers, and they probably never reached the extremes of absurdity common to the Negroes of the Lower Niger. Sorcery and magic have little influence with the ruling classes but are used by them to terrorize their subjects.[27]

Ceremonial Life.—Ceremonies are more numerous and elaborate in Uganda than elsewhere in Central Africa.[28] They are fostered by the political and economic inequalities,[29] the density of population, and the dullness of the life. Where the life is dull and the population dense there is a strong impulse in the privileged class to impress the masses through ceremony, and a readiness of the masses to join in them.[30] These ceremonies concern the preparing and eating of food, the family relations, the behavior of one class towards another, the proceedings at the court, the worship of the gods, and the interment of the dead. The sultan of Karagwé, observed Grant, would not drink out of a vessel that we or any commoner had used,[31] and no one would drink milk from a cow used by Grant for fear that his boiling the milk might bewitch the cow.[32] Besides the marriage ceremony,[33] wives and children must observe certain

27 Schweinitz, p. 104.
28 Stanley, "In Darkest Africa," I, p. 409.
29 Johnston, "Uganda Protectorate," p. 685.
30 Cooley, "Social Organization," p. 186.
31 Page 139.
32 Page 167.
33 Stuhlmann, p. 183.

formalities of respect to the head of the family. Friends and strangers have polite forms of greeting. "The salutation of the Uganda," says Long, "is very peculiar. As two persons meet, the word 'Ouangah' is responded to by 'Oh hi' which continues from an elevated voice to a lower tone until it becomes scarcely audible; then, and not till then, does the conversation commence."[34] A peasant passing an acquaintance says "Kulungi," meaning it is well. When strangers meet the greeting takes the form of a dialogue of inquiry about health, and news, and ends in a series of grunts.[35]. The natives of Uganda, says Tucker, display innate politeness. They express thanks for work done by slaves or other persons. A traveler is greeted by the expression, "I congratulate you on your journey."[36] Strangers, in order to secure fellowship with the natives of outlying tribes, must undergo the ceremony of blood-brotherhood.[37] Monarchs and chiefs go about with a good deal of state. "Thus the monarch," says Stanley, "has always about two score of drummers, a score of pipers, half a score of native guitar players, several mountebanks, clowns, dwarfs, and albinos, a multitude of errand boys, pages, messengers, courtiers, claimants, besides a large number of body-guards, and two standard bearers, either following or proceeding him wherever he goes, to declare his

[34] Page 128.

[35] Johnston, "Uganda Protectorate," p. 686.

[36] I, p. 97.

[37] Grant, p. 271; Stanley, "In Darkest Africa," I, pp. 132, 253.

state and quality. The chiefs, therefore, have also their followers, standard bearers and pages, and so on down to the peasant or cowherd, who makes an infantile slave trot after him to carry his shield and spears."[38]

Love of the spectacular goes along with love of ceremony. In the array of courtiers, and in the gaudiness of dress, the ruling class impress their superiority upon the populace. When Long visited Uganda he saw the king "dresssed in violet-colored silk, embroidered with gold, and wearing a new Egyptian fez."[39]

Æsthetic Life.—In the eastern part of the banana zone, on account of its elevation, the inhabitants wear more clothing than in the western part; and this fact perhaps explains why the tattooing and other mutilations of the body are less practiced in the former region. In Uganda the royal class make a slight cut below the eyes, but do not extract or file the teeth.[40] The same reason explains the less attention given to painting the body.[41] Among some tribes of Uganda, however, body-painting is highly artistic.[42] The body is greased, in some cases with butter, probably as a protective substitute for clothing. In the matter of decorations, the people of this zone vie with those of any other. Personal ornaments are not so generally worn, but where they

38 "Through the Dark Continent," I, p. 409.
39 Page 113.
40 Grant, p. 174.
41 Stuhlmann, p. 175.
42 Johnston, Lydekker, et al., p. 432.

are at all the fashion, they reach an absurd extreme. For example, important people wear huge masses of wire on their ankles.[43] A woman of Mpororo was seen wearing 216 rings on one leg.[44] Perhaps wire and iron rings are a kind of cash, and are carried round the limbs as a substitute for pockets and safety-vaults. At any rate, Carlile believes that ornament was the first money and savings bank.[45]

The decorative impulse seems to be more expended on tools, utensils, weapons, idols, etc., than is usual with the African Negro. The Uganda implements and ware are carefully and beautifully made.[46]

The dress approximates closely to that of civilized people. The natives wear mostly togas of white calico, but some of them preserve the traditional dress of goat-skins and native bark-cloth.[47] The men used to wear a toga of bark-cloth, varying in color from salmon to brick red,[48] and the women the same material, girded around the waist, and sometimes carrying a friezed cow-skin reaching from waist to ankle.[49] In both sexes, says Tucker, the dress "is extremely picturesque."[50] In the outlying districts the clothing seems to diminish in

43 Grant, p. 168.
44 Weiss, p. 328.
45 Page 293.
46 Stuhlmann, p. 176.
47 Grant, p. 186; Johnston, "Uganda Protectorate," p. 833.
48 Grant, p. 233.
49 *Ibid.*, p. 179.
50 I, p. 94.

quantity and quality. Among the Bavuma, an island people of Lake Victoria, the men still wear the bark-cloth, knotted over the shoulder and flowing gracefully to the ground, while the women wear only a banana leaf.[51] In some districts a skin loin-cloth is used, and in others, for instance, a district north of Lake Victoria, both sexes work in the field in a state of complete nudity.[52] The native cotton cloth does not penetrate the forest.[53]

Dancing seems not so fashionable here as among the West Africans, and is indulged in almost exclusively by the men. "The women form one line," says Cunningham, "and opposite them the men in another line with bells attached to their feet. The men prance about a bit, and do a good deal of bell-jingling; the women, standing in the opposite line, merely throw up their hands and clap at certain parts of the dance. This is kept up for hours at a time."[54]

Uganda is a land of music and musicians. It possesses a great variety of native musical instruments, such as the drum, horn, rattles, bells, flute, harp, etc.,[55] with many additions since the introduction of European civilization. "Every little goat-herd has his flute," says Tucker, "and almost every other man who walks along the road is playing on a

51 Cunningham, p. 130.

52 Johnston, "Uganda Protectorate," p. 47.

53 Ankermann, p. 62.

54 Page 35.

55 Long, p. 127; Johnston, "Uganda Protectorate," p. 113; Grant, p. 186.

reed flageolet."[56] Chaillé Long once charmed the court circles by a music box which played "Dixie," and "Tramp, Tramp, Tramp, the Boys are Marching."[57] The natives are very fond of singing,[58] and a professional class of singers is employed by the king to enliven his court. The æsthetic sense of the Negro seems to be strongest in regions of bountiful resources near the equator where there is little to occupy the attention.[59] In regions demanding more struggle for existence the attention is directed more into other lines. Civilized people are less æsthetic than savages, i. e., they are less absorbed in the sensitive life. In the character of the æsthetic manifestations the civilized people are, of course, far ahead of the savage. The æsthetic contrast between the high and low races is forcibly brought out in Ruskin's "Two Paths."

Psychological Life.—Information in regard to the cranial capacity of the people of this region is too meager for any positive statements. In a general way it may be said that the cranial capacity of the Central African Bantu is smaller than that of the southern branches of the same race. According to Shrubsall, the Central African cranium has a capacity of 1,430 c. c. and the Kafir cranium a capacity of 1,540 c. c.[60] Whether this difference has anything to do with the intelligence of the two peoples, it is

[56] I, p. 98.
[57] Page 114.
[58] Johnston, "Uganda Protectorate," p. 833.
[59] Johnston, Lydekker, et al., p. 473.
[60] "Notes on Crania," p. 257.

certain that the Kafir is far superior in intelligence to the Bantus of Central Africa. Among the Central African Bantus, however, the Waganda are superior to any other division; and this superiority is partly due to mixture of blood with the Bahima.

The Waganda generally show less pugnacity and more self-abasement than the Niam-Niam or Monbuttu, and fully as much of the gregarious instinct as any other Africans. They have less foresight than the people of the agricultural zones to the north and south of them. Thanks to the bounty of nature, they have little need of that faculty. In mechanical skill they show considerable aptness, and in cunning and fraud they exhibit the keenest intelligence. In the opinion of Stanley, "Their cloths are of a finer make, their habitations are better and neater; their spears are the most perfect, I should say, in Africa; and they exhibit extraordinary skill and knowledge of that deadly weapon; their shields are such as would attract admiration in any land, while the canoes surpass all canoes in the savage world."[61] At the time of Stanley's visit the emperor and his court could read and write in Arabic.[62]

The Waganda are more emotional than the Niam-Niam or Kafir. Their feelings and passions exercise a more despotic sway over conduct. What they will do, therefore, is not calculable, and it is on this

61 "Through the Dark Continent," I, p. 410.
62 *Ibid.*, p. 410.

account that they have to be governed despotically.[63] It follows from this emotionalism that the people have a weak inhibiting power. This deficiency is a common characteristic of the Negro everywhere, because of the dominion which his feelings exercise over his will. Several eminent scholars, however, have attempted to maintain, to the contrary, that the Negro has rather remarkable power of inhibition. They cite as evidence a long list of taboos on food, the customs of sexual abstinence by women during the period of gestation and nursing, etc. But it is difficult to see how these taboos and abstinences have any connection with the power of inhibition. In the first place, many of the food restrictions are prohibitions imposed by the king and aristocracy, in the interest of monopolistic privilege, and do not represent any voluntary inhibition by the abstainer. In the second place, the sexual continence of married women, and other customs of abstinence, are not inhibitions in the ordinary acceptation of the term. Among civilized people this power means the voluntary postponement of some enjoyment for a greater future satisfaction. We choose to inhibit our present desire or appetite, knowing that we are perfectly free to do so, and that the penalty for not doing so is want and suffering inflicted by ourselves. Contrary to this, the inhibitions of the savage are not voluntary, and do not arise out of measuring the present against the future. In every case the inhibition is either the re-

[63] Stanley, "Through the Dark Continent," I, p. 408.

sult of fear of immediate harm from some person or spirit. The savage believes that if he violates a taboo he will be immediately punished, probably by death.[64] Abstinence from women, says Sumner, is due to the fear of demons.[65] Of the Muganda people of Africa, Johnston says, "if they ate forbidden food they would suffer something like a loss of caste . . . become covered with sores."[66] Hence this suppression of the present desire does not represent any foresight or value placed upon the future. It no more illustrates inhibiting power than the refusal of a civilized man to put his finger in the fire, or to swallow a deadly poison. Lack of inhibition is not only characteristic of the Negro but of the inefficient elements of all races.

The imagination of the Waganda is very much inflamed by terror. It peoples the forest and streams with ghosts and demons, and these become the all-absorbing center of attention. Like a fever patient in delirium, the people see everything in an abnormal and distorted form. They attribute to their deities monstrous shapes and characteristics. Their imagination is constantly employed to invent myths to explain their deities and to devise means of conjuring them. Buckle would call this a case of the imagination predominating over the reason. But these two terms cannot be set in opposition, because all reasoning involves the play of

64 Marett, 202.
65 "Folkways," p. 511.
66 "Uganda Protectorate," p. 691.

the imagination. And the play of the imagination is a process of reasoning. Even dreams, according to some modern psychologists, are the effort of reason to put in logical connection the floating ideas that appear to man in his half-conscious state. The effort of the savage imagination to explain the phenomena around him, by the invention of myth and a world of spirits whom he must win over or circumvent, is the first beginning of that interpretation of nature which later results in the flowering of every science and philosophy.

The Waganda belong in Ribot's category of the emotional type,[67] or according to Giddings the idio-emotional type, characterized by lack of self-control and deliberation, and lack of the habit of attaining ends by indirect means.[68] Emotionalism is developed among a people whose struggle for existence is so easy that the higher faculties of the mind have no chance to develop.[69] Emotionalism is also favored among a people whose interests are few, and subject to very irregular excitement. A dull, inactive life, having few and rare excitements is sure to promote an explosive disposition; whereas an active life of varied and frequent excitements promotes discipline and control. The emotional excitement of the people, their fear of evil spirits, and of their neighbors, throw them frequently into a mood of agitation.[70]

67 Page 395.

68 "Inductive Sociology," pp. 139, 140.

69 Buckle, I, Ch. II.

70 Williams, p. 744; Ribot, pp. 388, 394.

In the family circle the people of this zone display the virtues common to human nature everywhere, and sometimes exhibit heroic devotion. An example of such devotion is mentioned by Swann in the case of the rescue of a boy who was seized by a crocodile while playing in Lake Tanganyika. "The lad's brother, who was standing on the shore, seeing his brother in trouble, without the least hesitation leaped into the water, amongst the screaming boys, and dealt the crocodile a heavy blow with his axe. This made him release the boy, who was promptly dragged on shore. Blood-poisoning set in and he died."[71] Lying is not common between members of the same group or rank.[72]

Outside the family circle there is little consideration for anybody. The poorness of communication prevents any consciousness of solidarity over a wide area, and, outside of a small circle of kin or neighbors, everybody is a stranger and enemy for whom there is little sympathy. It is not surprising, then, that the Waganda should be characterized as crafty, deceitful, thievish knaves, and as loving gain by robbery and violence,[73] and loving their enemies —cooked.[74] Vanity is a marked trait.[75]

The Waganda cannot be said to possess courage. They sometimes fall into a frenzy and act with desperation, but the cool courage that weighs the con-

71 Page 226.
72 Schweinitz, p. 106.
73 Stanley, "Through the Dark Continent," I, p. 408.
74 Cureau, p. 642.
75 Stanley, "Through the Dark Continent," I, p. 409.

sequences, and is spurred on by group sentiment, is absent. This deficiency is generally characteristic of the Negro, and differentiates him from the American Indian. The contrast is illustrated in the folklore of the two races. In the animal stories of the Indians, for instance, man nearly always overcomes the beast by a bold struggle; while in the similar stories of the Negro the beast usually gets the better of the man, or is outdone by magic. Stories of encounter between man and beast are, indeed, rare in Africa. Of the Central African folklore Hobley says, "The general type of the story is usually the meeting of a savage animal with a harmless one, and the eventual triumph of the harmless one by some simple trick."[76]

Contact with Europeans has done much to lift the Waganda from their savagery. It has diminished wars, human sacrifices, trial by ordeal, and reformed the administration of justice.[77] Many mission schools have Christianized and enlightened the masses. It is claimed that 200,000 of the natives can read and write. In religious, as in other innovations, however, the transformation has apparently been too sudden, and not always adapted to native psychology. Bishop Tucker of Uganda remarked that, "Were I asked to give my opinion as to what, in my estimation, has most hindered the development and independence of the native churches I should unhesitatingly answer, that deep-

[76] Page 337.

[77] Johnston, "Uganda Protectorate," pp. 277, 280.

rooted tendency which there is in the Anglo-Saxon character to Anglicize everything with which it comes in contact."[78] Every religion must be modified in form, if not in substance, to suit local conditions, says Montesquieu, "and when Montezuma with so much obstinacy insisted that the religion of the Spaniards was good for their country, and his for Mexico, he did not assert an absurdity."[79] What the final outcome may be of European influence upon the Waganda is difficult to predict. It will be an exception to the rule, however, if the native population does not die out as a result of civilized innovations. The Waganda were already on the rapid decline under the influence of Mohammedanism, and the European came just in time to prevent them from dying out from "premature debauchery."[80] Will the European civilization reverse the trend or hasten the extermination? Some writers claim that the Negroes of the tropics can never be exterminated because they are necessary to do the field work for which the white man is unfitted.[81] But the fact is that the white man, with his knowledge of sanitation, can live in any climate that any other race can live in.

78 Anti-Slavery Reporter, November-December, 1897, p. 259.
79 "Spirit of Laws," II, p. 127.
80 Johnston, "Uganda Protectorate," p. 640.
81 Semple, p. 114.

CHAPTER XIV

THE BANTUS OF THE WESTERN BANANA ZONE

General Description of the Zone.—The western banana zone is, in some important particulars, different from that of the east. In the first place, it is much lower in altitude, forming for the most part a low basin, little above sea level, except in the Kameruns where a few mountains rise to a considerable height. It is an area of great rainfall, and multitudinous rivers, and lakes of "inky-black slime" that lie "like a rotten serpent twisted between the mangroves."[1] Along the water courses and swamps vegetation takes the form of gigantic forests so interlaced and dark as to prevent any undergrowth.[2] "From the summits of trees," says Miss Kingsley, hang "great bushropes, some as straight as plumb lines, others coiled around and intertwined among each other, until one could fancy one was looking on some mighty battle between armies of gigantic serpents."[3] But the aspect of the forest is not altogether unpleasing. "Many of the highest trees," says Miss Kingsley, "are covered with

[1] Kingsley, "Travels in West Africa," p. 237.
[2] Kingsley, "Travels in West Africa," p. 200.
[3] *Ibid.*, p. 201.

brown-pink young shoots that look like flowers, and others are decorated by my enemy the climbing palm, now bearing clusters of bright, crimson berries. Climbing plants of other kinds are wreathing everything, some blossoming with mauve, some with yellow and some with white flowers, and every now and then a soft sweet breath of fragrance comes out to us as we pass by."[4] However, Miss Kingsley thinks that there are too many mosquitoes and sandflies in the scenery,[5] and too often the atmosphere is three-fourths solid stench from putrifying ooze.[6]

Along the river slopes, where the soil is drained, the vegetation is not so dense, and there the people can make a clearing and cultivate a few plants.

The fauna include the elephant, hippopotamus, crocodile, buffalo, antelope, porcupine, bear, gorilla, and many animals of the smaller kind.[7] Along water courses one sees crocodiles sprawling in all directions with mouth wide open, and in all of the pools, the hippopotamus snorts and wallows.[8] The country is full of birds, great and small. Flocks of pelican and crane rise out of the grass, says Miss Kingsley, "and the hornbills, about the size of a turkey-hen, carry on long confabulations with each other across the river, and I believe, sit up half the night and talk scandal."[9] If you walk across the

[4] *Ibid.*, p. 85.
[5] *Ibid.*, p. 90.
[6] *Ibid.*, p. 238.
[7] Ratzel, III, p. 117; Kingsley, "Travels in West Africa," p. 206.
[8] Kingsley, "Travels in West Africa," p. 182.
[9] "Travels in West Africa," p. 175.

forest, "jiggers" get in your feet, and if you wade the streams, leeches cling to you, and if you lie down to sleep large centipedes and scorpions drop on your bed.[10]

Inhabitants.—The inhabitants of this part of the banana zone are the Bantu, already mentioned in Chapter XII as occupying almost the entire area of Central and Southern Africa. They are homogeneous in the common linguistic characteristic of exclusive use of prefixes rather than by common physiognomy. A few tribes of this zone seem to show traces of Caucasian mixture. For example, the Balbua [11] and the Ababua, neighbors of the Zandeh, have some resemblance to the white race, and are lauded for their physical beauty.[12] The Balolo, in the bend of the Congo, show a refined type of face and light color of skin.[13] But the most remarkable people of the Central Congo (the northern bend) are the Bayanzi, Bangala, Ngombe, etc., who have very decided Caucasian features.[14] As the traveler goes inland from the West Coast he meets an improved type of men of a lighter color.[15] Probably this mixture of white blood has resulted from an invasion of the Libyans into this region in the remote past. The climate, no doubt, has had something to do with the lighter color of some of these tribes. The darkest

[10] *Ibid.*, pp. 150, 242, 173.
[11] Wolf, p. 728.
[12] Johnston, "George Grenfell and the Congo," II, p. 512.
[13] *Ibid.*, p. 525.
[14] *Ibid.*, p. 528.
[15] Ratzel, III, p. 106; Ward, p. 289.

Negroes are not found directly under the equator, but in the less forested regions where the sun's rays are less hidden by cloud and foliage.[16] The dark complexion is due to the thickening of the pigment of the skin as a protection against the injurious effects of the short rays of the sun.[17] The most interesting people of this zone are the Fan. They are a fine race, especially in the mountain districts of Sierra del Cristal, where one sees magnificent specimens of human beings, male and female. They are tall powerful people, of dark brown color, often with regular features.[18] Taking the Bantu as a whole, however, they form a decided Negro type, differing from the Nigritians by a somewhat shorter stature, (undeveloped legs among the riverain tribes, due to living much in boats), less elongated head, less prognathism, and less flattened nose.[19] They all resemble Alexander the Great in emitting a strong odor.[20] The Bantu race originated probably in the central western part of this zone somewhere southeast of Lake Chad. They were pushed south by invaders probably coming from the west. Johnston thinks that the dispersion began about 2,000 years ago.[21] Their original home was relatively a restricted area, which nowhere exceeded

16 Boshart, p. 98; Semple, p. 39.

17 Woodruff, "The Effects of Tropical Light upon the White Man," p. 88.

18 Kingsley, "Travels in West Africa," pp. 137, 266.

19 Deniker, p. 458.

20 Montaigne's Essay "Of Smells."

21 "British Central Africa," p. 480.

the limits of the banana zone. "The slighter the inner differences in an ethnic stock," says Semple, "whether in culture, language or physical traits, the smaller was their center of distribution and the more rapid their dispersal. The small initial habitat restricts the chances of variation through isolation and contrasted geographic conditions, as does also the short duration of their subsequent separation. . . . The distribution of the Bantu dialects over so wide a region in Central Africa, and with such slight divergences, presupposes narrow limits both of space and time for their origin, and a short period since their dispersal."[22]

Economic Life.—The people of this western banana zone are fundamentally vegetarians.[23] They subsist mostly upon the banana, plantain, and the oil-palm.[24] These plants grow spontaneously, though they are to some extent cultivated. In small clearings other products are grown, such as the yam, sweet potato, maize, pumpkin, pineapple, manioc, etc.[25] No natural races, however, are vegetarians from choice. They supplement their farinaceous diet by whatever animal resource is available. On account of the tsetse fly cattle and horses do not thrive, and the only domestic fauna are the goat, dog and

[22] Page 123.

[23] Wolf, p. 237.

[24] Overbergh, p. 67; Johnston, "George Grenfell and the Congo," I, p. 605; Milligan, p. 140; Kingsley, "Travels in West Africa," p. 151.

[25] Kingsley, "Travels in West Africa," pp. 151, 153; Overbergh, p. 68; Milligan, p. 115.

fowl.[26] None of these is plentiful or well treated. The eggs that a traveler is likely to find, says Miss Kingsley, are more fit for electioneering purposes than for anything else.[27] Some of the tribes eat the dog.[28] The chase is the main reliance for meat, and the chief joy and occupation of the men. On account of its hazards the men are obliged to hunt in large bands. When a herd of elephants or buffaloes is located the chief of the tribe sounds his drum and the men of the surrounding villages assemble for the hunt. The products of the chase are apportioned by the chief among the hunters, the lion's share, including the ivory, being retained by the chief himself. The big game, unfortunately, is not always abundant, and during the long intervals when it cannot be found the hunters fall back upon the small and timid fauna, such as the antelope, and even snakes and insects. The Fan eat stink-fish (dried-fish), snails, snakes, and a big maggot like the pupæ of the rhinoceros beetle;[29] and still not satisfied they eat human flesh. In this zone, as elsewhere in Central Africa, says Stanley, it is quite common for the natives to rush upon their enemies crying "meat! meat!"[30] A Belgian missionary of the Upper Congo wrote that, "on a market day, it is customary to take prisoners of war up and down with marks on their naked bodies, showing the parts the purchasers have se-

26 Hahn, Edward, p. 462.
27 "Travels in West Africa," p. 29.
28 Overbergh, p. 99.
29 Kingsley, "Travels in West Africa," p. 151.
30 "Through the Dark Continent," II, p. 201.

lected, as soon as the bodies are cut up. . . . One case is mentioned in which no purchaser could be found for the man's head, and the buyers of the arms and legs became impatient, and these were accordingly cut off, and the vender proceeded with his search for a purchaser of the head.''[31] Tribes on the Muhangi River used to breed slaves for the food-market.[32] The Fan often preserve some part of the people they have eaten as a memento. Miss Kingsley found in a hut, stinking and hanging up in a bag, three big toes, four eyes, two ears, and other parts of the human frame.[33] A Fan will eat his next door neighbor's relations, and sell his own deceased to his next-door neighbor in return, but he does not buy slaves and fatten them up for his table as some of the Middle Congo tribes do.''[34]

The Fan make a variety of rude pottery in the shape of cooking pots, palm-wine bottles, pipes, etc. They also make fish-hooks of bamboo, string made of pineapple fiber, fiber-plaited jugs, baskets and nets. They make excellent canoes, and do good work in iron, manufacturing knives, axes, spades and ornamental rings.[35]

Local trade is carried on at market towns on fixed days of the week, and attended by pretty much all

[31] *Missionary Review of the World,* I, p. 879.

[32] Johnston, "George Grenfell and the Congo," II, p. 686.

[33] "Travels in West Africa," p. 212.

[34] *Ibid.,* p. 299.

[35] Kingsley, "Travels in West Africa," pp. 258, 259, 260; Bennett, pp. 76, 83.

of the population.[36] Transactions are made by barter, cowry shells and beads.[37] Most natives are natural traders. Formerly ivory and slaves were the chief articles of commerce, but they are now superseded by rubber and palm-oil.

Many lines of steam launches serve commerce on the rivers, and several railroads, besides the Congo, connect the coast and the interior. These, however, concern mostly the white man. So far as the natives are concerned the highways are mostly goat tracks, and the transportation is by porters and canoes. In moving from one place to another a family needs no van. The "wives just pick up the stools and knives, and the cooking pots, and the box (for clothes), and the children toddle along with the calabashes."[38] In districts of much bush, tunnels have to be cut for the carriers.

Generally the women do all of the work except the hunting. They act as porters, carrying goods to market in baskets balanced on their heads. The men sometimes help to clear the fields, but the work of cultivation is left to the women.[39] The industrial limitations of the Fan are due to the bounty of nature, on the one hand, which renders economic development unnecessary, and on the other hand, to the ease of moving from place to place, thanks to the absence of any insuperable geographical bar-

36 Ward, Herbert, p. 290.

37 Johnston, "George Grenfell and the Congo," II, p. 796; Milligan, p. 141.

38 Kingsley, "Travels in West Africa," p. 99.

39 Overbergh, p. 68.

riers. A territory without natural boundaries, says Semple, "obviates the necessity of applying more work and more intelligence to the old area. Hence dispersion takes the place of intensification of industry."[40]

Slaveholding scarcely exists among the Fan or other nomadic hunters of this zone. Among the more settled populations, engaged somewhat in trade and agriculture, slaves may be found, but they are not relatively numerous, for the reason that there is no regular work for them. Since the recent exploitation of the country by the white man there has developed a considerable wage-class. Formerly war-captives were either eaten or sold. The chief often bought children from his own subjects in times of famine, and would resell them to the slave trader who came around periodically with his caravan of cloth, beads, rum and trinkets.[41] Among some of the settled tribes, who use slaves to cultivate the soil, we see the transition from the wandering life to a regular social order where production is systematic. Without slavery it is difficult to see how this transition could have been made. Slavery, therefore, as Sumner remarks, "is a part of the discipline by which the human race has learned how to carry on the industrial organization."[42] Dealey regards primitive slavery as a benevolent institution, because it arose as a substitute for cannibalism, massacre and torture.[43]

40 Page 213.

41 Préville, p. 184.

42 "Folkways," p. 263.

43 "Sociology," p. 101.

CHAPTER XV

THE BANTUS OF THE WESTERN BANANA ZONE (*continued*)

Family Life.—Marriage is often by capture,[1] but is more generally effected by gifts to the girl's parents.[2] For a fine Bangala girl the price is "two or three slaves, two or three necklaces of beads, and two or three empty bottles."[3] Near the West Coast girls of rare qualities, according to Milligan, sometimes command an exorbitant price, in some cases amounting to ten goats, five sheep, five guns, twenty empty trade-boxes, one hundred heads of tobacco, ten hats, ten looking-glasses, five blankets, five pair of trousers, two dozen plates, fifty dollars' worth of calico, fifty dollars' worth of rum, one chair and one cat. Men secure this dowry sometimes by the sale of a sister. Very young girls or infants are less expensive[4] and the marriage of these is frequent.[5]

As a rule marriage is not permitted between men and women of the same clan, and the Bulu do not

1 Johnston, "George Grenfell and the Congo," II, p. 676.
2 Ward, Herbert, p. 289.
3 Overbergh, p. 213.
4 Milligan, pp. 225, 227, 230.
5 Ward, Herbert, p. 289; Overbergh, p. 215; Kingsley, "Travels in West Africa," p. 165.

permit it within the village.[6] A Fan is obliged to marry into his own clan as no other clan is handy to marry into, and, in villages in touch with other clans, he has little chance of getting a cheap lady. All tribes look down on the Fans and they on all others. The Fans marry freely with people who closely resemble them, for example, the Bakele to the southeast.[7]

Polygamy is practiced by all the men who can afford it, but most men are able to possess only one wife.[8] The Fan, says Miss Kingsley, acquires rubber and buys a "good tough widow lady (they are cheap), who knows the lore of trade and art of adultery, and later buys younger wives to the number of six or seven." He settles down on an estate, and receives a percentage on the ivory trade.[9] The chiefs everywhere possess several wives.[10] Before marriage a girl bestows her favors pretty freely.[11]

The houses occupied by most of the families in this zone are made of banana leaves,[12] circular in form, with conical roof, but houses of the rectangular shape are common in the west. The Fan houses are of this latter kind, constructed of bark, fifteen feet long, ten wide and six high, and arranged along a

6 Milligan, p. 220; Johnston, "George Grenfell and the Congo," p. 676.

7 Kingsley, "Travels in West Africa," p. 256.

8 Milligan, p. 226.

9 "Travels in West Africa," p. 258.

10 Johnston, "George Grenfell and the Congo," II, p. 676.

11 Bennett, p. 70.

12 Johnston. "George Grenfell and the Congo," II, p. 752.

single street, closed at either end by a guard-house.[13] A special house is built in the middle of the town where goats are herded at night as a protection against leopards.[14] The surroundings of the Fan home are exceedingly filthy. One sees lying about, the remains of a crocodile eaten week before last, and piles of fish offal, and the decomposing remnants of the elephant, hippopotamus, etc.[15] The furniture most common consists only of a bed of pole framework, and several wooden pillows. A fire is built in the center of the house, and the smoke escapes through the openings between the roof and the wall.[16]

The support of the family devolves mostly upon the women, but in some tribes the men assist. A man of the Fan tribe, for instance, will chop wood, carry the baby, help build houses, weave baskets and make pottery.[17]

Affection between husband and wife in this zone is about as feeble as anywhere in the world. Intrigue and infidelity are the occasions of frequent palavers.[18] The wife is an artist in the use of poison,[19] and, for this or some other reason, the husband disdains to eat with her. He lends his wife to strangers, and in case of his illness he will ask a

13 Bennett, p. 72; Milligan, p. 220.
14 Kingsley, "Travels in West Africa," p. 213.
15 *Ibid.*, p. 188.
16 Milligan, p. 221.
17 Kingsley, "Travels in West Africa," p. 259.
18 Bennett, p. 70.
19 Milligan, p. 149.

friend to assume his marital relations. Husbands and wives often conspire together to tempt men to adultery. Custom requires the husband and wife to live apart during the lactation period, but both of them then intrigue with others.[20]

Parental love is ardent but of short duration.[21] Abortion is common, and children are often weaned rapidly for the purpose of killing them.[22] A woman rarely has more than two or three living children.[23] Children sometimes show a lasting love for their mother, but generally their regard for either parent is slight. On account of the hunting and fighting, boys are more under the control of the chief than of the parents. Old men are seldom met with. They are either sacrificed in witchcraft proceedings, or allowed to starve when unable to provide for themselves.[24]

Generally inheritance is in the female line, i. e., the property goes to the brothers or sisters.[25] In some cases a man's estate goes to his maternal uncle. In the northern bend of the Congo the property of a chief or freeman goes to his youngest son, and, under certain circumstances, to the eldest.[26]

Political Life.—Although the people of this zone

20 Milligan, pp. 224, 227, 232.

21 *Ibid.*, p. 223.

22 Johnston, "George Grenfell and the Congo," II, p. 671.

23 Overbergh, p. 201.

24 Ward, p. 290.

25 Kingsley, "Travels in West Africa," p. 259; Johnston, "George Grenfell and the Congo," II, p. 697.

26 Johnston, *Ibid.*, p. 699.

subsist principally upon vegetation, they do not live scattered as individual families, but in villages. The abundant food-supply permits this concentration. Along the river courses the villages have from fifty to one hundred inhabitants,[27] and in the more elevated districts, where the banana grows to better advantage, the population of a village runs up to two thousand.[28] The difficulties of communication hinder confederation or effective political control, so that in this zone the kingdoms, except in a few instances, are small.[29] There is often a lack of integration among members of the same tribe.[30] Riverain people know nothing of the country ten miles inland. Life here is largely a battle of individual with individual.[31] Tribal groups are held together by common totem rather than by mutual interest. The totem, says Tylor, has a great power "in consolidating clans, and allying them together within the larger circle of the tribe." [32] While there is considerable pressure of immigration from the zones north and south, it comes in the form of small unobtrusive bands, and does not excite a coöperative defensive movement. The forests, rivers and

27 Milligan, p. 220.

28 Ratzel, III, p. 112.

29 Johnston, "George Grenfell and the Congo," II, p. 700; Boshart, p. 101.

30 Wolf, p. 236; Milligan, p. 233.

31 Schrader, "Echanges d'activité entre la terre et l'homme." *Revue mensuelle de l'école d'anthropologie*, VI, p. 25.

32 "Remarks on Totemism," Jour. Anthropological Institute, I, n. s., p. 148.

swamps furnish a large measure of natural fortification. The same difficulties that impede invasion also serve to check aggression on a large scale. There is, therefore, no development of an efficient military system, and no foreign conquests.[33] The Fan protect their villages by poisoned splinters of reed stuck in the ground or in the forest streams.[34]

Government here is little above the primary group dominated by the male, but, as rudimentary as it is, it constitutes a discipline for its members, and leads to "that power of self-control and law-abidingness which was the essential condition of the progress of social organization."[35] Such government as exists probably arose from leadership in the chase. The chief, being youthful and lacking in wisdom, knows no discipline save that of tyranny. Stealing of women is a prime cause of war,[36] and when that event happens the chief sounds the same drum that summons the men to the hunt, and the signal is repeated from village to village.[37] The nomadic life, due to the caprice of the game and the exhaustion of the patches of cultivated ground, renders the kingdoms ephemeral and in a state of constant clash and disintegration. The kingdoms dissolve by dispersion and incursion made easy by the wide interstices between villages. "The rapid decline of the Indian race in America before the advancing whites," says Semple, "was due chiefly to

33 Ratzel, III, pp. 47, 136.
34 *Ibid.*, II, p. 398.
35 McDougall, p. 286.
36 Milligan, p. 238.
37 Préville, p. 181.

the division of the savages into small groups, scattered sparsely over a wide territory."[38]

The machinery of governments in this zone is, therefore, very imperfectly organized. Personal injuries are left to private revenge,[39] and violence is so common that all men go armed.[40] Each citizen carries on his left side a long two-edged sword-knife, sheathed in a python skin and suspended from a shoulder strap of leopard or monkey-skin.[41] Under these circumstances it is not surprising that old men should be scarce.[42] Among the Kamerun tribes a chief does not consider himself installed until he has killed one or more men, and distributed parts of their bodies among his kin and neighboring chiefs.[43] In case the government takes notice of an injury, the trial is before the chief and council of elders at the palaver house at the end of the street, and the decisions are often determined by ordeal or other device of chance.[44] Secret societies, very common in this part of Africa, are the right hand of government—a discipline of terror to keep women, children and slaves under subjection. The head of each of these societies is a magician who can discover witches or other culprits by his power of vi-

38 Page 80.
39 Kingsley, "Travels in West Africa," p. 231.
40 Ward, Herbert, p. 291.
41 Milligan, p. 134.
42 Bennett, p. 70.
43 Ratzel, III, p. 131.
44 Johnston, "George Grenfell and the Congo," II, p. 688; Milligan, p. 221.

sion or dreaming. When he points to the one he regards as guilty the verdict is arrived at by ordeal.[45] Secret societies probably originated from the too wide expansion of the clan, and the distribution of its members in localities separated from each other by geographical barriers. The clan or totem ceremonies of initiation, etc., were preserved by the isolated groups, and merged into a secret society to rule over those not belonging in the kinship group but belonging to the territory.[46] In some localities each village is held responsible for a wrong committed by any of its members.[47]

Hereditary chieftainship is exceptional, but where it exists the succession usually goes to the eldest son of the chief's sister.[48]

Religious Life.—The religion of this zone is a mixture of fetichism and polytheism. In the larger villages there are a few common gods, but in most localities the phenomena of nature are ruled by multitudes of spirits that have no general recognition.[49] In most localities the people do not conceive that their life depends upon the distant and uncontrollable forces of nature, as the sun, moon, the clouds, and overflow of rivers, but upon the forces close at hand, such as those which govern the movement of game, the behavior of dangerous beasts, reptiles, insects, the ripening of fruits, berries and vegetables. The important deities, therefore, are also near at

45 Milligan, p. 234.
46 Marett, pp. 177, 178.
47 Milligan, p. 236.
48 Ward, Herbert, p. 290.
49 Bennett, p. 85; Overbergh, p. 269.

hand instead of being far away in the sky, as is generally the case among pastoral and agricultural people. Some tribes have a sky god—a sort of supreme being, but he is too far off to care for humanity, and he leaves things pretty much to a host of mundane spirits who act with a will of their own.[50] The latter are mostly malevolent or mischievous. They are human, however, and can be coaxed into having creditable feelings like generosity and gratitude, but you can't trust them.[51] The reason that led the primitive man to give attention first to the wicked spirits was that he, "like ourselves, was apt to accept without wonder, without pondering and reasoning upon them, the beneficent processes of nature, the gentle rain, the light and warmth of the sun, the flowing of the river, the healthy growth of animal and vegetable life, but that his wonder was especially aroused by those things and events which excited also his fear, by disease and death, pestilence and famine, storm and flood, lightning and thunder, and the powerful beasts of prey."[52]

These multitudinous spirits have to be reckoned with in almost every transaction of life. They are controlled largely by charms whose power is, in fact, that of a counteracting spirit. A good supply of charms is consequently necessary for hunting, fishing, buying, planting, etc. Certain charms, for instance, will protect you from being seen by an ele-

[50] Johnston, "George Grenfell and the Congo," II, pp. 635, 636.
[51] Kingsley, "Travels in West Africa," p. 299.
[52] McDougall, p. 304.

phant.[53] Bells and rattles will scare away snakes when you are in the forest.[54] Other charms enable you to keep in the right path, to see things in the forest,[55] help you in love-making, etc.[56] It is to be observed that the rain-doctor is not needed in this zone. Having no rain to make, the magic-man can devote all of his time to making charms, and to conjuring the malfeasant spirits.

The peopling of the universe with spooks is due primarily to the inability of the savage to comprehend death as a natural fact. The most plausible explanation to the savage is that the spirit, which once animated the body, has escaped, or been driven or coaxed away by some other spirit. The spirit of the dead man, therefore, must continue to live. It is seen in dreams, and its voice is heard in strange sounds.

The attitude towards these spirits is that of fear, and to propitiate them food and drink are offered. This attention to the disembodied spirits leads to ancestor worship, though in its first stages it is characterized by fear of ancestors and not veneration for them. There are probably three stages in the development of ancestor worship. First, the spirits of the dead are feared and coaxed to stay away.[57] According to Miss Kingsley, the prayers of

[53] Kingsley, "Travels in West Africa," p. 304.
[54] *Ibid.*, p. 189.
[55] *Ibid.*, p. 338.
[56] *Ibid.*, p. 304.
[57] Milligan, "The Fetish Folk of West Africa," p. 151.

the people of this zone in substance say, "Go away, we don't want you."[58] Second, an effort is made to manipulate the spirits for some advantage. According to Milligan, some of the Congo tribes manifest an expectation of gain from their ancestors, but not a love for them.[59] The skull of the dead, says Frobenius, is not a *memento mori* of the ancestor, but a mere magic power.[60] Third, the spirits are venerated. This last stage is not reached anywhere in Negro Africa. Man is not very dependable in life, and his spirit is even less so because it is invisible. It is subject to bad influences, and may become positively vicious.

If the spirits of men live after them, so also the spirits of animals, and either may come back to life in the form of another man or beast.[61] Since the spirit in a man lives after he is dead, why may it not sometimes come out of a man while he is still alive, —for example, when he is dreaming? Then the spirits of the dead and the living have a general mix-up and cause trouble.[62] It is possible, says Johnston, "for spirits of dead or living men to enter the bodies of buffaloes, leopards or crocodiles, in order that they may inflict injuries on their enemies."[63] Wilkin thinks that transmigration of souls is the link connecting ancestor worship with to-

[58] "Travels in West Africa," p. 299.
[59] Page 253.
[60] "Die bildende Kunst," p. 4.
[61] Milligan, p. 255.
[62] Johnston, "George Grenfell and the Congo," II, p. 642.
[63] *Ibid.*, p. 632.

temism. When the soul of man comes back in a wolf, for instance, the man's descendants in the course of time naturally come to believe that they originated from the wolf, and they all thus become bound together by ties of totem kinship.[64] Frazer is of opinion that totemism grew out of an attempt to explain paternity before man learned of the part played by him in generation.

Disease and death are due to evil spirits, or witches who are persons in whom a malignant spirit has taken lodgment.[65] In case of a death the people rush into the streets, "with wild staring eyes, uttering imprecations and demanding blood." The witch-doctor is summoned, and indicates the person responsible for the death. The accused must pay damages to the relatives of the deceased, or face a trial by ordeal. A concoction is administered to him or her causing vertigo. If the victim falls it is a sign of guilt, and the bystanders at once cut the body to pieces.[66] In some cases the penalty is mutilation, or tying to a stake at low tide.[67] The Upper Ogowé people sometimes beat a corpse to a pulp to destroy an incarcerated spirit.[68] Even after the death of a cow or goat the witch-doctor is sometimes consulted.[69] Witches may inflict injuries in very mys-

64 Tylor, "Remarks on Totemism," Jour. Anthropological Institute, n. s. vol. I, p. 147.

65 Bennett, p. 95; Milligan, p. 268.

66 Milligan, p. 234.

67 Kingsley, "Travels in West Africa," p. 316.

68 *Ibid.*, p. 330.

69 *Missionary Review of the World*, n. s. VIII, p. 160.

terious ways. They may obtain power over an enemy by possessing a bit of his hair or finger nail.[70]

The medicine man is consulted in all cases of sickness, and his method is, first, protective or prophylactic, i. e., making charms to keep away evil. The charm or fetich is a kind of magic object employed to frighten off obnoxious men and beasts. If a man steal anything where a fetich is placed it will enter into him, and cause him to "swell up and bust."[71] The second method of the medicine man is therapeutic, i. e., administering drugs, and practicing magic rites to exorcise the demon of disease. His method is experimental, like that of the European physician, and in his way he has blazed the path of real medical science.[72]

According to Spencer, the profession of the philosopher, judge, scientist, etc., arose from the primitive medicine man. This theory is plausible but seems to be of doubtful validity. While the medicine man may have taken the lead in these fields of knowledge, he was not alone concerned in them. In this connection Thomas remarks, that "the first form of philosophy is the mythology growing out of the attempt of primitive man to understand such phenomena as echoes, clouds, stars, thunder, wind, shadows, dreams, etc. The creation of a mythology is not the work of a medicine man alone, but the work of the social mind in general. Among the first forms of science are the number, time and

[70] Milligan, p. 263. [71] Milligan, p. 262. [72] Bordier, p. 54.

space conceptions, and a vague body of experimental knowledge growing out of the general activities of the group or the individuals of the group, and essential to the control of these activities, and the development of new and more serviceable habits. The first decision of cases was by old men, and later by men in authority, particularly those to whom preëminent ability, particularly in war, gave uncommon authority; and these were first of all rulers rather than priests.''[73]

The great powers attributed to charms, and to all animate and inanimate objects, indicate that the people of this zone rank both kinds of objects on a level with themselves. And as Lang suggests, perhaps the irrational element in the myths of civilized people is the survival of an epoch in which nature occupied this exalted estimation.[74] According to some African legends, all animals were once men who were turned into beasts because they refused to work.[75]

The wicked spirits are so numerous and busy in this zone that the people cannot afford to employ a medicine man every time one of them becomes harassing. So, as a matter of economy, the people try to pacify the spirits by offering them a place to dwell and some food and drink. An image (mask) or idol is, therefore, made as a lodging place, and near

73 "Source Book for Origins," p. 301.
74 "Myth, Ritual and Religion," p. 41.
75 Richter, p. 180.

it is placed a supply of nourishment. These idols are almost as thick as the forest.[76]

To propitiate the gods human sacrifices are sometimes offered, but more commonly such sacrifices are made for the purpose of furnishing attendants for the deceased in the other world.[77] They are not so common as among the Nigritians of the western part of this zone, probably because the smaller and more nomadic groups do not develop that degree of fear which leads to such practices. The sense of fear grows by contagion of the crowd. A striking difference is found in the fear element in the superstitions of the Fan, and in those of the more sedentary people living in the large villages. "The Fans," says Miss Kingsley, "though surrounded by intensely superstitious tribes, are remarkably free from superstition themselves, taking little or no interest in speculative matters except to get charms to make them invisible to the elephant," etc.[78] An extreme attention to the supernatural is never found among people like the Fan who are mostly nomadic hunters and have to struggle and overcome nature. Another explanation of the more rational conceptions of the Fan is to be found in the fact that they are the descendants of the Gallas of the eastern plateau where superstition is less mixed with terror.

76 Ward, Herbert, p. 288; Milligan, p. 249; Bennett, p. 86; Johnston, "George Grenfell and the Congo," II, p. 637.

77 Overbergh, p. 253.

78 "Travels in West Africa," p. 338.

The myths of the people of this zone pertain to familiar and near objects with which the people have to cope. Remote phenomena such as the sky, the sun and moon, are of little concern. Hunting life is nowhere characterized by the cosmogonic myth but by the myth pertaining to plant and animal.[79]

The daily activities of the Fan are inextricably entangled with their religion, i. e., with their spirit world; and this fact seems to confirm the view of McDougall that in its beginning religion and morality are inseparable. "For the essence of moral conduct," says he, "is the performance of social duty, the duty prescribed by society, as opposed to the mere following of the promptings of egoistic impulses. If we define moral conduct in the broad sense, and this is the only satisfactory definition of it, then, no matter how grotesque and, from our point of view, how immoral the prescribed codes of conduct of the societies may appear to be, we must admit conformity to the code to be moral conduct; and we must admit that religion from its crude beginnings was bound up with morality in some such way as we have briefly sketched; that the two things, religion and morality, were not at first separate and later fused together; but that they were always intimately related, and have reciprocally acted and reacted upon one another throughout the course of their evolution."[80] In Volume I of this

[79] Dewey, "Interpretation of the Savage Mind," quoted in Thomas' "Source Book for Origins," p. 183.

[80] Page 313.

series the author gives his reasons for the belief that religion and morals develop together.[81]

Notions about the after life in this zone are vague. All tribes, however, believe in some kind of future existence. Some of the Kamerun tribes think that it takes nine days for the soul of the deceased to reach the place of eternal rest, and consequently the funeral is not held until the lapse of that time.[82] Some souls go to the sky, some to a dark forest, and some to the bottom of the sea.[83]

81 Page 319. Read on this question Marett, pp. 206, 213.
82 Ratzel, II, p. 373.
83 Johnston, "George Grenfell and the Congo," II, p. 643.

CHAPTER XVI

THE BANTUS OF THE WESTERN BANANA ZONE (*concluded*)

Ceremonial Life.—Ceremonies are not highly developed in this part of the banana zone, on account of the relative smallness of the groups, and the great attention to hunting. Boys on attaining their maturity go through the ceremony of initiation.[1] Strangers entering into a community must submit to the ceremony of blood-brotherhood before they can be considered friends.[2] "A native offering one drink or food always tastes it first himself in your presence to show that it is not poisoned."[3] Some of the social forms are a little odd. For instance, describing the ceremony of greeting among the Fan, Miss Kingsley says that a native woman "took my hand in her two, turned it palm up and spat in it."[4] This spitting formality obtains over a wide area in Central and Eastern Africa. The most elaborate and spectacular display in this zone is found in connection with the many secret societies. They operate to "reënforce the functions of control," or

1 Johnston, "George Grenfell and the Congo," II, p. 665.
2 Ward, Herbert, p. 291.
3 Milligan, p. 270.
4 "Travels in West Africa," p. 227.

rather to take the place of an orderly government.[5] Funerals excite the people to a high degree of emotion, and lead to more or less impressive and prolonged ceremony. In some villages, after the burial of a husband, the widow is driven through fire and flagellation, which ceremony was originally designed to free her from the ghost of her late husband.

Æsthetic Life.—The practice of body mutilation for æsthetic or other purpose is wide-spread in this zone. For instance, the Fan and many tribes of the Congo file to a point their incisor teeth.[6] Tattooing is universal. Sometimes it serves as a tribal mark, and again only as a decoration.[7] In some tribes only the chiefs tattoo. A practice also common among the chiefs is that of wearing long nails as a mark of superiority.[8] The Dwallas pull out their eyelashes which they think sharpens their vision. Piercing the ears for pendants is a popular fashion[9] and women often wear a bamboo or porcupine quill pin in the cartilage of the nose.[10] The human body, not needing a protective dress, is used as a frame for hanging any kind of shining object, or as a background for artistic touches of the paint-brush. Women wear necklaces of gorilla teeth, and loads of

[5] Webster, p. 107.

[6] Ratzel, III, pp. 136, 138; Johnston, "George Grenfell and the Congo," II, p. 571.

[7] Kingsley, "Travels in West Africa," p. 380.

[8] *Ibid.*, p. 170.

[9] Johnston, "George Grenfell and the Congo," II, p. 572.

[10] Bennett, p. 72.

brass bracelets and armlets.[11] The wife of a Bangala chief, Upper Congo, once wore a brass collar weighing twenty-five pounds.[12] The women sometimes wear girdles of woven grass but rarely wear flowers.[13] Painting the body is common in the Congo and elsewhere, the favorite color being vermilion or red.[14]

Barring a few tribes, who go entirely naked (the Bopoto for instance), the dress of the people of this zone consists of bark-cloth or skins.[15] In some localities, while the men dress in bark-cloth, the women scantily clothe themselves with a banana leaf in front, and a reddish-brown tail of fibers behind, a costume resembling that of the Bongo and Niam-Niam,[16] and these garments, says Miss Kingsley, are held together largely by "capillary attraction."[17] Now and then, a native gets a chance to adorn himself with a suit of European goods, and he then reaches the acme of æsthetic happiness. Milligan tells us of a chief who bought a suit of European blue denim, and the next Sunday at the divine service "The old man wore the coat, his wife followed with the trousers, and a grown daughter brought up the rear with the vest."[19]

[11] Kingsley, "Travels in West Africa," pp. 128, 209.

[12] Johnston, "George Grenfell and the Congo," II, p. 588.

[13] Kingsley, "Travels in West Africa," p. 162.

[14] *Ibid.*, p. 121; Johnston, "George Grenfell and the Congo," II, p. 562; Schweinfurth, II, p. 19; Bennett, p. 72.

[15] Ward, Herbert, p. 293; Schultz, p. 144; Bennett, p. 72.

[16] Ratzel, III, p. 137.

[17] "Travels in West Africa," p. 17.

[19] Page 154.

In addition to decorating themselves the people of this zone ornament all of their handiwork—tools, weapons and implements. Among some tribes Stanley observed ivory-tipped oars.

Singing and dancing are enthusiastically enjoyed. The Fan dance to a "rump-a-tump-tump tune-beat of the drum," and singing usually accompanies the dance.[20] The songs are monotonous repetitions of some such phrase as "The leopard caught the monkey's tail."[21] The sexes rarely dance together. The women sing and dance standing in a circle, while the men form a double line and march up and down the streets with bells jingling on their ankles.[22] The Bulu dance is "an amazing and rapid succession of extravagant gestures, grotesque poses, and outrageous contortions."[23] Dances are provided for a betrothal, a marriage, victory in war, for the new moon, for the end of the mourning period,[24] and sometimes they take the form of sport in which rival dancers contest for supremacy. They often last all night.

The chief musical instrument is the drum, and it is used for the dance, and to summon men to hunt and fight. Other instruments are the harp, a lyre, the strings of which are made of palm-leaf fibers, a Pan's pipe carved from wood, a bugle made of a

20 Kingsley, "Travels in West Africa," p. 121; Johnston, "George Grenfell and the Congo," II, p. 714.

21 Milligan, p. 243.

22 Milligan, pp. 244, 246.

23 *Ibid.*, p. 135.

24 Bennett, p. 71; Milligan, p. 245.

buffalo horn or the tooth of an elephant, a zylophone made of a palm-stock, and a variety of rattles and whistles.[25]

Some efforts are made at sculpture and painting. The Kameruns paint the interior walls of their houses, and make and paint figures of clay. The Dwallas used to carve in ivory. Small sculptured amulet figures are common and also sculptured figures of ancestors.[26] Attempts at drawing are rare and very poor.[27]

Psychological Characteristics.—All Bantus show a striking uniformity of skull formation,[28] but, if conditions of life modify the development of the skull and brain, we should expect to find the capacity of the skulls of this zone to be below the Bantu average, on account of the relative uniformity of the environment, and the ease of obtaining a livelihood. And we should also expect the Fan to show a superior capacity to the surrounding aborigines, since they are probably mixed largely with immigrants from the eastern plateau. In fact, the people of this zone appear to represent a variety of types with corresponding differences in intelligence and mental traits.

Generally speaking they show only a moderate

25 Milligan, p. 243; Johnston, "George Grenfell and the Congo," II, p. 722.

26 Frobenius, "Die bildende Kunst der Afrikaner," Mittheilungen der Anthropologischen Gesellschaft, XXVII, pp. 2, 6, 7, 8.

27 Bennett, p. 80.

28 Shrubsall, "A Study of A-Bantu Skulls and Crania," Jour. Anthropological Institute, n. s. V, p. 88.

degree of pugnacity, except in case of the Fan; a strong instinct of repulsion, manifesting itself in hatred of strangers and of neighboring groups; and a strong gregarious instinct. The acquisitive and constructive instincts seem to be almost absent. The sedentary groups are less aggressive and shrewd than the nomadic, and their emotions predominate more over their reason. They are, therefore, more superstitious, and show more self-abasement.

The Fan are a good example of the nomadic type. "Their countenances," says Miss Kingsley, "are very bright and expressive, and if once you have been among them you can never mistake a Fan." They are full of fire and temper, quick to take offense, and utterly indifferent to life. They have shrewd sense, and are unimaginative.[29] With some reservation they may be classified, after the methods of Giddings, as the idio-motor type in which "Intellect does not develop much beyond perception and conjecture. Relief is determined mainly by instinct, habit, and auto-suggestion."[30] Their predominant mood seems, to the author of this book, to be that of the agitative rather than the forceful. Lacking true courage, they attack their enemies in ambush, or assassinate a defenseless man or woman working in the field or carrying water. Such acts are considered meritorious.[31]

29 "Travels in West Africa," p. 331.
30 "Inductive Sociology," p. 87.
31 Milligan, "The Fetish Folk of West Africa," p. 266.

The people of this zone are violent rather than courageous, and their incessant conflicts, together with the enervating climate, keep them in a constant state of irritation. Their weary and agitative character causes them to seek relief in amusements, or diversions, that sink them deep in the instinctive life, because the narrowness of the activities do not permit of a variety of wholesome expansive pleasures, which among civilized people, lift man out of the sensuous mire.[32] The value of wholesome diversions is especially great for people who are subject to the agitative mood, and also for individuals who work excessively, and are subject to weariness. When the civilized man, through weariness or anxiety, falls into an agitative mood his self-assertive instinct reaches out for forceful or expansive images, and these sustain him, and lift him out of his despondency; but the self-assertive instinct of the uncivilized man is weak,—his imagination, instead of soaring, sinks to the carnal, and he can contemplate nothing in the future to compensate for his existing disquietude. He therefore does not rise out of it.[33]

Imitativeness, as opposed to creativeness, is a characteristic of all the people.[34] Improvidence is also a universal characteristic. The Dwallas, though belonging to the more settled and industrious populations, scarcely produce enough bananas and yams, with the help of their slaves, to keep the wolf from the door, and their country is noted for dear-

[32] Williams, p. 755. [33] *Ibid.*, p. 752. [34] Cureau, p. 685.

ness of provisions.[35] While savages generally have not enough foresight many of the most civilized people have too much. *"Calamitosus est animus futuri anxius."*[36]

As a rule the level of culture rises as we go inland,[37] which may be accounted for by the more open and elevated country, the greater possibility of settled industry through confederation, and the infiltration of culture from Northeast Africa.[38] The Bangala are the most intelligent of the interior tribes, and this is attributed to their confederation.[39]

Within the family circle the virtues common to all races are manifested, such as affection, kindness, and mutual helpfulness. Love between husband and wife, parents and children is obvious, though of less intensity and stability than among better organized people.[40] Outside the family group the primary virtues extend somewhat to the tribe or village, but not so effectively here as in other parts of Africa, because of the lack of incentive to coöperate. Beyond the tribe or village, regard for others scarcely exists. Fellow-feeling is weak, and individualism, so characteristic of the hunting life, reaches here an extreme development. The groups are separated by natural barriers of river, swamp and forest, and, instead of coöperating, they meet only to contest for choice hunting and gathering grounds. All strangers are enemies. The ceremony of blood-brother-

[35] Ratzel, III, p. 122.
[36] Seneca, "Epistolae," 98.
[37] Cureau, p. 691.
[38] Semple, p. 280.
[39] Overbergh, pp. 77, 79.
[40] Cureau, pp. 645, 648, 650.

hood is the only passport to friendship for outsiders.[41] Of the Central African, Wolf says, "Er ist ein Krasser Egoist und unertraglicher Realist wie ihn Peschuël ganz rechtig nennt."[42] He lacks the constructive imagination necessary to enter into the feelings and situation of others. He will waylay, kill and eat a stranger with the same indifference that he would slay a wild beast. According to Milligan, nineteen out of twenty of the natives die by violence. Strife between individuals and loosely organized groups is chronic, and this keeps the people in a resentful and malignant state of mind which reacts within the village group and family, preventing the normal development of the primary virtues. The aged, the sick and incapable are left to die.[43] Altruism is shown only among those of a group who are united by ties of protection and alimentation.[44] The same is, however, pretty largely true of civilized people. "Our sense of right," says Cooley, "ignores those whom we do not, through sympathy, feel as part of ourselves, no matter how close their physical contiguity. To the Norman conqueror the Saxon was an inferior animal, whose sentiments he no more admitted to his imagination, I suppose, than a farmer does those of his cattle, and, towards whom, accordingly, he did not feel human obligation. It was the same with the

[41] Johnston, "George Grenfell and the Congo," II, p. 687.
[42] Page 236.
[43] Cureau, p. 651.
[44] Cureau, p. 651.

slaveholder and the slave, and so it sometimes is with employer and wage-earner. The behavior of the Europeans toward the Chinese during the recent invasion of China showed in a striking manner how completely moral obligation breaks down in dealing with people who are not felt to be of kindred humanity with ourselves.''[45]

The fiery temper and hostile attitude of the people of this zone are due in part to the natural instinct of self-display or love of distinction, which having no other outlet, finds vent in the destruction of human life. Here is a very striking illustration of the baneful working out of a human instinct among savages, which produces among civilized people the most happy results. The instinct of self-display in a cultured society finds its satisfaction in defeating a rival at golf, cricket, football, chess or in the competitive game of commerce, science and art. It becomes a factor of socialization like pugnacity.

The political and economic conditions, and also the climatic conditions, tend to excite personal violence and malignancy. A uniform climate, such as that of the tropics, has a tendency to produce emotional instability, and, at the same time, the moist warm winds induce general lassitude, irritability, ill humor and quarrelsomeness.[46] Man in the forest is neither very gay nor droll. He is rather melancholic. His humor is sad and morose.

45 "Human Nature and the Social Order," p. 362.

46 Ward, Robert, p. 247; Dexter, pp. 23, 26.

He laughs little.[47] If the native sometimes bursts into laughter, and always seems to love fun, it is rather because of the rarity of the occasions which excite his risibilities. Anger is more often manifested than good humor, but the former is short lived and seldom reaches the intensity of revenge.

As to the effect of European contact upon the people of this zone, it is difficult to judge. Before pronouncing judgment it would be necessary to decide what it is that constitutes progress or regression, and on these points there is the widest divergence. Many of the natives in the vicinity of the mission schools have given up their fetich religion, and formally adopted Christianity; they have put on European clothes, learned to eat with a fork, and to read and write. Some of them have been sent to European universities, and attained to a marked degree of culture. But can these be regarded as anything more than isolated examples? Many explorers and administrators in Africa think not. Much of the missionary and civilizing efforts merely destroys the restraints of fear in the native religion and substitutes for them abstractions beyond their grasp, causing a loss of equilibrium and a moral descent.[48]

One of the subtile evils of missionary work is that it removes from the native mind the stimulus of the mysterious. The unsophisticated African, being surrounded as he thinks by a host of spirits, contemplates them with constant curiosity and a

[47] Cureau, p. 684. [48] Cureau, p. 687.

sense of the mysterious. The mystery in their phenomena thus gives interest to life and prevents a lapse into mental and moral torpor. The missionary destroys this stimulus by undermining the belief in spirits. If the natives could substitute, for this interest in the spirit mysteries, an equal interest in the play of natural law in the social and economic phenomena, the result might be different. But the social condition of the savage is too simple to awaken this interest.

If the missionary influence is good that of the exploiting white man and trader largely counteracts it. At any rate, we look over this African territory and see the natives dying out from disorganization and disease,[40] and fleeing from the white man, leaving behind abandoned fields and empty villages.

[40] Bennett, p. 70.

CHAPTER XVII

BANTUS OF THE MANIOC ZONE

Description of the Zone.—The zone of the manioc is a broad area about 15° wide, stretching somewhat diagonally across the continent, and lying mostly below the equator. The line marking its northern boundary begins at the Rio del Rey River, which flows into the Gulf of Guinea, and then follows an irregular course to Lake Tanganyika; thence northeast to the vicinity of Lake Victoria, and thence running a circle southward and northeastward to the coast. The southern boundary begins about Benguela, on the West Coast, and extends eastward to the mouth of the Zambesi River.[1] The zone takes in a part of the Lower Congo, and the higher altitudes of the southern lake regions. It varies in elevation from sea level to a height of 3,000 feet.[2] Much of this area is covered with forest, but, since it lies below the equator, the rainfall is not so great as in the banana zone, and the vegetation is not so luxuriant or rank. Here and there are large areas of open park-like country, or plains covered with high grass and weeds. Between Lake Tan-

1 Stanley, "How I Found Livingstone," p. 549.

2 Livingstone, "Last Journals," I, p. 266.

ganyika and the coast the zone is bisected by the pastoral plateau and its forest borders. The temperature is not so high upon the average as in the zone above. It ranges during the twenty-four hours from 60° to 90°. This variation is enough to make both the heat and the cold painful.[3] In the higher altitudes of the interior the mercury in the early morning often drops to 43°.[4]

Wild game such as the elephant, buffalo, antelope, lion, etc., were formerly abundant but their zones have been much restricted and their numbers depleted within the last century.[5]

The Inhabitants.—The natives are all of the Bantu stock except the few scattered groups of Pygmies described in the preceding volume. They comprise the Gabunese, Mpongwe, Bateke, Baloa, Bakalai, Baluba, Barotse, Angolese, Kazembe, Wanyamwezi, etc. They are all, with few exceptions, decidedly negroid in type but differ notably in color and features. Two constrasting types may be broadly distinguished. One, dark, prognathous, thick-lipped, and flat-nosed, forms the substratum. The other, lighter in color, less prognathous and less negroid in features, forms the ruling classes. The existence of these two classes is explained by the invasion of the pastoral tribes from the east and south.[6] In British Central Africa the population

[3] Hahn, p. 055, Boshart, p. 88.

[4] Livingstone, "Last Journals," I, p. 259.

[5] *Ibid.*, p. 259.

[6] Livingstone, "Last Journals," I, p. 259; Stanley, "Through the Dark Continent," II, p. 80.

is decidedly black, and none of the tribes has the oblique eyes as are occasionally found in the Congo. The hair of the infants is distinctly brownish.[7] The Banyansi are of lighter color and well formed.[8] The Bateke of Stanley Pool are described as having a Greek physiognomy.[9] These contrasting types are due to differences of climate and race intermixture.

Economic Life.—This zone was no doubt once a great hunting ground,[10] but its open character facilitated the extermination of the game, superinduced by the demand of the white man for ivory. As hunting on a large scale declined the people resorted to rats, mice, caterpillars, worms, etc.[11] The scarcity of wild game probably led to, or extended, the practice of eating human flesh. In the last century, however, cannibalism has declined partly on account of the regularity of the food supply furnished by agriculture. The cultivation of the soil not only arrested cannibalism by supplying food but by giving employment to war captives.

The domestic animals are the goat, sheep, hog, dog, cat, fowl and pigeon.[12] The elephant could not be domesticated here on account of the costliness of feeding him.[12a] Cattle are killed in many regions

7 Johnston, "British Central Africa," pp. 393, 396, 398.

8 Johnston, "On the Races of the Congo and the Portuguese Colonies," Jour. Anthropological Institute, vol. XIII, p. 474.

9 Boshart, p. 99.

10 Johnston, "British Central Africa," p. 435.

11 Ratzel, II, p. 557.

12 Johnston, "George Grenfell and the Congo," II, pp. 429, 616.

12a Boshart, pp. 93, 95.

by the tsetse fly, and in others they are destroyed by a certain poisonous bush.[13] In rare localities may be found a few cattle belonging to a chief.[14] The fowl are scrawny and scarce, and their eggs are eaten mostly in a state of advanced preservation. The natives like their eggs "full of meat."

Whether the natives resorted to agriculture as a result of dearth of game, or because forced to it as a result of conquest, is a debatable question. Préville believes in the latter theory, and also Richter who says that man has to be coerced in order to work at all in this oppressive climate.[15] The Bantu, as pretty much all Central Africans, are fundamentally vegetarians, and when they fail to get sustained by nature they cultivate the soil. Nothing is so characteristic of the people as the hoe,[16] which is the only implement of agriculture.[17]

A dry season permits the ripening of a variety of grains of which the chief is manioc (tapioca) which was introduced in the sixteenth century by the Portuguese in Angola. Its cultivation rapidly spread over a wide area of Central Africa.[18] Along with manioc the people use maize, millet, sorghum

[13] Kallenberg, p. 52; Johnston, "On the Races of the Congo and the Portuguese Colonies," Jour. Anthropological Institute, XIII, p. 466.

[14] Burton, II, p. 282; Richter, p. 68.

[15] Richter, p. 123.

[16] Hahn, "Die Haustiere und ihre Beziehungen zur Wertschaft des Menschen," p. 571.

[17] Johnston, "British Central Africa," p. 426.

[18] Morgan, p. 235; Livingstone, "Last Journals," I, p. 262; Boshart, p. 92; Weule, p. 84; Schweinfurth, I, p. 527; Johnston,

(a small grain), and in some places the banana and plantain. The banana is rare in the elevated districts where it is found only on the slopes and in the valleys. Other products of the soil, varying according to locality, are ground nuts, melons, beans, sugar-cane, peas, yams, pumpkins, eleusine, rice, cotton and tobacco.[19] The fields or gardens usually have a high hedge around them to keep off the wild beasts.[20] The depredations of the monkey and the elephant in some districts discourage the cultivation of the cereals.[21] In connection with each house there is a granary for storing the manioc, etc.[22] It is a huge circular basket-work, plastered with mud, and set on a raised platform as a protection against rats and ants.[23] Wooden mortars for preparing the manioc may be seen in front of all the huts. The natives are fond of fermented drinks which they make from the banana, maize, manioc and honey.[24] Dried fish is a common food near the coast, and dried rats in the interior.[25]

This zone is characterized by a higher development of handicrafts than is found in the banana zone. The houses are more carefully built. The

"George Grenfell and the Congo," II, p. 605; Hahn, "Afrika," p. 115; Richter, p. 95.

[19] Ratzel, II, pp. 550, 557; III, p. 114; Kallenberg, p. 52.

[20] Livingstone, "Last Journals," I, p. 307.

[21] Burton, II, p. 57.

[22] Stanley, "Through the Dark Continent," II, p. 86.

[23] Johnston, "British Central Africa," p. 456; Ferree, p. 156.

[24] Johnston, "George Grenfell and the Congo," II, p. 513; Livingstone, "Last Journals," II, p. 127.

[25] Ratzel, III, p. 98.

articles of manufacture are more varied, including cotton and bark-cloth, woven vessels, baskets, mats, string, pots, nets of fiber, garments of skin, iron spears and knives, hoes, sickles, needles, awls, bells, wire circlets, etc. The cutlery has often been compared to that of Sheffield.[26] Each village has its smelting house, charcoal burners and blacksmiths.

Along the West Coast, as far south as Benguela, trade is carried on by a special professional class of men. On the eastern slope the Wanyamwesi are celebrated traders, and they monopolize the carrying of goods from the coast to the interior. They were called by Stanley the "Yankees of Africa."[27] At the interior markets the trading is frequently assigned to the women. The business of the market is limited to fixed days of the week. On the Lower Congo every fourth day a market is held at some particular village where people come in boats or afoot, bringing pottery, palm-oil, fish, fowl, pigs, flour, salt, hoes, mats, grass-cloth, wooden statuettes, etc.[28] The traders adulterate and give short weight like civilized people.[29] Sometimes three thousand people attend a market, and they make a terrible din, mingling the roar of haggling voices with the crowing of the cocks and squealing

26 Ratzel, III, pp. 44, 45, 132; Johnston, "British Central Africa," pp. 456, 457, 459; Burton, II, p. 71; Weiss, p. 111; Weule, p. 275; Stanley, "How I Found Livingstone," I, p. 545; Werner, pp. 196, 201, 202; Richter, pp. 91, 95.

27 "How I Found Livingstone," I, p. 540; Burton, II, p. 29.

28 Cameron, p. 265; Weule, p. 274.

29 Cameron, p. 376.

of the pigs.[30] Cowries pass as money in some places and in others iron hoes,[31] and in still others coins of foreign governments. In towns where Europeans are settled trade is diversified and the means of transportation modernized. Railroads and steamboat lines connect the east and west coasts with various points in the interior.

The work of production is divided between the sexes with some degree of equality. The women do the field work but are assisted sometimes by the men.[32] They also build houses, weave, grind corn, brew beer, and make pottery.[32a] The men work in iron, repair fences and houses, weave cloth, and make and mend the garments of the women.[33] There are specialists for all handicrafts.[34] Among the Barotse there is considerable coöperation in building, planting and hunting.[35]

Slaves are in much demand for field work. They usually live in hamlets apart from their masters. The ruling class turn over all agricultural work to the slaves. In most tribes the free and slave classes are very distinct. Perhaps nowhere else in the world can be found a clearer example of one class

30 Livingstone, "Last Journals," II, pp. 123, 125.

31 Stanley, "Through the Dark Continent," II, p. 88; Johnston, "George Grenfell and the Congo," II, p. 796.

32 Johnston, "George Grenfell and the Congo," II, p. 520.

32a Richter, p. 96.

33 Werner, pp. 135, 195; Johnston, "George Grenfell and the Congo," II, p. 675.

34 Stanley, "Through the Dark Continent," II, p. 82; Weiss, p. 111; Macdonald, p. 102.

35 Richter, p. 95.

living upon the labor of another. Of course civilized people are much horrified at slavery because under that system the incidence of the burden of supporting the population is clearly visible. Yet under our modern economic and political system the burden is often as heavily pressed upon certain classes as in savage society, but in the disguised form of inherited wealth, shifted taxation, monopolies, pensions and other forms of exploitation.

Many of the slaves in the manioc zone are war captives, but numerous others have been purchased from parents in times of famine.[36]

The people seem to have a clear idea of property rights. Plantations and enclosures belong to the people who made them, and so also movables.[37]

Family Life.—Family life in this zone is somewhat more elevated than that of the banana zone, although in some localities, as in the Lower Congo, it is on the same level. The more sedentary life of the population permits the children to live longer with their parents, and facilitates a better transmission of tradition. Girls being serviceable as field workers are not given in marriage without a valuable consideration, and the greater usefulness of women causes them to be somewhat better treated. Wives are sometimes obtained by capture but more generally by purchase, and the bargain is sometimes made before the child is born. The price is paid in goats, hides, cloth, etc., and varies much according to local-

[36] Werne, p. 273.

[37] Johnston, "British Central Africa," p. 471.

ity and family rank.[38] In the Congo the "intended husband buys the young girl of her father. He is obliged to supply the dowry, his wife's trousseau, and to provide her with a house with all cooking and cleaning utensils. Further, he has to defray the cost of the feast to which the relatives of both families are invited. The day of the wedding there is a banquet at which pork forms the main dish. The feast is accompanied by songs and dances."[39] The custom in some districts demands that the suitor consult the bride's maternal uncle.[40] In certain tribes marriage is patrilocal, i. e., the wife goes to live in the house of her husband, and in other tribes matrilocal, i. e., the husband goes to her home.[41]

Polygamy is not so universal in the manioc as in the banana zone, perhaps owing to a better balance between the sexes. The men do not die so rapidly from violence; and not many of them can accumulate the purchase price for more than one wife. The chief, however, often has many wives, and among them, not infrequently, some of his own daughters.[42]

Chastity is esteemed a virtue but is rarely practiced. "Over nearly the whole of British Central Africa," says Johnston, "chastity before puberty is

[38] Johnston, "British Central Africa," pp. 412, 415; Werner, p. 129; Milligan, p. 52.

[39] Johnston, "George Grenfell and the Congo," II, p. 679.

[40] Stigand, p. 122.

[41] Johnston, "British Central Africa," p. 413; Burton, II, p. 24; Macdonald, p. 121.

[42] Cameron, p. 307.

an unknown condition." Girls rarely remain virgin after about five years of age.[43] After puberty young girls assemble together and live apart from their parents in a separate hut where they receive their friends without interference.[44] It is common for both sexes to bathe together naked.[45]

Each family occupies a suite of huts, one for each adult.[46] The custom of living separated probably grew out of the necessity of making the huts conical in form to turn the rain. The people did not know how to make a waterproof roof for a large house. In the Lower Congo region large square houses have come into use through the influence of white immigrants.[47] In many villages the boys live in a common house until they are married.[48]

The work of maintenance does not fall so heavily upon the women here as in the banana zone. The men assist in the field work, and have a large share in the handicrafts, including the making of garments for women. Husband and wife have their individual property.[49]

Married life seems to run about as smoothly here as in most other parts of the world. Yet many marriages are what might be called failures. Intrigues

43 "British Central Africa," p. 409.
44 Burton, II, p. 24.
45 Richter, p. 78.
46 Richter, p. 107.
47 Johnston, "British Central Africa," pp. 453, 455; Livingstone, "Last Journals," II, p. 25; Guessfeldt, p. 212; Ankermann, p. 56; Hahn, "Afrika," p. 117.
48 Webster, p. 13.
49 Richter, p. 100.

and adultery are not uncommon,[50] and divorces are frequent.[51] Among the Barotse separations are so common that the sex relations practically amount to free love. It is rare that a Barotse man of middle life is found living with his first wife.[52] Women having a dowry and property of their own often assert their independence. Children are welcomed and loved with a true maternal instinct, even if the love is not so lasting as among civilized people. Abortion is often practiced but not through objections to children *per se.* It is done by young wives to escape from the custom of living apart from their husbands during the period of gestation and lactation.[53] This separation of husband and wife is the result of some kind of superstition. Men sometimes exchange their wives, or divorce them. If a wife's children die the husband is entitled to divorce, and she is entitled to divorce "if the husband neglects to sew and mend her garments."[54] Mothers often show a deep and abiding love for their children. Werne instances the case of a woman, living some distance from a mission house, who, hearing that her son, a pupil there, was ill, walked in and carried him home on her back. He was a big lad of thirteen or fourteen.[55] Among some tribes, however, parental affection scarcely exists. A Bar-

[50] Johnston, "British Central Africa," p. 412.
[51] Milligan, p. 53.
[52] Richter, p. 103.
[53] Johnston, "British Central Africa," p. 417.
[54] Macdonald, p. 109.
[55] Johnston, "British Central Africa," p. 146.

otse father thinks nothing of his children, and the mother's love for them is feeble. She does not hesitate to kill them if they stand in the way of a new marriage.[56]

Children in most cases take the name of the mother, but they are sometimes claimed as the property of the father.[57] Where there is property to transmit, or where goods come to have a high value, there is a tendency for the father to dictate their disposal, and for the children to take the name of the father. The transition from the matrilineal to the patrilineal family is generally effected chiefly through the development of property and positions of honor which cause the father to prefer his sons as inheritors. Blood-brotherhood, secret societies, totemism and religious dedication are devices by which men, consciously or unconsciously, escape from the bonds of the maternal system. Migration, militancy and wife purchase also have a tendency to break down that system.[58] In Loango and in many other regions of this zone children are considered the exclusive property of the wife. In case of her death they may be bought by the husband from the wife's relatives.[59] Inheritance is, with few exceptions, in the female line. Among the Anyanja the sons inherit, and among the Yao a

[56] Richter, p. 105.

[57] Burton, II, p. 23.

[58] Thomas, "Sex and Society," pp. 89, 90, 92, 93; Ellwood, Chas. A., "Sociology," pp. 83, 84.

[59] Ratzel, III, p. 124.

woman's property goes to her sons and daughters.[60]

Political Life.—Before the introduction of agriculture in this region the population was probably scattered in small groups, on account of lack of sufficient game or spontaneous production. These groups, by reason of the often open character of the country, would come into collision, resulting in temporary consolidations or confederations, facilitated by common language and race. After systematic agriculture was begun the groups probably enlarged by multiplication and intertribal warfare. The impetus to consolidate was then powerfully aided by a great immigration from the southeast. These new arrivals were the outcasts or rebellious elements from the pastoral regions, and their coming is explained by the fact that the best organized and most military tribes lived in the far southeast in the most favored pastures. Now, when a rebellion was organized, or a restless surplus population sought an outlet, the only open way was northward. Later, when rebellions in the more northern tribes broke out and sought new pastures they also could advance only in a northward direction, since the stronger tribes were behind them and the weaker ones in front. Each step north was marked by less favored pastures, less military governments, and more timid and peaceful people. When finally the emigrants reached the zone of manioc they found there the tsetse fly which destroyed their cattle.

[60] Johnston, "British Central Africa," p. 471.

They were obliged now to turn back against a stronger host, or give up the pastoral life, and invade the territory of the hunters and cultivators of the soil. Pressure of circumstances compelled the latter course. So the emigrants pressed across the line, conquered the natives, forced them to field work, and henceforth lived upon the products of the soil. Often several communities thus became united by conquest under one government, the rulers of which were lighter in color and less negroid than the masses. Geographical obstacles seem to have diverted this invading movement from the regions of the east, Lake Nyassa and the northern lands of the Upper Zambesi. There the mass of the people and the rulers remain of the same color and type.[61]

Each state organized under this immigration movement became at once aggressive towards its neighbors.[62] The rather open nature of the country and the apparent possibility of assembling a large fighting force would seem to have favored wide conquests and the formation of large empires; but, in fact, few of such empires developed.[63] The more conspicuous among these are the Lunda, the Barotse, Bakongo, and Baluba.[64] At one time a single empire is said to have included Bakongo, parts of French Gaboon, Portuguese Kabinda and Angola,

61 Johnston, "British Central Africa," p. 394.

62 Macdonald, p. 111; Stanley, "In Darkest Africa," II, p. 273.

63 Johnston, "On the Races of the Congo and the Portuguese Colonies," Jour. Anthropological Institute, vol. XIII, p. 468.

64 Weiss, p. 110.

and the Congo Free State, to which may have been included Mpongwe on the north, a branch of Bangala on the south, and the Balunda and Mabunda and other groups more inland.[65] The existence of such an empire seems to the writer altogether incredible.

There are two obstacles to large kingdoms. One is the frequency of natural barriers of river, forest, and great fields of high, almost impenetrable grass, intervening between settlements. The other obstacle consists in the absence of any means of rapid communication, or beast of burden for transportation, that would enable widely separated groups to be held together. The small groups have the advantage of being able to hide and this renders political cohesion almost impossible, and at the same time prevents war from being very destructive.[66]

On some accounts we should expect to find less despotic governments in this than in the banana zone. For instance, property is more general, and the people more linked to the soil. These conditions would seem to foster some spirit of independence. Furthermore, the time devoted to war is much less than in the banana zone, and the military organization is less powerful. But since the governments are the outcome of conquest, and since the conquered have to be constrained to till the soil, those

[65] R. H. Fox Bourne, "Civilization in Congoland," London, 1903, p. 4.

[66] Johnston, "British Central Africa," p. 470.

who rule can do so only by striking terror into the hearts of their subjects.[67]

Between rulers and subjects there is a jealously maintained barrier, and the distinction between master and slave is more closely drawn than in the banana zone.[68] The subjects have not the chance of rising to the top common to hunting or pastoral people. Unless large numbers of the population have an opportunity to accumulate property, or otherwise distinguish themselves, classes always tend to become fixed.[69] The contrasts in types do not favor free social intercourse; and the economic life is so uniform and simple, and the facilities for communication so imperfect, that there is no opportunity for innovations in methods and ideas that would favor emergence from the understratum. "Unlikeness in the constituents," says Cooley, "a settled system, and a low state of communication and enlightenment favor the growth of caste, and *vice versa*.[70]

The governments of this zone though despotic are rarely personal. Generally there is a council composed mostly of royal connections which decides questions of peace and war.[71] The Barotse empire, however, is decidedly personal, and contrasts with

67 Richter, p. 113.

68 Werne, p. 255; Johnston, "George Grenfell and the Congo," II, p. 685.

69 Sumner, p. 163.

70 "Social Organization," p. 217.

71 Werne, p. 261; Johnston, "George Grenfell and the Congo," II, p. 697.

that of Lunda, which has an elective monarch and a popular assembly in which every one can freely express his views. The monopoly of trade, claimed everywhere by the chief, gives him great power over his subjects.

The administration of justice within each government varies from that loose state in which grievauces are left to private revenge to a system of rigid legal control.[72] Murder, adultery and theft are the chief offenses noticed by the governments. The punishments consist of amputation of ears and hands, or execution by throwing from a precipice, beating or stoning to death, throat-cutting, and administration of the poison ordeal. The death penalty is, however, rarely inflicted if the accused can pay damages.[73] In some cases torture is visited upon the accused to force confession.[74]

The revenues of the governments are derived from ivory, slaves, salt, cloth, skins, grain, fruit, etc.[75] Formerly the kings claimed all of the ivory, and bought slaves from starving families to resell to the slave trader, but since the arrest of the slave trade the resources of the kings have diminished, and also their power over their subjects.[76]

72 Werne, p. 264.

73 Johnston, "George Grenfell and the Congo," II, p. 696; Macdonald, p. 110.

74 Macdonald, p. 110; Johnston, Lydekker, et al., p. 504; In the opinion of Welling torture represents a higher stage of evolution than the ordeal, as the former is applied only on strong evidence of guilt. "Law of Torture," p. 197.

75 Ratzel, II, p. 559.

76 Burton, II, p. 31; Livingstone, "Last Journals," I. p. 265.

Lack of economic interdependence, and consequent lack of spirit of coöperation, give an uncertain tenure to all kingdoms. "A temporary failure of food-supply, cruelty, or excessive exaction of tribute on part of the chief, occasions an exodus. The history of every negro tribe in Africa, gives instances of such secessions, which often leave whole districts empty and exposed to the next wandering occupant."[77]

[77] Semple, p. 81.

CHAPTER XVIII

BANTUS OF THE MANIOC ZONE (*continued*)

Religious Life.—Religion is of the same general character as that of the banana zone. It seems to arise out of the notion of ghosts as the survival of the soul after death, and leads to ancestor worship.[1] The offerings to the idols are intended as gifts to the departed father or mother.[2] The surviving spirits may assume human, animal, or other form, and pass to the rank of a god. Among many tribes there is a belief in a supreme being but he is far away and receives little attention. The open character of much of the country, and free intercommunication, tend to acquaint the people over a wide area with the divinities that may have developed local significance. Usually there are gods of the sky, sun, moon, lightning, etc., along with multitudinous minor spirits concerned with phenomena closer at hand. More attention is given to distant or cosmic gods than is the case nearer the equator. When man locates in an environment where the warmth of the sun is necessary to personal comfort, and to the growth and ripening of crops, his interest is likely

1 Johnston, "British Central Africa," p. 449.

2 Livingstone, "Last Journals," I, p. 353; Werne, p. 54.

to be drawn towards the gods of the heavens. Sun-worship and fire-worship are to be expected in such a region. In this manioc zone fire-worship is very general, and increases in the direction of the temperate climates.[3] Attention to fire is likely to lead to sun-worship as the heat of the sun naturally suggests that terrestrial fire originated from the celestial, as in the Greek myth of Prometheus's bringing fire from heaven.

Probably the notion of beneficent gods arose first in connection with those most remote from man's habitation, since the notion of local spirits, even including ancestral spirits, is generally associated with malevolence and evil.[4]

The gods, big and little, take a zealous interest in human events. They display their powers in charms, in the storms, in the behavior of animals, in the growth of vegetation, etc. They make the luck in all undertakings. The blacksmith gets a better result by placing a bit of human flesh in his forge.[5] The Mpongwe keep in miniature houses chests containing lime, ochre, etc., to rub on the skin as protection against the dangers of hunting and fishing. Crops are everywhere guarded by medicine sticks.[6] Man must consult an oracle before going on a journey. The magician in charge pours flour on a flat stone, and if it forms a perfect cone

3 Frobenius, "Die Weltanschauung der Naturvölker," Beiträge zur Volks-und Volkerkunde, Vol. VI, pp. 281, 285, 290.

4 Macdonald, p. 114.

5 Ratzel. II, p. 351.

6 Kingsley, "Travels in West Africa," p. 305.

the omen is good; or he pours beer on the ground, and if it sinks in one spot the gods are propitious.[7] In any expedition if a rabbit crosses the road it is a sign of death to the leader.[8] The Mpongwe can make strangers more friendly by giving them food mixed with the scrapings of a human skull.[9] The ordeal sometimes takes the place of a troublesome and expensive judiciary.

Human sacrifices are common only in a few localities. They are rare in French Congo, and do not exist south of the Quanza River.[10] In a few places wives and slaves are immolated upon the death of a chief, or human sacrifices are made sometimes to appease a god.[11] More generally sacrifices are limited to animals, food and drink, and even these are not offered in a very serious spirit. The flesh of sacrificial animals is eaten.[12]

Diseases here, as elsewhere in Africa, are caused by wicked spirits and witches. Deaths are mostly attributed to witchcraft, but sometimes to accident. A death in war is always the work of the gods.[13]

There are two kinds of medicine men; one is a genuine healer, and the other a wizard who makes

[7] Macdonald, p. 103.
[8] *Ibid.*, p. 104.
[9] Ratzel, III, p. 131.
[10] Kingsley, "Travels in West Africa," p. 306; Johnston, "On the Races of the Congo and the Portuguese Colonies," *Jour. Anthropological Institute*, Vol. XIII, p. 468.
[11] Cameron, p. 333; Macdonald, pp. 106, 112; Kallenberg, p. 115.
[12] Macdonald, p. 106.
[13] Johnston, "British Central Africa," p. 439; Ratzel, II, p. 351.

charms and ferrets crime.[14] Both do a general practice, and the patient decides which he wants.[15] The protective charms, says Miss Kingsley, contain all manner of nastiness, including a large percentage of the dung of fowl.[16] In Central Africa the wizards are almost as thick as the forest. They are of both sexes, the women usually taking over the medical part of the profession.[17] This fact supports the view of Thomas that the profession of the physician did not arise entirely from the medicine man, as Spencer believed, but arose partly from lay practitioners.[18]

Persons accused of witchcraft must undergo the poison ordeal at which the wizard performs magic rites with portions of human bodies.[19] In French Congo the wizard, after a variety of ceremonies, induces the disease-causing spirit to enter an antelope horn, snail-shell or nut kernel.[20] Some doctors make incisions in the flesh and rub in ashes to kill the demon of disease.[21] The wizard is often put to death if his prescriptions do not cure, or his predictions fail, or some calamity be charged to his art.[22]

14 Macdonald, p. 104.
15 Johnston, "British Central Africa," p. 442.
16 "Travels in West Africa," p. 303.
17 Burton, II, p. 350.
18 "Source Book for Origins," p. 284.
19 Ratzel, III, p. 130.
20 Kingsley, "Travels in West Africa," p. 302.
21 Macdonald, p. 104.
22 Burton, II, p. 351; Stanley, "How I Found Livingstone," I, p. 245.

Idols are common but diminish in number with the distance from the equator.[23]

Ceremonial Life.—The large groups of this zone, with their division into a free and slave class and their rather despotic forms of government, monotony of existence and interest in supernatural spirits, favor a high degree of ceremonial. The people have fixed rules for eating,[24] ceremonials for the birth of children,[25] for initiation into manhood,[25a] for marriage,[26] for the purification of women in case they give birth to twins,[26a] for deaths, funerals, and for those who handle a corpse.[27] In the Congo region the interval between death and burial, and the quantity of cloth wrapped around a corpse, mark the differences in the rank of the people. The body of a great person is wrapped in voluminous folds of cloth, pieces of which are almost daily added to, so as to conceal any signs of decomposition. When too large for the house in which it is contained the building is taken down and a larger one erected. In some cases eight years elapse before burial.[28] Funerals are celebrated with intoxication, music, obscene songs and lascivious dances, continuing until late in the night.[29] In the Lunda kingdom the new

23 Cameron, p. 308; Kingsley, "Travels in West Africa." p. 307; Ratzel, II, p. 352; Livingstone, "Last Journals," I, p. 353.

24 Ratzel, III, p. 116.

25 Johnston, "British Central Africa," p. 439.

25a *Ibid.*, p. 410.

26 *Ibid.*, p. 413.

26a *Ibid.*, p. 418.

27 *Ibid.*, p. 443.

28 Romer, p. 172.

29 *Ibid.*, p. 173.

ruler attends the funeral of the deceased followed by a concourse. The corpse is borne in a chair, adorned as for a festival, to the Kalangi River where the procession performs all sorts of ceremonies and magic rites. New fire is made by rubbing a stick, and a boy and girl are slain as sacrifice.[30] The custom generally prevails of placing utensils, bottles, food, and so forth upon the graves.[31] Fear that the spirit of the dead may come back and do mischief causes the banana trees of the deceased to be cut down, his pots broken and his hut abandoned.[32] Sometimes mock funerals are held to deceive the demons that hover about the sick.[33]

"The life of an African," says Johnston, "is rigidly ruled by custom. He is more of a slave of custom than the average European. . . . All the important phases and functions of their lives are attended with special customs, almost invariably expressed by much dancing, and brewing, drinking, and libations of native beer. At the beginning of the hoeing season feasts are held. In some cases there is a hoe dance wherein the dancers carry hoes which they strike together with a musical clang, in rhythm with the beating of the drums. . . . No important journey is undertaken without small sacrifices to ancestors and consulting the oracle by means of the small divination sticks."[34]

30 Ratzel, II, p. 567.
31 Johnston, "British Central Africa," p. 445.
32 *Ibid.*, p. 445.
33 Macdonald, p. 114.
34 "British Central Africa," p. 452.

In Lunda people greet each other by hand-clapping, and in the presence of a great personage they prostrate and strew themselves with dust. Whistling and howling are also demonstrations towards the great. Courtiers wipe up the saliva where the sovereign spits, and when he sneezes they yell, whistle and pop their fingers.[35] In some localities it is disrespectful to allow your shadow to fall on any part of another person.[36] Spitting in the face is a mark of esteem east of Tanganyika.[37]

Mourning is "by a persistent beating of drums by night and by day, and also by a continual howling kept up by relatives and others of whom many may be hired for the occasion. . . . Relatives shave their heads."[38] "Women kneel when addressing men, and go off the public path into the grass or bush when they meet any of the opposite sex, as a sign of subordination and subjection."[39] "In the southern part of British Central Africa," says Johnston, "the natives kneel and clap their hands. In the countries bordering on the Portuguese possessions and in Makualand, the natives clap their hands and simultaneously scrape their feet backwards along the ground, one foot at a time. In the northern districts of Nyassa and thence westward, the position in salutation is most extraordinary, especially if it is an inferior saluting a superior. The man who is

35 Ratzel, II, p. 557.
36 Livingstone, "Last Journals," I, p. 291.
37 Cameron, p. 315.
38 Macdonald, p. 112.
39 *Ibid.*, p. 118.

greeting you will throw himself on his stomach and smack himself violently on the hinder parts." Women kneel with their hands placed over the knees and sometimes wallow at a man's feet and endeavor to place his foot on their necks. Suppliants often use a phrase "to catch the leg," which means to place the foot of a superior on your neck. This phrase was once used by a chief who had been defeated in war with the British. He sent to his conqueror a message which literally translated meant that he wanted to catch the Queen's leg.[40]

Court ceremonies and other spectacular rites are much displayed by the larger kingdoms.[41]

Æsthetic Life.—Mutilation of the body, in one form or other, is common in this zone, but seems to diminish in the direction of the south. The Ovampo of both sexes knock out one of the upper incisors. Other tribes knock out the lower incisors or file their teeth to a point.[42] Tattooing or cicatrisation is also common, and is sometimes used as a tribal mark.[43] It diminishes towards the south, and is absent on the West Coast below the Quanza.[44] Some women wear a nose ornament of bone, ivory or silver.[45] Livingstone observed a man sewing feathers on his arrow

40 Johnston, "British Central Africa," p. 407.

41 Ratzel, III, p. 126.

42 Ratzel, II, pp. 542, 545; III, pp. 130, 555; Werner, p. 38; Johnston, "British Central Africa," p. 424.

43 Ratzel, III, p. 132; Johnston, "British Central Africa," p. 422.

44 Johnston, "On the Races of the Congo and the Portuguese Colonies," *Jour. Anthropological Institute*, XIII, p. 468.

45 Weule, p. 49; Johnston, "British Central Africa," p. 423.

who was using the hole in the cartilage of his nose to hold his needle.[46] Sometimes metal ornaments are worn in the upper lip.[47] Much attention is given to hair dressing which takes on a variety of styles including the plastering of the hair with mud.[48] The Barotse use their matted hair as a pin-cushion or substitute for a pocket.[49] Like all other savages the people love to bedeck themselves with necklaces, rings, bracelets and anklets.[50] The ornamentation of weapons and utensils, in many places, reaches a degree of excellence.[51] In British Central Africa pottery is not much ornamented, but in the Upper Congo it takes on an artistic finish. "The Baluba and Bakuba peoples of the south-center," says Johnston, "are steeped in artistic feeling, which finds its expression in the carving of masks out of solid blocks of wood, exquisite iron metal-work, the beautiful patterns of their pile cloths, and the fantastic designs and coloration of their pottery."[52] The Barotse paint animals and men in a variety of aspects.[53]

The dress of the people has undergone considerable change since the importation of European

[46] "Last Journal," I, p. 289.

[47] Johnston, "British Central Africa," p. 423.

[48] Stanley, "Through the Dark Continent," II, p. 82; Cameron, p. 376.

[49] Richter, p. 79.

[50] Johnston, "George Grenfell and the Congo," II, p. 585; Stigand, p. 119.

[51] Ratzel, "History of Mankind," II, p. 550; III, pp. 44, 45, 126.

[52] "George Grenfell and the Congo," II, p. 811.

[53] Richter, p. 162.

goods. Formerly it was limited mostly to a loin-strip of bark, native cotton-cloth or skin, and this is still the dress over a large area,[54] but the prevailing dress is of imported calico.[55] The Mpongwe belles step proudly in white stockings. On the Congo Coast the natives wear a cap made of dry grass or a handkerchief worn as a turban.[56] The Barotse wear sandals for long journeys.[57]

Dancing takes on a variety of forms. As soon as dark comes the people assemble to enjoy this exercise.[58] Evidences of the drama seem to be lacking. The musical instruments include the guitar, harp, drum, horn, banjo, reed, flute and a sort of piano called the marimbo.[59] Among the Zambesi tribes the musicians are organized into bands, and in some of the kingdoms the royal musicians live in a special house.[60] Herbert Spencer advanced the theory that the professional musician and dancer evolved from the medicine man or priest, but there seems to be no evidence to support this theory in Africa. They probably originated independently as clearly shown by Thomas.[61] Weapons and imple-

54 Schweinitz, p. 141.

55 Weule, p. 274; Schweinitz, p. 141.

56 Johnston, "George Grenfell and the Congo," II, p. 597; Milligan, p. 34.

57 Richter, p. 78.

58 Johnston, "British Central Africa," p. 411; Weule, p. 181; Stigand, p. 121.

59 Milligan, p. 77; Gressfeldt, p. 215; Stanley, "How I Found Livingstone," I, p. 549.

60 Ratzel, II, p. 550.

61 "Source Book for Origins," p. 287.

ments are generally ornamented.[62] In several districts carving in wood and ivory is well developed.[63] Human and animal figures are cut on pipes and knobkerries.[64] The Baluba and Bakuba are especially good carvers.[65]

Psychological Characteristics.—Both the cranial capacity and the conformation of the skull seem to improve somewhat as one goes south from the equator.[66] Whether this is true or not there is a decidedly higher mental development in the manioc than in the banana zone. The superiority is due partly to the greater amount and variety of mental work imposed by the environment, and partly to the infusion of the blood of the pastoral people of the south.

The instinct of pugnacity here, as in the banana zone, is not conspicuous, because of the terrifying aspects of nature. Agricultural life rather makes people timid or averse to personal antagonisms.[67]

The instinct of curiosity is stronger here than in

62 Richter, p. 88.

63 Werne, p. 203.

64 Ratzel, II, p. 543.

65 Johnston, "George Grenfell and the Congo," II, p. 811.

66 "The cranial capacity of the Bantu

In Corisco is	1,225 c. c.
In Congo is	1,400 c. c.
In Loanda is	1,670 c. c.
In Angola is	1,510 c. c.
In Massamedes is (Hottentot mixture)	1.235 c. c."

Shrubsall, "A Study of A-Bantu Skulls and Crania," *Jour. Anthropological Institute*, n. s. Vol. I, p. 75.

67 Milligan, pp. 36-37.

the banana zone. In the lowest societies it is latent, because there is little to excite it, but, as the life of the people becomes more complex and the work more varied, there arise more occasions to be inquisitive, to speculate, and more mysteries appear, calling for explanation. The wealth of myths of the people of this zone attests their curiosity.

The instinct of fear is somewhat less pronounced here than in the banana zone, for the reason that nature is less antagonistic, and human life not so much exposed to violence. All restraints, however, that enter into the moral system of the people seem to be based upon fear. Sexual continence, respect for property, and obedience to law and the gods are more the outcome of fear than of any abstract considerations. Of the petitions of the natives to their gods, Dr. Nassau says, "these are distinctly prayers, appeals for mercy, agonizing protests, but there is no praise, no thanks and no confession of sin."[68]

The acquisitive instinct is more noticeably developed in this zone. The great social power connected with slaves and grain is especially stimulating to man's love of possessions. This instinct, according to McDougall, is more pronounced among agricultural than among pastoral people. "Among pastoral nomads," he says, "the working of the instinct is manifested in the vast herds sometimes accumulated by a single patriarchal family. But it was only when agriculture began to be extensively practiced that the instinct could produce its greatest

68 Kingsley, "Travels in West Africa," p. 308.

social effects. For grain of all sorts lends itself especially well to hoarding as a form of wealth.''[69] The great social value of this instinct is that it does not stop at the satisfaction of one's needs but spurs man to continuous activity. Neither savages nor civilized people cease striving when they have enough to satisfy their practical needs, if the climate does not enervate. A certain physical vitality as well as the stimulus of possession is necessary to arouse men to activity.[70] In modern civilized societies the acquisitive instinct is rather over-stimulated.[71] In the manioc zone the climate restrains it.

In foresight, inhibiting power, rational interpretation and general intelligence the superiority of the manioc people is conspicuous. They are keen and clever in trade.[72] ''The Abunda, or Quanza'' says Johnston, ''are remarkably smart and intelligent.''[73] Witchcraft and magic play a diminishing rôle as one goes south from the banana zone,[74] and also human sacrifices diminish.[75] In the treatment of disease there is less hocus-pocus and more drugs and concoctions.[76] The imagination of the people is fantastic and picturesque rather than gross.

69 Page 313.

70 Bain, p. 193.

71 Ellwood, "Sociology in Its Psychological Aspects," p. 227.

72 Stanley, "How I Found Livingstone," I, p. 541.

73 "On the Races of the Congo and the Portuguese Colonies," *Jour. Anthropological Institute*, XIII, p. 466.

74 *Ibid.*, p. 468.

75 *Ibid.*, p. 468.

76 Johnston, "British Central Africa," p. 440; Richter, p. 191.

This is shown in their animal legends wherein the hare wears the head of a man, marries an elephant, and is made to eat flesh; the lion to cook bread, the frog to hoe corn, and men and beasts to intermarry.[77]

The feelings of the manioc people are not so explosive as those of the banana zone people. The sedentary agricultural life is not so full of strong excitements as that of the hunting and fighting life, and the climate is not so irritating in its oppressive heat, nor so violent in its manifestations; but the number and variety of excitements are greater, and this accustoms the people to some degree of control over their feelings. Occasional and severe demands upon feeling everywhere explain its excess. The predominant mood of the people is that of expansiveness, induced by the relatively quiet and contented life. This mood is shown in the great attention to music.

The morals within the kinship group appear to differ little from those of similar groups elsewhere in Africa. As these primary groups are often protected by the larger political organization, the relations of individuals within them should be more refined. The elemental virtues of affection, sympathy, and truthfulness towards each other are prominent.[78] Latrobe Bateman said of the Bashilange, "They are thoroughly honest, brave to foolhardiness and faithful to each other. . . . They are warm-hearted and affectionate toward their friends

[77] Richter, p. 168.

[78] Milligan, p. 36; Cameron, p. 248.

and especially their kinfolk, and are the only African tribe amongst whom, in their primitive state, I have observed anything like a becoming conjugal affection and regard."[79] Parental love is probably as deep here as among civilized people but of shorter duration. Under the simple African life children soon learn to shift for themselves, and they separate early from their parents. An indifference thus grows up between them which shows itself in the frequent abandonment of the aged. Of the people about Luebo, Rev. De Witt Snyder says, "parental love is here merely an instinct to protect and provide for their children, like that of dumb brutes for their offspring. The aged and sick are left to take care of themselves and die unattended."[80] Inattention to the sick is often due more to ignorance and superstition than to coldness of heart.

Man is a little more cheerful and light-hearted here than in the equatorial regions.[81] "In an open country," says Cureau, "man is gay, exuberant and loves noise and music."[82]

The Bantu of this region have a lively sense of humor but it is not of a high order. Among civilized people there is a humor, well illustrated in the person of Abraham Lincoln, that fortifies against adversity and despair. It belongs to a forceful type of character, and is the work of the imagination

79 Page 6.

80 *Missionary Review of the World*, XVI, n. s., p. 185.

81 Johnston, "British Central Africa," p. 408; Macdonald, p. 109.

82 Page 648.

in calling up images to compensate for a vexatious state of mind.[83] The Negro lacks the mental energy or constructive imagination for this fortifying task.

The people of this zone are more hospitable and considerate of strangers, and show more fellow-feeling towards those outside the kinship groups than is common among the Negro peoples of Africa.[84]

Most of the traits manifested in this zone bear a closer resemblance to those of the people in the zone of the banana than the conditions of the environment would seem to justify, and the explanation is to be found in the fact that the fundamental population of this zone migrated from the zone above where they received their impress.

Contact with the white man has scarcely improved the status of the natives. Crime among them has increased at a frightful rate,[85] and the high mortality is depopulating whole districts.[86] Of the white man's influence in the Congo, Bourne says, "From the first the predominating influences and achievements have been degrading, not elevating. Whatever advantages to the natives may have resulted from missionary efforts and scientific inquiries and travelers' pastimes, the chief aim and the chief attainment of the white man's intrusion in Congoland have been not the natives' profit but their own. So it was in the early days, when only the otherwise unin-

[83] Williams, p. 753.

[84] Cureau believes that an open country causes man's nature to expand and become more generous and loyal. (Page 648.)

[85] Boulger, p. 203.

[86] Milligan, p. 42.

viting coasts were scoured in order to provide American and other sugar plantations and cotton fields with slaves, for whom the payment, if any was paid, principally consisted of poisonous liquors and more immediately destructive implements of war. So it is now, when all accessible regions in the interior are scoured for ivory and rubber and so forth; with tools and textile fabrics added to the rum and rifles, the gin and gunpowder which were the former staples of trade. If the over-sea slave traffic has been suppressed and the enslavement of one native by another forbidden, the old forms of slavery have been succeeded or supplemented by new, more grinding and hateful to the victims, and for the satisfaction of white instead of black oppressors. Savage customs and institutions have been condemned and interfered with in so far as they proved inconvenient to the usurpers of land and its produce, but for the most part with nothing but increase of savagery. Under Congo State rule, if nowhere else, the tribes most prone to killing and eating their neighbors have been allowed to continue and extend their cannibalism; and the Congo State has only been more reckless and unscrupulous than its British, French, German and Portuguese associates in training and arming the most warlike for fighting and slaughtering purposes of their own."[87] The poor results of missionary work have been due, partly to the evil influences of European governmental action and of industrial exploiters, and partly to lack of

[87] Page 300.

understanding of Negro psychology which has led to a wrong method of education. The way to influence character is to begin with the practical life, not with the theoretical and abstract; with conduct and feeling, and not with belief and book-learning. "Our faith in the power of book learning," says Sumner, "is excessive and unfounded. It is a superstition of the age. The education which forms character and produces faith in sound principles of life comes through personal influence and example. It is borne on the mores. It is taken in from the habits and atmosphere of a school, not from school text-books." . . . "Book learning is addressed to the intellect, not to the feelings, but the feelings are the spring of action."[88] One difficulty in the education of children in Africa is that at the age of puberty they tend to "fall into disappointing nullity," on account of their absorption in sexual interests.[89]

"Think of the thousands of noble-minded men and women," says Miss Kingsley, "who since 1490 have gone and lived and died in Africa, in the cause of evangelisation of Africa. Call these missionaries what you may—you have no right to deny that their constant aim has been the elevation of the African. Look back at the effects of similar efforts made by Christianity on the Teutonic tribes of Europe and you see its success—then look at the history of the Roman Catholic mission to Congo, a mission that for 200 years held these Africans com-

88 Page 630.
89 Johnston, "British Central Africa," p. 408.

pletely in its arms, and look at the Congo native to-day in the regions that mission ruled. The missionary attempt to elevate the African mass seems like unto cutting a path through a bit of African forest: you can cut a very nice tidy path there, and, as long as you are there to keep it clear, it's all a path need be, but leave it and it goes to bush.''[90]

The most recent book on Africa (1912), by Joseph K. Goodrich, speaks of the present status and future of the Negro as follows:

"Yet the march of civilization, if it has not actually displaced the blacks by whites, has so transformed the conditions under which they lived that there is little left of the old life; and it is a lamentable fact that the present status of the natives is, all things considered, worse than was the former. It is an unfortunate concomitant of European civilization that its first impress has, almost without exception, been disastrous to the people of a lower degree of culture than the European standards, or essentially different from them in kind, even when there was a reasonable comparison in degree. If we look at any part of the world to which the adventurous European explorers and navigators went in the fifteenth, sixteenth and seventeenth centuries we must admit, if we are honest, that the first touch of that civilization was blighting. For every sincere bearer of the banner of the Prince of Peace there were a hundred reckless buccaneers, without one thought of the physical or spiritual welfare of

90 Symposium on "British Africa," II, p. 374.

the 'savage heathen' whom they met; whose sole object was to get wealth, the means being unimportant; whose fierce lust held no woman in respect, and whose determination to seize slaves was stopped by nothing. It was so in the case of Africa. Down both coasts the European civilization marched, one missionary disposed to recognize the brotherhood of man, and a hundred freebooters insistent that to the victors belonged the spoils, and they took them in any way they could and in every shape they found them,—gold, ivory, slaves, whatever there was that could be converted into money. . . .

"Again, it seems to the native that it is very easy to earn, by doing some little odd task for the European, the pittance which suffices to keep him alive for a few days. That much secured, there is no occasion to worry about the future, and he 'knocks off' all work until his purse is once more empty and his stomach calling for food. The same statement which has been made about the Fulas may be repeated here as applicable to both sides of the continent as well as all across the broad zone in which the true negroes are found: the people are examples of bad results arrived at when a strange civilization has become dominant and yet is not properly assimilated by the natives. The present state of the African Negro is, in nearly every respect, decidedly worse than was the first. The exploiting of this country, the establishing of steamboat lines on the rivers and lakes, the building of railways all over the continent, have made it easier for the people to gratify their natural fondness for moving about—simply to be on the go, for business they have none—and they yield most readily; but the assimilation of the civilization that all this development connotes has not attained the level which those who wish the negro well would like to see. Of other conditions, such as the horrors of the Belgian Congo, and other places where they are somewhat similar, yet not quite so bad, we will not speak further here. It is enough to say that it is the influence of the acts of Europeans which has brought about such conditions, and which would keep them alive indefinitely were it not for public sentiment, of which the African negro, who is the real sufferer, knows nothing. All this must do more to counteract the altruistic efforts of missionary and teacher than has been accomplished for permanent good in the way of evangelisation at all the mission stations throughout Central Africa put together. Nominally the slave trade has been abolished, but it is true that festering spots still exist—a disgrace to our vaunted Christian civilisation.

"Of the future for the blacks in Africa it is difficult to speak. Pessimistic as it sounds, the present writer looks upon it as likely to be hopeless in the extreme."[91]

[91] Pages 228-231.

CHAPTER XIX

THE BANTUS OF THE SOUTHERN CATTLE ZONE

Description of the Zone.—The cattle zone lies immediately south of the manioc zone, and, before the white man's appearance, it included all of South Africa except the Kalahari desert. In contour South Africa exhibits the character common to the whole continent, in that it is an elevated plateau in the center surrounded on the coasts by irregular ranges of mountains.

The amount of rainfall in the interior diminishes according to distance from the equator, and at the line marking the entrance into the cattle zone it is very slight and limited mostly to the winter season. Then downpours flood the country, filling all of the streams, lakes and pools. Many of the rivers, on account of the general level of the country and the burning rays of the sun, lose their moisture by evaporation before reaching a perennial coastward effluent. Near the coast on all sides the rain is more abundant, feeding numerous streams and giving great fertility to the soils near which they traverse.[1] The climate of the coast districts is temperate, while that of the interior is marked by extremes of heat and cold and more sudden changes.[2]

1 Hahn, p. 135.

2 Reclus, IV, pp. 225, 254.

Vegetation in the various districts varies with the amount of rain and the moisture along the rivers and lakes. In the mountains bordering the coasts and on the coast plains vegetation is abundant and even often luxuriant, with great areas of woodland; but inland, trees follow the streams and depressions, and rarely assume the aspect of forest. Much of the country resembles a boundless prairie with here and there a few wooded islets rising above the tall waving grass. In some places nothing can be seen except thorny plants and dreary wastes of sand.[3]

This part of Africa once abounded in game, such as the lion, buffalo, giraff, rhinoceros, hyena, jackal, antelope, elephant, and hippopotamus.[4] The larger game is now disappearing under the advances of the white man and the use of modern guns.

The Inhabitants.—All of the Negroes of this zone belong to the Bantu except the Hottentots, who resemble in language and type the Bushmen of the Kalahari desert. The chief subdivisions are the Zulu, Kafir, Makololo, Matebele, Bechuana, Bakalahari, Mashona, Basuto, Damara and Ova-Herero. The term Kafir is often used to cover all Bantus of South Africa.

The Zulu are the best physical type of the southern tribes. They are above the mean Negro height. Their figures are shapely and muscular, and their face-features very little negroid. In many cases their nose is regular instead of flat. Their skin

[3] *Ibid.*, pp. 240, 242. [4] Moffat, pp. 163, 523.

varies from a light, clear brown to blue black.[5] The superiority of the Zulu is due mainly to the Galla blood infused by immigration from the north.

The Bechuana are more or less mixed with Hottentot blood, and represent a more negroid type, while the Bakalahari show a still more marked Hottentot mixture.[6]

The Herero show a marked approximation to the Caucasian. Their heads are less elongated, the cheek-bones less prominent, and the lips less everted than is the case with the average Bantu.[7] The superiority of the Herero is due to their probable immigration from the Galla tribes of Central Africa.

The other tribes of South Africa show varying degrees of mixture between the invading Galla type and the aboriginal Negro. Almost everywhere the substratum of the population is a darker and more negroid type. Generally the lighter colored tribes are near the coast and more distant from the equator, and this fact would seem to indicate that the climate had had some effect in bleaching the skin.

Economic Life.—The life of the people of this zone revolves about the cattle pen.[8] In the center of each village is a circular inclosure for cattle.

[5] Keane, "Man: Past and Present," p. 100; Fritsch, pp. 13-25; Deniker, p. 467.

[6] Deniker, p. 465.

[7] Ratzel, II, p. 467; Johnston, "On the Races of the Congo and the Portuguese Colonies." *Jour. Anthropological Institute,* Vol. XIII, p. 464.

[8] Theal, "History and Ethnography of Africa," I, p. 154; Conder, p. 82.

The huts of the people are arranged around the inclosure. The cattle are prized mainly for their milk, which is used generally in a sour state. When occasionally an ox is slain for food it is consumed gluttonously. A family of four or five people can eat a whole carcass in a day and a half. Some tribes have in addition to the cattle a quantity of sheep and goats, while other tribes have neither sheep, goats nor cattle.[9] The invading hordes of Zulu, Matebele and Makololo that swept over a great area of South Africa destroyed or captured the cattle in many tribes and left in their devastated path only a few dogs and chickens.[10] The natives so bereft were forced to take up agriculture.

The pastoral people supplement their diet of milk by a variety of vegetables and fruits. The cultivation of the soil is imposed upon slave men and women, or serfs who live in villages to themselves.[11] Near the cattle kraal are patches of ground for raising maize (Kafir corn), millet, rice, melons, pumpkins, hemp, tobacco, etc.[12] The season for planting is fixed by the chief, and the women sow the grain to the accompaniment of shouts and singing.[13] The grain harvested is stored in holes dug in the middle of the cow pen, or in baskets or in clay jars. The latter are eight to twelve feet in diameter, about the

9 Ratzel, II, pp. 416, 455.

10 Ratzel, *Ibid.*, p. 505.

11 Moffat, p. 390; Reclus, IV, p. 229.

12 Theal, "History and Ethnography of South Africa," I, p. 147; Bent, p. 258.

13 Ratzel, II, p. 433.

same height, and they rest upon a circle of stones. Grain doesn't often last to the next season on account of the weevil.[14] Vast areas of rich soil have gone to waste on account of the devastating hordes of cattle-lifters that have overrun the country.[15] Some tribes, owing to the loss of their cattle and the undependable character of agriculture, have been reduced to desperate extremities for food, and are glad to subsist upon mice, caterpillars, or kernels that pass undigested from the elephant.[16] The Tongas, having lost their cattle by raiders, "consult the flight of vultures in order to take part in the carrion feast."[17] In the far interior where water is scarce it sometimes happens that men, women and oxen, coming unexpectedly upon a pool or creek, enter into a general scramble for the refreshing draught.[18] A popular drink among the prosperous tribes is a beer made of millet or maize.[19]

In the industrial arts the pastors are behind the tribes of Central Africa, except that in iron-work they maintain the general average of excellence. The Zulu cutlery is sometimes ranked with that of England.[20] The pastors manufacture their kaross from various skins; they make sacks of ox-hides for milk, make pottery, plaited dishes, baskets, mats,

14 Bent, p. 86; Moffat, p. 399.
15 Moffat, pp. 269, 523; Reclus, IV, p. 236.
16 Ratzel, II, p. 476.
17 Reclus, IV, p. 230.
18 Moffat, p. 387.
19 Bent, p. 58; Conder, p. 82.
20 Ratzel, II, pp. 421, 430.

stools, hoes, lances, axes, knives, etc. Excellent wood carving is done in Mashonaland.[21]

The pastoral groups are so far self-sustaining that there is little development of trade. Where untouched by European innovations they have no regular roads and no bridges, and the only instruments of transportation are porters and oxen.[22] River navigation is almost unknown. There is scarcely a canoe from the Cape to Lake Ngame.[23] Of course, since the intrusion of the white man into this region, many vehicles have come into use and thousands of miles of railway.

The division of labor is well marked. The women generally do the field work, but in some cases the men assist.[24] Women make the pottery, tan skins, spin and weave, make clothes, cook, and sometimes tend the cattle.[25] The men as a rule look after the cattle, do the milking, the smith-work, carving, etc. The Zulu have a division of labor into the armourer, brazier, tanner, shoemaker, pipe-maker, etc.[26]

Among the Kafirs uncultivated land is held in common, but is assigned annually by the chief to his headmen. Cattle are not held in common.[27] Each freeman has his individual herds, and often in

[21] Goodrich, p. 211; Chapman, I, p. 172; Moffat, pp. 471, 494; Conder, p. 90; Theal, "History and Ethnography of South Africa," I, p. 156.

[22] Theal, "History and Ethnography of South Africa," I, p. 83.

[23] Semple, p. 298.

[24] Ratzel, II, p. 507.

[25] *Ibid.*, p. 415.

[26] Kidd, "Savage Childhood," p. 39.

[27] Theal, "History and Ethnography of South Africa," I, p. 82.

the same family property is held in severalty. Among the Herero a child acquires from his father, uncle, or cousin his individual cattle, and does not live on the common property of the family.[28] The chief has his oxen and the people theirs.[29] Every man owns the land he cultivates.[30]

The industrial life of the natives of this zone has been revolutionized in many districts by the intrusion of the white man. In the sphere of the white man's activities, mining predominates over stock-raising or farming. The labor problem as it affects the natives is to be discussed in another volume of this series.

Family Life.—Wives are purchased in terms of cattle and their sale is a source of wealth to their parents.[31] The transaction is not regarded as a purchase by the native but as a dowry or pledge of good conduct on the part of the husband.[32] If the wife give birth to no children the husband may demand a return of the cattle. Young girls go through a ceremony of initiation at puberty which announces that they are ready to be applied for in marriage.[33] The arrangement of marriages is usually made by parents[34] but matches from mutual love are not uncommon.[35] In recent years with the increase of

28 Ratzel, II, p. 416.
29 Kidd, "Kafir Socialism," p. 10.
30 *Ibid.*, p. 17; Macdonald, p. 276.
31 Kidd, "Kafir Socialism," p. 9.
32 Macdonald, p. 270.
33 Theal, "History and Ethnography of South Africa," I, p. 116.
34 Macdonald, p. 270.
35 Theal, "History and Ethnography of South Africa," I, p. 117.

agriculture women have become more important economic factors and consequently more and more expensive. In Zululand young boys have to bestir themselves by going on long journeys to the coast, seeking employment of the white man, in order to earn the wherewith to buy a wife.[36]

Polygamy is common and also concubinage. Men of importance sometimes have an hundred wives. Concubines are obtained by military conquests.[37] The introduction of the plow has tended to diminish the extent of polygamy by enabling one woman to support the family.[38] The Kafirs marry within the tribe but not within the clan or circle of blood kin.[39] Virginity is prized but not much in fashion before marriage, and married women even are very unchaste. On days of public celebrations sexual license is shocking. Illegitimacy among the Zulu is rare on account of the abortion produced by the medicine man.[40]

The huts of the people are made of brush, sticks and mats, and are mostly conical in form. The Kafir, like a true nomad, says Ratzel, "first puts up the cattle pen, *isibaya,* by surrounding a circular space with a fence and hedge, or, in districts where wood is scarce, with a wall of stones or turf. The huts, one apiece for the husband, for each of his

36 Cunningham, p. 168.

37 Ratzel, II, pp. 443, 544.

38 Conder, p. 86.

39 Kidd, "Kafir Socialism," p. 12; Macdonald, p. 270.

40 Macdonald, p. 270; Theal, "History and Ethnography of South Africa," I, p. 123.

wives and for each adult member of the family, are erected in a semi-circle around the cattle pen. The man gets some two hundred pointed laths twelve feet long and sticks them in a circle in the ground. The woman binds them together at the top with liana fibers, fastens grass or reeds over them, and spreads the space within with a mixture of earth and cow-dung. Newly built huts look like haycocks."[41] Among the northern Kafirs the round hive-shaped hut gives way to the quadrangular. Generally round huts with cone-shaped roof predominate in the east and beehive huts in the west.[42] In some localities the hut is built upon poles, seven feet or more from the ground, or in trees, to escape the attack of lions.[43]

The burden of supporting the family does not rest so much upon the women as in the zones near the equator. The men do a liberal share of the work, especially in tending the cattle.

Family ties are stronger in this zone than among the agricultural people of the north. The father, however, is master of the family, and the position of the wife is not elevated. The wives of kings shuffle on their knees in the presence of their lord.[44] The Zulu is fond of his wives,[45] and parents are wonderfully kind to their young children.[46] It is

[41] II, p. 431.
[42] Ankermann, p. 56.
[43] Moffat, pp. 519, 520.
[44] Reclus, IV, p. 175.
[45] Macdonald, p. 218.
[46] Kidd, "Savage Childhood," p. 95; Weiss, p. 113.

not uncommon to see a mother embrace her sons.[47] The father also often shows a deep affection for his sons. Moffat instances the case of a man who walked two hundred miles and offered all of his beads and ornaments to redeem his two sons who had been stolen by the Matebele.[48] Twins, however, are abhorred and put to death.[49] Infanticide is a national institution among the Zulu.[50] The Bechuana put to death albinos, the deaf and blind.[51] Among some of the debased tribes it is not uncommon for parents to sell their children.[52] When boys cut their second teeth they cease to sit with the other sex. They must live in a separate hut to themselves till married.[53] The aged parents are respected and cared for; even grandparents are respected.[54] Kidd thinks that the constant relations of the people with the spirits of their ancestors tend to strengthen family ties.[55] A Kafir married woman must cut off all communication with her husband's kin; she must not pronounce their names.[56]

Descent is generally in the male line. The eldest son inherits the cattle and his father's wives.[57]

47 Moffat, p. 547.
48 Page 547.
49 Kidd, "Savage Childhood," p. 45; Bent, p. 316.
50 Ratzel, II, p. 435.
51 Reclus, IV, p. 158.
52 Moffat, p. 390.
53 Webster, p. 12; Kidd, "Savage Childhood," p. 84.
54 Kidd, "Savage Childhood," pp. 36, 39, 98, 145.
55 "Kafir Socialism," p. 28.
56 Avebury, p. 14.
57 Bent, p. 315; Fritsch, p. 135; Macdonald, pp. 277, 278.

CHAPTER XX

BANTUS OF THE SOUTHERN CATTLE ZONE (*continued*)

Political Life.—In making the transition from the narrow plateau of East Africa to the south, the pastoral people have to pass through regions not suitable for grazing, and at the same time infested with the tsetse fly. Once across these regions the pasture lands become more and more inviting. In order to occupy these favored areas, in the first instance, it was necessary for the invaders to mass themselves together. The cattle had to be kept in an enclosure in the center protected by a circle of huts. Each clan was divided into two groups, one of which comprised the army made up of the young unmarried men. The pastoral resources did not permit of very large communities, the Kafir villages varying in size from 500 to 2,000 persons. In a few favored sections were villages of several thousand each. Moffat says, that "riding into the center of the large fold, which was capable of holding ten thousand head of cattle, we were rather taken by surprise to find it lined by 800 warriors, besides 200 which were concealed in each side of the entrance as if in ambush."[1] The Bechuana, who combine considerable

[1] Page 530.

agriculture with their pastoral life, contrast with the Zulu in forming larger groups. Their towns are often fortified by stone walls, and their cattle are kept in an outlying post.[2]

Once organized for defense, the temptation to aggression becomes irresistible, in view of the prospect of booty from weaker tribes. Among the Zulu, marriages were not permitted to the military groups and no children allowed in them. Unlimited concubinage, however, was allowed, and the offspring of the fighting group were killed. Hence aggression became necessary to prevent a decrease in the supply of women.[3]

The fact of common race, language, and an open country would seem to favor large federations, but such is the geography of South Africa that pasture fields are intervened by forests, waste lands and mountains, and therefore do not, as the steppe lands of the Sudan, favor a great empire like that among the Fellatahs. Indeed, the process of federation never advanced as far as the geographical conditions or fighting strength of the people seemed to warrant. The few tribes that confederated lacked cohesion, on account first, of the despotic form of government which excited rebellion and, second, the open nature of the country which facilitated the escape of disaffected elements of the population. If expansion had been a matter only of military leadership there would have been mighty empires in South Africa; for it has produced many men of

[2] Conder, pp. 87, 88. [3] Ratzel, II, pp. 442, 443.

military genius. The fighting ability of the rank and file would also have favored the success of empire building; for the whole male population was trained from infancy in the art of war. But, in fact, the different communities were so loosely bound together that they could scarcely understand each other's dialect.[4]

The conquering tribes always dispossessed the conquered of their cattle, and either reduced them to a servile class of peasants, or killed all of them except the boys and girls. The chief, in peace, as in war, held his subjects together by tyranny.[5] The process of absorption by conquest brought together an alien mixture of men and women who had little common sympathy as a basis for unity. Of Mosilikatsi's government, Moffat says, that it was "the very essence of despotism. His word was law and he had only to lift his finger, or give a frown, and his greatest nobles trembled in his presence. No one appeared to have a judgment of his own, none dared to negative an opinion breathed by his sovereign."[6] Among some of the more agricultural and less military tribes, government took on a milder form.[7] For example, the Bechuana (the name means equals) were ruled by a council of elders,[8] but even their government was based upon a rigid caste system in

[4] Theal, "History and Ethnography of South Africa," I, p. 76.

[5] Macdonald, p. 290.

[6] Page 543.

[7] Macdonald, p. 288.

[8] Livingstone, "Missionary Travels and Researches," pp. 200, 201; Theal, "History and Ethnography of South Africa," I, p. 77.

which the rich class alone possessed rights.[9] The Bechuana had not until recently emerged from the pure tribal state. They were divided into the crocodile, fish, monkey, buffalo, lion and other tribes. They sang about their totem at feasts, and the crocodile tribe marked the ears of their cattle with an incision which resembled the open jaws of that creature. The modern coat-of-arms of civilized people probably had its origin in some such markings.[10]

In the Kafir tribes the people are the property of the rulers. It used to be that when a man died his nearest relative was required to report the circumstance to the head of the clan, and to take a present of some kind with him as consolation for the loss sustained.[11] At the present time injuries or wrongs are not left to private revenge.[12] An offense against any one is atoned for by a fine paid to the chief.[13] "Children are responsible to the father, he is responsible to the headman, who in turn is responsible to the petty chief; while the petty chiefs are responsible to the king."[14] Rulership among the Kafirs is generally hereditary, except among the Zulus where the leader is chosen or self-appointed.[15]

About 1853 the Zulus were divided into regiments of 900 men. They embraced 78 tribes, each averag-

[9] Conder, p. 89.
[10] Lang, "Myth, Ritual and Religion," p. 71.
[11] Theal, "History and Ethnography of South Africa," I, p. 79.
[12] Kidd, "Kafir Socialism," p. 20.
[13] Kidd, *Ibid.*, p. 9.
[14] Kidd, *Ibid.*, p. 4.
[15] Macdonald, p. 289.

ing about 367 huts and 1,500 souls.[16] Each soldier wore an ox-hide shield, covering his whole body, and carried a club and short spear, his brow being adorned with a profusion of feathers.[17] In times of war the women and prisoners followed the army, driving the cattle, cooking, bringing water, and carrying mats.[18]

In the long-continued wars of South Africa each tribe deprived of cattle was obliged either to perish or rob others, and hence the whole region was set in motion like a storm-tossed sea.[19] The Zambesi and Kubango basins, which might support a population of 200,000,000, were swept bare by devastating wars.[20] Even the countries north of the Zambesi, and on the borders of Lake Nyassa, perished economically and politically from the Zulu invasions.[21] The weaker tribes took refuge in localities difficult of access and enclosed by palisades.[22] One tribe, the Ba Silika, escaped destruction by occupying a bluff, near the Limpopo, protected by a zone of tsetse fly. Their herds were kept in the upland valleys. Other tribes deprived of their cattle took to the woods to live by hunting, or to die of hunger.[23]

The inception of the Zulu invasion into the north is related by Theal as follows: "About the year 1783, or perhaps a little later, one of the wives of the chief of a small tribe, living on the banks of the

16 Ratzel, II, p. 336.
17 Moffat, p. 553.
18 Ratzel, II, p. 443.
19 Moffat, p. 372.
20 Ratzel, II, p. 236.
21 *Ibid.*, II, p. 506.
22 *Ibid.*, p. 509.
23 Moffat, p. 415.

river Umvolosi, gave birth to a son, who was named Tshaka (more often written Chaka). Before he was fully grown the boy excited the jealousy of his father, and was obliged to flee for his life. He took refuge with Dingiswayo, head of a powerful tribe, who in his early years had gone through many strange adventures, and had by some means come to hear of the European military system. When Tshaka fled to him, Dingiswayo was carrying on a war with his neighbors, and had his followers regularly drilled and formed into regiments. The young refugee became a soldier in one of these regiments, and, by his bravery and address, rapidly rose to a high position. Time passed on, Dingiswayo died, and the army raised Tshaka, then its favorite general, to supreme command. This was the origin of the terrible Zulu power.

"Tshaka was a man of great bodily strength and of unusual vigor of mind, but he was utterly merciless. He set himself the task not merely of conquering but of exterminating the tribes as far as he could reach. With this object he greatly improved the discipline of the army, and substituted for the light assegai a short-handled, long-bladed spear, formed either to cut or stab. With this weapon in his hand, the highly trained Zulu soldier, proud of his fame and his ornaments, and knowing that death was the penalty of cowardice or disobedience, was really invincible.

"Tribe after tribe passed out of sight under the Zulu spear, none of the members remaining but a few of the handsomest girls and some boys reserved to carry burdens. These boys, with only the choice before them of abject slavery or becoming soldiers, always begged to be allowed to enter the army, and were soon known as the fiercest of the warriors.

"The territory that is now the colony of Natal was densely peopled before the time of Tshaka. But soon after the commencement of his career, various tribes that were trying to escape from his armies fell upon the inhabitants of that fair land, and drove before them those whom they did not destroy. As far as the Umzimvubu River the whole population was in motion, slaughtering and being slaughtered."[24]

About this time one of Chaka's captains, Sebituane, became fired with ambition to found an empire of his own. He escaped from Chaka and established the kingdom of the Makololo.[25]

In 1827, not long after Sebituane began his rebellion, another of Chaka's captains, Mosilikatsi, dreaming also of empire, escaped, marched northward to the neighborhood of the Makololo, and there in 1834 established the kingdom of the Matebele.[26] "The country over which he marched," says Theal, "was covered with skeletons, and literally no human beings were left in it, for his object was to place a desert between Tshaka and himself. When he considered himself at a safe distance from his old home, he halted, erected military kraals, after the

[24] Page 164.

[25] Richter, p. 15.

[26] Richter, p. 17.

Zulu pattern, and from them as a center his regiments traversed the land north, south and west in search of spoil."[27] . . . "While the Matebele were engaged in their career of destruction, other bands were similarly employed farther north, so that by 1828 there was not a single Bechuana tribe left intact between the Magalisberg and the Limpopo."[28]

In 1829 the missionary Moffat visited Mosilikatsi, whose kraal was then 100 miles east of the Marikwa. "When the Matebele conquered a town," says Moffat, "the terrified inhabitants were driven in a mass to the outskirts where the parents and all the married women were slaughtered on the spot. Such as have dared to be brave in defense of their town, their wives and children, are reserved for a still more terrible death. Dry grass, saturated with fat, is tied around their naked bodies and then set on fire. The youths and girls are loaded on beasts of burden with the spoils of the town. If the town be in an isolated position the helpless infants are left to perish either with hunger or to be devoured by beasts of prey."[29]

The country within the sweep of the Matebele was rapidly depopulated.[30] "On the side of the hills and Kashan mountains," says Moffat, "were towns in ruins where thousands once made the country alive amidst fruit vales, now covered with luxuriant grass, and inhabited by game. The extirpating invasions of the Mantatees and Matebele had left to beasts of

[27] Page 169.

[28] Page 169.

[29] Page 555.

[30] Bent, p. 269.

prey the undisputed right of these lovely woodland glens."[31] The havoc wrought by Chaka the Terrible was nothing comparable to that of Mosilikatsi.[32]

The story of the struggle of the Boers and English with the Matebele and other Kafir tribes is a long and tragic one. It may be briefly summarized as follows: In 1836 a band of invading Boers, under Potgieter and Maritz, surprised one of Mosilikatsi's camps near the present Wiuberg (Vet River). After a hot fight the Matebele retreated leaving 400 men dead on the field. The Boers burnt the kraal and carried off 7,000 head of cattle.[33]

A short time afterwards, a second attack upon the Matebele was made by the Boers under Potgieter and Pieter Uys. Mosilikatsi was found on the Marikwa, fifty miles north of Mosega, and he had about 12,000 warriors. "But the advantage of the farmers in their guns and horses was so great that the hundred and thirty-five did not hesitate to attack a force which was to theirs as ninety to one."[34] After a nine days' onslaught by Mosilikatsi he was so badly crippled in men that he gave up the contest and fled to the north, and, in the country beyond the Limpopo, commenced to destroy the southern Bechuana. The Boers contented themselves by seizing six or seven thousand head of cattle.[35]

"In September, 1828, Tshaka was murdered by two of his brothers, one of whom—Dingan by name

[31] Page 518.

[32] *Ibid.*, p. 526.

[33] Theal, "South Africa," p. 200.

[34] *Ibid.*, p. 202.

[35] *Ibid.*, p. 203.

—succeeded as chief of the Zulus. The new ruler was equally as cruel but not so able as his predecessor."[36] When the white colonists began to move towards Natal, their leader, Pieter Retief, negotiated with the Zulu chief, Dingan, for permission to enter. When all of the terms and conditions seemed to be agreed upon, Dingan caused Retief and his escort, now in Dingan's camp, to be seized and executed. A few hours later about 10,000 Zulus set out and, after eleven days' march, fell upon the most advanced immigrant encampment, near the present village of Weenen. "Forty-one white men, fifty-six white women and one hundred and eighty-five white children, and about two hundred and fifty colored servants perished in the dreadful massacre. Needless to say, the wagons and their contents were utterly destroyed."[37] A camp of immigrants farther on had barely time to draw their wagons around them when the Zulus appeared. After attacking the laager without success, and losing a great number of men, the Zulus retired and drove away a large herd of cattle.[38]

The colonists were now in a high fever of revenge. Three hundred and forty-seven of them assembled and rode directly towards the Zulu capital under Potgieter and Uys. After a five days' march they came in sight of a division of the Zulu army. A fight ensued. The Zulus, feigning retreat, drew the invaders into a skillfully planned ambuscade. In a gorge between two ranges of hills the immigrants

[36] *Ibid.*, p. 167. [37] *Ibid.*, p. 208. [38] *Ibid.*, p. 209.

were surrounded and attacked. Only the most desperate fighting enabled the immigrants to cut their way through the rear and escape, leaving behind them a large number of horses, all of the baggage and ammunition, and ten of their men slain, of whom one was their commandant Uys.

"A few days later seventeen Englishmen left Port Natal with about fifteen hundred blacks, of whom between three and four hundred were armed with muskets. A few miles south of the Tugela they came upon a Zulu regiment which pretended to take flight, leaving food cooking on fires and even throwing away a number of shields and assegais. The Natal army pursued with all haste, crossed the Tugela, took possession of a kraal on the northern bank, and then found it had been drawn between the horns of a Zulu army fully seven thousand strong." The battle was fought April 17, 1838, one of the most desperate in the history of South Africa. Repeated rushes of the Zulus finally cut the Natal army in two, and put it to rout. The retreat across the river was intercepted by a Zulu regiment. "Thirteen English lay dead on the field of battle, with a thousand Natal blacks, and probably three times that number of Zulus."[39]

In November, 1838, Andrew Pretorius arrived in Natal and was elected commander-in-general. He at once organized a force of 460 men, and on December 16 routed Dingan's army, but could not then follow with his cavalry into the districts where

[39] *Ibid.*, p. 213.

Dingan had retired. In January, 1840, Pretorius again set out to find Dingan's army. Through the treachery and assistance of a large force of Zulu deserters he located the army and defeated it. Dingan with a remnant of his force fled northward to the border of the Swazi country where he was soon afterwards assassinated. Thereafter, the terror which the Zulu name had inspired in South Africa was a thing of the past.[40]

. . . . . .

Many of the Bechuana tribes lived in an ill-watered steppe which afforded little inducement to agriculture and supported a sparse population. They were politically weak and not able to contend successfully against the Zulu, Matebele and Makololo. Raiding in this region, however, on account of the distance between villages and watering places, meant long marches and a precarious existence. The invaders were hardly paid for their efforts. Moffat observed, that "With all their conquests, and the many thousands of cattle which they must have captured, they were dying of hunger. Their march for hundreds of miles might have been traced by human bones." [41]

The Basuto occupied the Drakensberg mountains and were little affected by the Zulu movement. This region, the Switzerland of South Africa, is a plateau about 5,000 feet above sea, rising like a gi-

[40] *Ibid.*, p. 217. [41] Page 369.

gantic billow in successive waves of mountains until the summit of the Drakensberg is reached, the highest peak of which is over 11,000 feet.[42]

It was not until 1867 that Basutoland was conquered. Moshesh, then the leader of the native army, after a brilliant strategic defense, was at last overcome by the Boers, and his men were scattered among the hills. By the interference of Sir Wodehouse the Basuto were proclaimed British subjects, and in 1871 their territory was annexed to Cape Colony.[43]

All of the territory formerly held by the Bantus of the cattle zone, except that of German West Africa and Portuguese East Africa, now belongs to the Union of South Africa.

Religious Life.—In this prairie region nature is not manifested in that violent form which overcomes the people with terror. Subsistence arises here, not from the bounty of nature, but so palpably from labor and foresight that the people are not greatly concerned with the play of external forces. Nevertheless, the people are surrounded by enough that is mysterious to fill their minds with superstition. Spirit belief is as strong here as elsewhere in Africa, but it is less fantastic and fear-inspiring. The fundamental conception of the people is that the spirits of men live after them. These departed spirits get hungry and thirsty; they are subject to moods like the living, and they interfere in a vexatious way with

[42] Theal, "South Africa," p. 263. [43] *Ibid.*, pp. 321-330.

the course of human events.[44] This conception leads naturally to ancestor worship. "The clan worships the spirits of the ancestors of the chiefs, and the tribe worships the spirits of the ancestors of the paramount chief."[45] Sometimes the spirits of the dead visit their friends and descendants in the form of animals, and hence a sort of animal worship.[46] The Ova-Herero worship certain trees supposed to be their ancestors.[47] Generally speaking, the people of this zone do not pay much attention to animals in their religious thought, and do not believe in reincarnation and transmigration of souls to the same extent as the equatorial Negroes.

A distinctive characteristic of the Kafir religion is that it is concerned with the spirits of human beings rather than with the spirits of nature; and, in consequence of this, the idea of beneficence in spirits is more observable than among the natives of the manioc and banana zones. Religious rites are entered into with joy, not with terror. The gods are invited to be present and partake of the repast. This is but a step to the festal thanksgiving and acknowledgment of benefits.[48]

In addition to the ancestral spirits, there are others personifying nature. A god of lightning is

[44] Kidd, "Kafir Socialism," p. 28; Theal, "History and Ethnography of South Africa," I, p. 84.

[45] Macdonald, p. 286.

[46] Theal, "History and Ethnography of South Africa," I, p. 90.

[47] Ratzel, II, p. 481.

[48] Brinton, p. 181.

common among the Zulu and Bechuana.[49] Sky gods are found everywhere, and probably are connected in their origin with the fire cult which is widespread in South Africa.[50] "The sun is supposed to travel under the earth after it sets. It is then warmed up —boiled in a pot of fat—and sent up at dawn next day."[51] The Zulu conceives of thunder, clouds and lightning as actual creatures capable of being herded like cattle. A cloud herd is like a cow herd, except that only a sorcerer can manipulate the former.[52] Some tribes believe in a supreme being who was once a man.

The gods or spirits, good and bad, are inextricably entangled in the social life of the people. Kafir children are washed in a medicine mixed with the dirt scraped from the father's body, in order to impart the spirit of the grandfather or clan.[53] Sneezing is caused by the ancestral spirit and it is a sign that the spirit is taking care of the child. Bleeding at the nose is also the work of the ancestral spirit and indicates the purging of the child of bad blood.[54] To catch two mice in one trap causes a man's wife to have twins.[55] Food of certain kinds

[49] Conder, p. 82; Macdonald, p. 295.

[50] Brinton, p. 142; Theal, "History and Ethnography of South Africa," I, p. 94; Frobenius, "Die Weltanschauung der Naturvölker," Beiträge zur Volks-und Volkerkunde, VI, pp. 287-289.

[51] Kidd, "Savage Childhood," p. 147.

[52] Lang, "Myth, Ritual and Religion," p. 110.

[53] Kidd, "Savage Childhood," p. 12.

[54] Kidd, *Ibid.*, p. 106.

[55] *Ibid.*, p. 48.

must not be eaten lest the ire of an evil spirit be awakened.[56] Milk must not be brought in contact with iron lest evil comes to the cattle. Certain plants are supposed to be lucky and others unlucky. The Makololo will not plant maize for fear of immediate death, but whoever plants coffee will be ever happy.[57] A vessel that breaks has lost its spirit, or is bewitched. A Bechuana smith once tried to hammer a cast-iron pot that had been stolen. As he struck it upon the anvil it flew to pieces. He did not doubt that it was bewitched.[58] The Namaqua protect themselves from lightning by shooting poisoned arrows at it.[59] The Bechuana used to eat the flesh of an enemy to add his courage to their own.[60]

Human sacrifices occur only in rare cases. Sometimes when an important chief dies several of his wives and slaves are sacrificed and also his favorite dog.[61] On the occasion of the death of Chaka's mother, two maidens followed her into the other world.[62] Most generally spirits are propitiated and made to serve the living by offerings of cattle, sheep, goats, corn, etc.[63] In case of sickness a Zulu will sometimes offer an ox to appease the offended spirit.[64] The people always eat any animal or fowl

[56] Reclus, IV, p. 159.
[57] Ratzel, II, p. 371.
[58] Moffat, p. 290.
[59] *Ibid.*, p. 259.
[60] Reclus, IV, p. 160.
[61] Theal, "History and Ethnography of South Africa," I, p. 88.
[62] Ratzel, II, p. 374.
[63] *Ibid.*, II, p. 412.
[64] Macdonald, p. 267.

used as a sacrifice.[65] Idols are not found in South Africa.[66]

Diseases are not always due to evil spirits. For instance, death from starvation is not attributed to any occult source.[67] But spirits do cause much sickness and many deaths. A spirit that causes the death of one person, may, like our microbe, enter into another person and take his life also. Formerly the custom prevailed among the Herero of cutting through the spine of the deceased to kill the worm or spirit, *otjivura,* which was supposed to reside there, and which after death would become an evil spectre.[68]

Magic-men, sorcerers or witch-doctors are very numerous, and their work is highly specialized.[69] There are magic-men who detect witches, protect crops and people from evil, etc. Then there is a special class of doctors who make rain, and keep off lightning and thunder.[70] Finally there is the medicine man proper devoted to curing sickness.[71] The work of the magic-man is not regarded by the Kafir as supernatural, but in the same light as we regard our chemist or electrician.[72] The war-doctor makes the soldiers brave and invincible by sprinkling them

65 *Ibid.*, p. 106.
66 Moffat, pp. 236, 243; Conder, p. 83.
67 Moffat, p. 437.
68 Ratzel, II, p. 468.
69 Macdonald, pp. 293, 294.
70 Macdonald, p. 295.
71 *Ibid.*, p. 273.
72 Kidd, "Kafir Socialism," p. 21.

with a concoction of roots and herbs, and smearing them with portions of the bodies of slain enemies.[73] "A sorcerer," says Moffat, "will pretend he cannot find out the guilty person, or where the malady of another lies, till he has an ox or goat to manœuvre by cutting out certain parts. An ox is usually required of the rich."[74] The Herero doctor takes auguries from the coils and glands in the mesentery of a slaughtered wether, like any Roman auspices,[75] or, as a sovereign remedy, smears hyena dung on the patient's mouth and forehead.[76] To bring rain when the skies are unpropitious is a trying ordeal for the magic-man, especially if he have to respond to a call 200 miles distant.[77] To gain time he calls for a baboon, or the heart of a lion—both scarce and difficult to get.[78] When the matter can be delayed no longer he assembles all the people of the town, who pass in succession before him, when each is sprayed with drippings of a zebra's tail dipped in water.[79] In case of failure sundry excuses are offered. Sometimes the resident missionary is blamed, or the church bells.[80] But the people get angry and take revenge, so that "a rain doctor seldom dies a natural death."[81] The Zulu doctor is a self-made man. He wanders in the woods, comes back daubed with clay and festooned with snakes, and claims to have lived in a pool with the rainbow.

[73] Macdonald, p. 284.
[74] Page 277.
[75] Ratzel, II, p. 412.
[76] *Ibid.*, p. 480.
[77] Moffat, p. 309.
[78] *Ibid.*, p. 318.
[79] *Ibid.*, p. 317.
[80] *Ibid.*, p. 320; Conder, p. 84.
[81] Moffat, p. 325.

If he can now guess where things are hid he is a diviner by acclamation.[82] He sometimes has presentiments, hears voices and songs, and sees people at a great distance, like our modern clairvoyants and spiritualists.[83]

The Kafirs have no idea of reward or punishment in the after-life.[84]

82 Gallaway, p. 179.
83 *Ibid.*, pp. 169, 170-2-3.
84 Theal, "History and Ethnography of South Africa," I, p. 85.

CHAPTER XXI

BANTUS OF THE SOUTHERN CATTLE ZONE (*continued*)

Ceremonial Life.—Ceremony in this zone is very marked, but pertains to acts of minor importance, and does not seem to be inspired to any great extent by religion or political terror. It seems rather to be the expression of an effort to compensate for monotony of life. There are no ceremonies connected with sowing seeds, plowing or harvesting.[1] Most of the ceremony seems to relate to the sexual life. There is a ceremony of initiation into manhood,[2] and a ceremony of blood-brotherhood.[3] Among the Bechuana the entrance of a youth upon maturity is accompanied by ceremonies of circumcision, instruction and seclusion which last for months and often for several years.[4] Parleys in connection with marriage often last two or three months. "The wedding ceremony," says Ratzel, "which takes a similar course among all South Kaffirs, consists among the Zulus of the ceremonial transference of the bride to the bridegroom's hut, escorted by the relations

[1] Macdonald, p. 282.
[2] Livingstone, "Travels and Researches," p. 163.
[3] Ratzel, II, p. 380.
[4] *Ibid.*, II, p. 370; Macdonald, p. 268.

and friends in great numbers."[5] The second day after marriage, among the Bechuana the witch-doctor scratches both bride and groom, and their blood is reciprocally rubbed into their wounds.[6] Women in labor are assisted by some wise old women of the kraal. One of them performs the duty of twisting the neck of a child if it should be born feet-foremost, and of performing a like ceremony in case of twins. The new-born babe is brought to the door of the father's hut. The father then "takes the feather of a vulture, singes it in a flame, and holds the smouldering feather under the nose of the babe. The vulture is supposed to be a valiant and brave fighter, and the babe is supposed to imbibe the qualities of the bird.[7] Then the medicine man performs a magic rite to see if the ancestral spirit is pleased with the child.[8] Among the Bechuana, the third day after delivery, the mother's breast is scratched and rubbed with medicinal roots. Both husband and wife go through a purification by sitting crosswise opposite each other on an amulet stick, after which they are smeared with medicinal ointment. The witch-doctor then makes them drink healing water. A husband will swell up and die if he omits this process.[9] Among the Kafir, about the fourth week after a child is born, an ox is sacrificed as a thanks-

[5] II, p. 436.
[6] *Ibid.*, p. 370.
[7] Kidd, "Savage Childhood," p. 21.
[8] *Ibid.*, p. 22.
[9] Ratzel, II, pp. 369, 370.

giving, and all of the clan rejoice in the feast.[10] A forest bird causes children to grow their second teeth, and on this account a child will throw his first loose tooth into the air and call upon the bird to give him another one.[11] An infant may not leave the hut until a month old. Then it is sprinkled with magic powder on its head, and the doctor says, "God spare this child to us." It is also scratched in many parts of the body and has a fetich medicine rubbed in.[12]

Chiefs of equal rank try to avoid meeting, because a salutation of one to the other would mean subordination.[13] When a Zulu chief dies, his funeral is accompanied by a large concourse of mourners who devour hundreds of slaughtered cattle, and drink copiously of palm-wine, beer, and spirits brought in enormous quantities for the carnival.[14] When a member of a Bechuana tribe dies, his grave is bathed in medicine water, and the footprints of the bearers of the corpse are sprinkled with water from a consecrated horn; and their fingers are scratched and medicine rubbed in the wounds. The relations kneel on the grave. No cow is milked on the day of death. Each member of the kraal eats one grain of the deceased's corn with some dry cow-dung. All the mourners return to their huts and enter head last.[15] It is very common for food, ornaments and articles of apparel to be placed on graves.[16] The Kafir generally bury with respect only the chiefs. Common

10 Kidd, "Savage Childhood, p. 25; Macdonald, p. 26.

11 Kidd, "Savage Childhood," p. 83.

12 Ratzel, II, p. 370.

13 Macdonald, p. 266.

14 Ratzel, II, p. 373.

15 *Ibid.*, p. 371.

16 Macdonald, p. 275.

people are thrown into an open ditch as a feast for hyenas and jackals.

Æsthetic Life.—Nearly all of the cattle people scar their bodies.[17] The Kafirs cut short lines across their nose, forehead, cheeks and breasts.[18] The Nyambanás wear a row of pimples or warts, the size of a pea, from the forehead to the tip of the nose. A Bachapin Kafir, who has distinguished himself, may wear a long scar on his thigh.[19] The facts stated in this book in regard to tattooing do not bear out the theory of Hirn that it arises from the notion that it gave magic strength to fighters. Knocking out or filing the upper front teeth is common among the Herero and Batoka, but is not practiced among the Zulu.[20] Puncturing the ears, and using the openings as a substitute for a pocket, is a common practice. Sometimes snuff boxes are carried in these openings.[21]

The tonsorial art reaches fantastic and dizzy heights of æsthetic expression. The northern Kafir, after puberty, wears a tuft made hard with a mixture of charcoal and grease.[22] Sometimes it stands upright to a great height resembling the Eiffel Tower,[23] again it is cut short resembling a paint brush,[24] or it is spread out like the horns of a buffalo.[25]

17 Fritsch, p. 15.
18 Macdonald, p. 267.
19 Avebury, p. 60.
20 Ratzel, II, pp. 466, 551.
21 Bent, p. 355.
22 Ratzel, II, p. 427.
23 Bent, p. 258.
24 *Ibid.*, p. 90
25 Ratzel, II, p. 507.

The natives often disguise the natural color of their skin by paint. The Bechuana smear their bodies with an ointment of a metallic luster; and the Zulu in time of war rub their bodies with grease and red ochre. Body painting is also practiced by the Zulu in connection with the ceremony of circumcision.[26]

Personal decorations are used in profusion. Warriors wear a round cockade of ostrich feathers on their heads, and often as many as eight copper rings around their necks, besides rings of similar material on their arms, legs, and in their ears.[27] Iron rings often take the place of copper, but copper is preferred, and is sometimes obtained from the brass hooks of old boots.[28] Zulu kings bestow heavy bronze arm rings on their successful warriors. Decorations play even a greater rôle among the women than the men.[29]

Tools, weapons and houses are often ornamented with admirable taste. Knives have carved ivory handles.[30] Spoons are ornamented with a carved giraff, or hog, or other animal.[31] The Bechuana excel all other Kafirs in originality, elegance, and fineness of wood carving.[32] In some of the Bechuana houses the walls and doors are ornamented

26 Ratzel, II, p. 427; Johnston, Lydekker, et al., p. 432.

27 Moffat, p. 363.

28 Bent, p. 251.

29 Fritsch, p. 62.

30 Moffat, p. 535.

31 *Ibid.*, p. 509.

32 Ratzel, II, p. 430.

with a kind of architectural effect. "Pillars supporting the roof in the form of pilasters projecting from the walls, and, adorned with flutings and other designs, showed much taste in the architectress."[33] The seats inside of the houses are supported by carved figures of men and animals—often degenerating into grotesque designs. The seats are difficult to distinguish from the neckrests.[34] The Bechuana show taste in their pottery and in the weaving of mats and baskets.

Of the dress of the people little is to be said. The Zulu men and women of the commonalty wear only a leather apron, often adorned with cat-tails. The wives of chiefs wear an ox-hide toga reaching to the feet.[35] The Bechuana are not so nude. The women wear an apron before and behind, the fore one adorned with leather fringes, beads, etc. The aprons of the rich are made of the furs of the jackal, wild cat, or other animal. The chief's apron is made of leopard skin. The poor wear cow skin, or goat skin. Some tribes wear bark-cloth made from the fig tree, and others wear fabrics woven from flax or cotton.[36] The Matebele wear caps made of the tiger-cat or zebra skin. The Bechuana wear a small straw hat.[37] The Herero are the only people who

33 Moffat, p. 524.

34 Frobenius, "The Origin of African Civilizations," "Report Smithsonian Institute," 1898, p. 644.

35 Ankermann, p. 62.

36 Ratzel, II, pp. 507, 508, 545; Theal, "History and Ethnography of South Africa," I, p. 156; Schurtz, p. 140.

37 Conder, p. 87.

cover their feet with sandals.[38] The élite of the Bechuana carry a parasol made of black ostrich feathers.[39]

Some of the Kafir tribes display skill in sculpture, but none in drawing or painting. They have even difficulty in understanding a drawing, while perspective is altogether beyond them.[40] They pay little attention to the aspect of things and never admire the scenery.[41] Upon the whole, the pastoral people of this zone do not give so much attention to the beautifying of themselves and their workmanship as the peoples nearer the equator.

Psychological Characteristics.—In cranial capacity the Kafir stands above the inhabitants of the manioc or banana zone,[42] and shows a corresponding superi-

38 Ratzel, II, p. 470.

39 Moffat, p. 504.

40 Avebury, p. 44.

41 Kidd, "Savage Childhood," p. 126.

42 "Of the tribes below the Zambesi," says Shrubsall, "we find the skulls of this race are large, heavy and of good capacity, while the range of individual variation is greater than that between different tribes." The average capacity of all male Kafirs is 1540 c. c. "The capacity of the Kafir skulls is considerably larger than that of other African Negroes, the average being

West African negro	1420 c. c.
Central Lakes negro	1430 c. c.
Koranna negro	1425 c. c.
True Hottentot negro	1365 c. c."

"A Study of A-Bantu Skulls and Crania," *Jour. Anthropological Institute*, n. s. Vol. I, p. 57.

Viewed from above the skulls of the Zulu (Xosas) present an oval outline, varying between the Forma ovoides and the Forma ellipsoides of Sergi. . . . Both the frontal and parietal eminences are prominent. (Page 57.)

ority in mental power and intelligence.[43] They have a degree of energy, spirit and audacity uncommon in the Negro. They are credited with courage in war,[44] and the spirit of overcoming is shown more in their folklore than in that of other branches of the Negro race.[45] And also they "do not live in everlasting dread of spirits." The thought of evil spirits is not even a terror to children.[46] Their military life and habit of manipulating men has developed a degree of constructive imagination far beyond that of any other races of Africa. Their strategy in war and diplomacy in politics would do credit to any race; and some of their military leaders have been not inaptly compared to Cæsar. In 1852, when Sir George Cathcart invaded Basutoland, his army was led into

The Bechuana are intermediate between the Xosas and the Negroes of the Great Lakes. (Page 71.) Their crania are ellipsoidal and less in capacity than those of the Xosas. The average is about 1420 c. c.

In the western branch of the Kafir, the Ova Mpo and Ba-kalahari show a larger capacity. The Herero average about 1640 c. c. and the Ova Mpo about 1512 c. c. (Page 71.)

"South of the Vaal the Basuto and Kafir skulls are more infantile and seem to show intermixture with the Bushmen and Hottentot race, which still survives in the western corner of the African continent. Such intermixture is indicated by the diminished height, capacity, and prognathism of the skull." (Page 88.)

"To the east, the type is modified and softened down, the crania becoming more leptorrhine, leptoprospic and microseme, while the cephalic index is slightly raised." (Page 88.)

43 Conder, p. 81; Livingstone, "Travels and Researches," p. 20.

44 Conder, p. 81; Livingstone, "Travels and Researches," p. 38; Ratzel, II, p. 424.

45 Kidd, "Savage Childhood," pp. 228, 249.

46 *Ibid.*, p. 132.

a trap by the simple stratagem on the part of the native leader, Moshesh, of exposing an immense herd of cattle in a position on the Berea mountain where their capture appeared easy. The British army was surprised, defeated and forced to retreat.[47] These military leaders are of great value to the people in that they serve as models for the aspiring youth. They incite a spirit of rivalry and of hero worship. To have any kind of hero indicates a decided advance over a state in which the people are bound by habit and tradition. Great men in any community are evidence of departure from conventionality. A higher form of leadership, not attained by the uncivilized, is that based upon examples belonging to art and history. Our highest ideals come to us from people whom we do not chance to know in the flesh.[48] The Kafir has less fear and is less a slave to custom than the Negroes of the north. Fear always breeds custom.[49] The Zulu are especially pugnacious. Their characteristic expression is defiance. They have a firmer will and more rapid decision than their neighbors.[50] They maintain a forceful mood and constitute a forceful type. The Herero are self-willed and sullen, hard to approach, and more moved by reason than emotion.[51] The Bechuana are of a softer and more gentle stamp

47 Theal, "History of South Africa," p. 265.
48 Cooley, "Human Nature and the Social Order," p. 361.
49 Ross, "Social Psychology," p. 203.
50 Ratzel, II, pp. 423, 425.
51 *Ibid.*, p. 466.

but very versatile.[52] The Kafir have numerals extending to one hundred, and their language is "adequate for the expression of any ideas whatever."[53]

The feelings of the Kafir are characterized as excitable and explosive.[54] So long as a Kafir's passions are not excited he is as merry and innocent as a child, loving songs and dances, and is as sociable as an ant.[55] But he is easily provoked into outbursts of violence. He, however, is not so much swayed by feeling as the average Negro. He acts more on reason and his will has more consistency.

The inhibiting power of the Kafir is, therefore, more developed than that of the people of the equatorial region. This power is built up by the social struggle and favorable conditions of climate. Variable and trying climates, says Dexter, train and educate the mind to self-control.[56]

Within the family group the Kafir show the virtues of affection, kindness and mutual helpfulness characteristic of all peoples; and these virtues extend in a great measure to all the members of the tribe. Any member within a tribe may stop wherever he may chance to be and partake of food and drink without invitation.[57] Honesty within the

52 *Ibid.*, p. 425; Fritsch, p. 165.

53 Theal, "History and Ethnography of South Africa," I, p. 76; Crawford, "Numerals as Evidence of the Progress of Civilization," *Transactions of the Ethnological Society*, n. s. Vol. II, p. 89.

54 Fritsch, p. 56.

55 Ratzel, II, p. 425.

56 Page 26.

57 Kidd, "Kafir Socialism," p. 30.

group seems to be prevalent,[58] and parents punish their children if they lie.[59] The lying and stealing charged against the Kafir are probably traits manifested only towards strangers.[60] There is one respect in which the conduct within the primitive group is very inferior to that of the civilized. The individuals of the primitive group are susceptible to deeper envy. Any Kafir who rises above the commonalty in possessions is liable to decapitation, and confiscation of his property, through a charge of witchcraft. This envy among the Negroes renders progress towards civilization exceedingly difficult.[61] For all people outside the group, connected by alimentation and blood, there is little consideration. The attitude towards strangers, however, varies much in different localities. The Bechuana who live under hard conditions seem to have a wider human sympathy. Conder remarks, that "There is a good deal of hospitality between the tribes. Thus the Batlaping, who were starving at Taung, went with their families in 1885 to visit Mafeking, when the Barolong had a good harvest. These visitors were fed a month and sent home with bags of mealies in their wagons."[62] Among the Zulu and eastern tribes, incessant raiding, pillaging and fighting have intensified their cold-heartedness towards strangers. There is no wrong in stealing from a rival

58 Livingstone, "Travels and Researches," p. 219.
59 Kidd, "Savage Childhood," p. 128.
60 Conder, p. 81; Fritsch, p. 53.
61 Theal, "History and Ethnology of South Africa," I, p. 103.
62 Page 87.

tribe[63] or stranger, and any man who injures a member of another tribe does a meritorious act.[64] The chief ambition of a Matebele is to kill his first man, and each aspiring youth is required to pass through human smoke.[65] The Kafir, though ranking above most Negroes, have less power of sympathizing with others than a European. They are slow in locating pain in their own bodies, and also in imagining what others suffer.[66]

Tribal wars have tended to unify and socialize members within the groups, and to intensify hostility towards those outside.[67] The general effect of war everywhere has been to socialize within the group. According to McDougall, wars "have developed in the surviving groups just those social and moral qualities of individuals which are essential conditions of all effective coöperation and of the higher forms of association."[68] . . . "And the more the pugnacious instinct impelled primitive societies to warfare, the more rapidly and effectively must the fundamental social attributes of men have been developed in the societies which survived the ordeal."[69] In the light of this principle, the Zulu groups, on account of their more pugnacious activities, should have become more highly socialized

[63] Moffat, p. 289; Kidd, "Kafir Socialism," p. 67.
[64] Kidd, *Ibid.*, p. 18.
[65] Ratzel, II, p. 350.
[66] Kidd, "Savage Childhood," p. 64.
[67] Kidd, "Savage Childhood," p. 75.
[68] Page 287.
[69] Page 288.

than the other tribes of South Africa. Their failure to become so socialized must be attributed to the absence of a varied economic field of conflict into which the fighting impulse could be carried over. In countries more favored with natural resources and climate for individual development the pugnacious instinct can be converted into a social asset.[70]

The instinct of repulsion among the Kafirs is not manifested in the unsocial manner in which it is displayed by the people of the banana zone. This instinct which, in the lower stages of culture, is spent blindly and injuriously against individuals within the group, tends to be transformed by warfare into resentment against foreigners, and against any action within the group detrimental to the general good. It becomes an important factor in moral consciousness. The failure of this instinct to foster morals among the Kafirs is due to the same cause as that which prevents the socializing effects of tribal conflicts, to wit: the absence of a complex social medium in which natural instincts may be diffused.

In fact, the Kafir has very little moral consciousness. In all things he is so much governed by tradition and habit that he is rarely thrown on his private judgment. He has no sense of "I ought."[71] This sense develops under conditions which give rise to new and unexpected situations.

The Kafir differs from other Africans in posses-

[70] McDougall, p. 293.

[71] Kidd, "Savage Childhood," p. 121.

sing more idealism. He finds models for this in his military heroes and in the great spirits of his ancestors. The climate is somewhat favorable to it and he has also the constructive imagination necessary to its formation. Kafir idealism, however, is feeble compared to that of civilized people. The present realities greatly predominate in his consciousness.[72]

Contact with civilization has been in a large measure a poison to the Kafir. A few of them, raised and educated under the personal examples of Caucasians, have attained to a high degree of mental and moral culture, but such opportunities of contact come only to a very limited number. The masses are isolated from the whites, and have no chance to assimilate culture by intimate association. They therefore imitate of the white man's culture only that which is observed in the street, i. e., his vices rather than his virtues. "Close relations to a few people," says Ross, "as in the well-knit family and joined to a vivid sense of obligation to the community, seem to be more favorable to stable character than the loose touch-and-go associations of general intercourse."[73] The superficial and external aspects of civilization the Kafir can assume, and in this half adoption, he loses the best of his native traits.

Especially deplorable is the physical degeneracy which inevitably follows contact with civilization.[74]

72 Fritsch, p. 51.
73 "Social Psychology," p. 88.
74 Conder, p. 80.

"The fate of the black man," says Cole, "is written in the history of the past: slowly but surely he passes away from the face of the earth—year by year his numbers diminish—his race is exterminated. The Kafir's time is well-nigh come."[75] Speaking in general of savage peoples, McDougall says, that they "are rapidly dying out, owing to the failure of the social sanctions to give sufficient support to the parental instinct against developing intelligence. It is largely for this reason that contact with civilization proves so fatal to so many savage peoples; for such contact stimulates their intelligence, while it breaks the power of their customs and social sanctions generally and fails to replace them by any equally efficient."[76]

Even the good things of civilization do not always suit the Negro; for instance, our dress, diet, school-strain and individualism. "The virtues and arts of civilization," says Sumner, "are almost as disastrous to the uncivilized as its vices. It is really the great tragedy of civilization that the contact of the lower and higher is disastrous to the former, no matter what may be the point of contact, or how little the civilized may desire to do harm."[77] Sometimes harm comes solely from a too rapid introduction of new culture.[78]

Now, to summarize some of the most general con-

[75] Page 49.
[76] Page 270.
[77] Page 111.
[78] Ulysses G. Weatherly, "Race and Marriage," *Am. Jour. Sociology*, XV, No. 4, p. 452.

clusions of the study of the Negro in Africa, it should be said, first, that the Negro races respond to environment in the different zones of Africa just as the Caucasian and Mongolian races form different types in their respective localities. If there is a difference of races in plasticity and responsiveness to external phenomena it is probably in favor of the Negro. There are probably greater diversities of the Negro in Africa than of the Caucasian in Europe and America. The African Negro varies from the shortest to almost the tallest of men, from a very dark color to a complexion lighter than that of many Caucasians, from the flat to the straight nose, from the thick to the thin lip, from the prognathous to the orthognathous jaw, from the receding to the almost prominent forehead. And the contrasts in psychological characteristics are not less striking.

The backwardness of the Negro in Africa is not due directly to lack of mental capacity but to unfavorable environment. Natural selection has adjusted the mental capacity to the conditions. If any other race had peopled Africa in early neolithic times, and remained there until now, it would have advanced no higher than the present culture level of the Negro. "The map of isotherms," says Ellen Semple, "shows Africa quite enclosed between the two torrid lines of 20 Centigrade, except for a narrow sub-tropical belt along the Barbary coast in the north, and in the south an equally narrow littoral extending east and north from the

Cape of Good Hope. At first glance, the large area of South Africa, lying on the temperate side of the Tropic of Capricorn, raises hopes for a rich economic, social and cultural development here; but these are dashed by the examination of the isotherms. Excessive heat lays its retarding touch upon everything, while a prevailing aridity (rainfall less than ten inches), except on the narrow windward slope of the eastern mountains, gives the last touch of climatic monotony. The coastal belt of Cape Colony and Natal raises tropical and subtropical products, like all the rest of the continent, while the semi-arid interior is committed with little variations to pastoral life. Climatic monotony, operating alone, would have condemned South Africa to poverty of development, and will unquestionably always avail to impoverish its national life.''[79]

The question naturally arises, Could the Negro race, under a favorable environment, develop to the same degree of culture as the Caucasian or Mongolian? A correct answer to this question can be given only by history. The experiment is being made, by the Negroes transplanted to America, of which the third volume of this series will deal. In view of the known modifiability of races it seems reasonable to assume that the Negro would be thoroughly capable of evolving a civilization, but such a result would require a long process of natural selection, and freedom from the antagonistic influences of the more fortunate races.

79 Page 623.

Race traits and tendencies are very slow to change whether looked at from the standpoint of heredity or social environment. "Character," says Patten, "is formed by the long series of environments in which a race has lived. Each change to a new environment brings out new traits by creating new motor adjustments, but it does not of necessity destroy the earlier traits. Many of them abide and are brought out more clearly by the new conditions."[80] At present the most conspicuous characteristic of the Negro is an excessive emotionalism. A change of environment may modify suddenly and radically the activity and habits of a people, but their temperament, which is a part of their organic nature, can be changed only by a slow process of evolution. An individual who inherits a choleric temperament may, according to opportunity and stimulation, become superstitious and degraded, or a distinguished artist, poet or musician, but he could not, under any circumstances, transform himself into a phlegmatic or melancholic temperament. Races, as individuals, have inherited emotional characteristics, and these must always color the products of their intellects. "The character," says Ribot, "sends its roots down into the unconscious, i. e., into the individual organism: this is what makes it so difficult to penetrate or modify. The intellectual dispositions can only exercise an indirect action in its constitution."[81]

Furthermore, the instincts of the Negro differ

[80] Page 4. [81] Page 392.

from those of the Caucasian in intensity and direction. Under changed conditions they would, no doubt, be greatly modified, but they would never behave in the same way as those of the Caucasian. A Negro civilization, therefore, would be unique and unlike that of any other race.

The great mistake of the statesmen, missionaries, philanthropists, and sentimentalists is in supposing that it is desirable to make over all races in the likeness of the white man. Races of men, as species of plants, should be cultivated along the lines of their special endowment. It is variation and differentiation that characterize progress in mankind as in all other forms of life.

It would be a great loss to the culture of the world if the races of men should ever become homogeneous. For instance, it would be a misfortune if all races should come to have the meditative, introspective and phlegmatic disposition of the Germans, or the active, daring, and intensely practical disposition of the English and Americans, or the rollicking, emotional and volatile disposition of the Negro. Great superiority of mental development in one direction implies inferiority in other directions.[82] A race living an out-door life, and receiving most of its stimulations through the medium of the eye, will necessarily develop a kind of emotionalism that produces in the mind pictorial and artistic imagery.[83] A race living an in-door life, in a climate overcast with cloud, will tend to develop the powers

82 Bain, p. 95. 83 *Ibid.*, p. 100.

of abstraction and reflection at the expense of the emotions. It cannot be strongly affected by that concrete imagery which favors the growth of the most beautiful sentiments.[84]

A deplorable error of missionary work in Africa and elsewhere has been the effort to reconstruct the natives in the likeness of the Europeans. Besides not being desirable it is impossible. The introduction of European civilization among the Negroes of Africa has had a tendency to disorganize the race and bring about its extinction. This has been so, not because the Negro lacks the capacity for higher culture, but because the methods of introducing it have been bad. Either the process of undermining the old culture has been too rapid, or the elements of new culture have not been imparted in their proper order, or they have not been the kind suited to the psychological and environmental conditions of the race. Only a radical change in the methods thus far employed by the administrators and missionary workers in Africa can overcome this tendency.

The final outcome of the white man's invasion of Africa, is, therefore, not promising for the Negro. If the issue depended solely upon the work of the missionaries the present injurious effects of their activities might be corrected by a change of policy. But, unfortunately for every missionary in Africa, there are thousands of white exploiters who teach the natives all the vices of civilization and infect

[84] *Ibid.*, p. 100.

them with deadly diseases, thus counteracting whatever good the missionaries may do.

The European Powers dominant in Africa hope that the natives may incidentally become civilized through the efforts of the missionary and the schoolhouse; but they forget that more of the natives are imitating the exploiters than the exhorters. What can be expected but ruin for the Negro in view of the examples of robbery, oppression, and vice of every kind furnished by the representatives of the European Powers in Africa? Thus far the interest of the Caucasian in the backward races has been that of exploitation for his own advantage. There are no foreign policies primarily in the interest of the subject peoples. The African Negro has had the benefit of many examples of heroism and self-sacrifice on the part of missionaries and other workers in his behalf, but will these avail in his sensitive nature against the spectacle of the stronger race's invasion of defenseless territory with sword and cannon, the usurpation of land, products and labor, and the pollution of morals and religion through avarice of trade and insolence of depravity?

CHAPTER XXII

THE NEGROES OF THE EAST

The Negro peoples east of Africa are as follows: The Andamans or Mincopies in the islands of the sea of Bengal west of India; some forest tribes in the Malay Peninsula; the Aket of Sumatra; the Aeta of Luzon, Philippine Islands; the Papuans of New Guinea, and the natives of the Black Islands extending from New Guinea to Fiji; the Sakalavas of Madagascar, and if we may believe recent reports a small group of Negritos in the highlands of Ceylon. A Negrito tribe of very ape-like features until recently lived in Java but it is now extinct. The Australians, and now extinct Tasmanians, do not properly belong to the Negro races. Their hair, in form and quantity, their skull formation and color of skin, mark them off from the Negro and place them in a class by themselves. They belong to what Tylor calls the Brown Race.

A sociological interpretation of these peoples is omitted in this study of the Races of Mankind for the reason that the conditions of their existence are so similar in many particulars to those of the Negroes of Africa that a discussion of their psychological characteristics and institutions would be a tiresome repetition of what has been said of the Africans.

Something, however, should be said of the ethnological relations of these eastern Negroes.

Several ethnologists take the view that the Bushmen, Hottentots and Pygmies of Africa are of the same race as the Negritos of the Andaman Islands, of the Philippines, of the Malay Peninsula and of other scattered tribes of the East. It is claimed that they represent an aboriginal population once occupying a vast area of the equatorial continent which in a former geological epoch connected Africa and Asia; that the now predominant taller Negroes represent a variation from the original pygmy, being a superior type which survived in competition with the parent stock. Some support to this theory is found in the statement of Sergi, based upon archeological and anthropological research, that in the Neolithic age a pygmy race not only existed in Africa, but spread round the Mediterranean shores and extended even as far north as Russia.[1] While this question is one for the anthropologists, among whom there is little agreement, the author ventures the opinion that the scattered pygmy Negroes represent only variations, from the larger and more numerous type, arising from local conditions, especially conditions of scant food supply, imposing a severe struggle for existence. There appears to be no general uniformity in physiognomy among these scattered groups to justify the theory of their racial unity.

[1] Page 234.

CHAPTER XXIII

ORIGIN OF THE NEGRO RACE

Evidences of man's existence upon the earth reach to such great antiquity that the time can be measured only in geological epochs. If we begin in the oldest and lowest geological stratum, and search upwards for evidences of the existence of animal life on the earth, we shall pass through the palæozoic and mesozoic epochs without finding any traces of man. In these two epochs, however, we observe a gradual ascent in animal life from the lowest forms of marine life to animals of a type such as mollusks, amphibians, reptiles and a few birds and mammals. Now, glancing upward through the kainozoic epoch, we find in the lowest subdivision of that epoch, the eocene, the appearance of the ancestor of the horse, the four-toed orohippus; and in the next subdivision, the miocene, we find the monkeys, and in the next subdivision, the pliocene, we find the anthropoid apes which correspond almost exactly to man in number and form of bones and general anatomy. Whether man existed at this early time is uncertain. At the close of the pliocene period the glacial age had set in —covering northern Europe and America with a great sheet of ice. This ice age lasted probably three or four thousand years.[1]

Coming now to the geological epoch known as the Quaternary or Post Tertiary, and examining the strata belonging to the subdivision, post-pliocene, we find that the first ice age has receded and a second one developed. Between these ice ages evidences of man's existence is undoubted. From that epoch down to the beginning of the metal age, man's existence upon the earth is divided by anthropologists into three sub-periods: the eolithic (dawn of stone), the palæolithic (old stone), and neolithic (new stone), based upon the character and variety of man's implements.

The eolithic and palæolithic periods are divided into several subdivisions, according to country, for instance, Chellean, Mousterian and Magdalenian, etc. These early periods belong to the interglacial epoch following the great ice age,[2] when the geography of the earth was very different from what it is now. The continents of Asia and America were then joined together, England was joined to the continent of Europe, and Africa and Asia were joined by a continuous land area. Immediately following the great ice age, Chellean period, the climate of Europe was mild and moist, affording a home for tropical life. Europe harbored such animals as the smooth-skinned, two-horned rhinoceros, the great hippopotamus, and the straight-tusked ele-

1 Keane, "Ethnology," p. 57.
2 Deniker, p. 305.

phant, allied to species now found in Africa. It has been conjectured that the migration of animals at this time must have been from south to north. The irregular extension of the ice sheet would have prevented migration from the east to the west or the contrary. The fact that the horse, native of Asia, was not in Europe at this time lends additional probability to the supposition that the movement of men and other animals was from the south.[3] At this epoch we find the implements and other evidences of man, but no unquestioned skeletal remains of him.[3a]

Later when the ice sheets again advanced southward and the climate of Europe became dry and cold (Mousterian period), we discover in various parts of Europe caves containing not only the implements of man but his skeleton, and that also of the animals he hunted and ate, such as the thick furred mammoth, the reindeer, etc.[4]

The first man, according to the fragments of his skeleton found in this second period, was short in stature, having a long, narrow head, receding forehead, heavy, prognathous jaw, and prominent brow ridges.[5] If this be accepted as the type of the first man, and if the migrations of animals in palæolithic times was from the south, the connection between the palæolithic man and the African Negro is very

[3] Deniker, p. 304; Keane, "Man: Past and Present," p. 455.

[3a] Since the above was written a skull and jaw of man have been found in England associated with eolithic implements. See Chapin's "Social Evolution" for an up-to-date discussion of this subject.

[4] Deniker, p. 305; Marett, p. 46.

[5] Deniker, p. 311; Marett, pp. 37, 77.

apparent. Darwin, Keane, and many other scientists claim that the first man was developed in Africa or in the Indo-African Continent.[6]

The African Negro seems to be a survival of the first human inhabitants of the earth. Perhaps the first man differed from the present Negro in color of skin, hair and minor features, as, according to the opinion of Quatrefages, based upon the theory that the evolution of the individual recapitulates the evolution of the race, the first man had a yellow skin, and somewhat reddish hair.[7] The palæolithic men, who remained in Africa, may have there developed the black skin and woolly hair, while those migrating north and east may have developed in transit the Caucasian and Mongolian types. That the white race originated in Africa is now generally conceded. Sergi traces its origin to the Atlas Mountains and the Great Lakes.[8]

At the beginning of the neolithic period, when the climate and geology of the earth assumed its present state, the Negro was probably in possession of all Africa except some districts in the north. Then began the pressure of other races into the domain of the Negro. The Hamites or Berbers, originating about the Great Lakes, or in the Atlas Mountains, mixed with the Negroes forming the Ethiopians and probably the Egyptians, who then drove the Negroes

[6] Darwin, "Descent of Man," New York, 1903, p. 158; Keane, "Ethnology," p. 375; "Man: Past and Present," pp. 5, 458.

[7] "History of the Human Species," p. 242.

[8] "The Mediterranean Races," pp. 41, 43, 252.

towards the south. Later the Semites, having developed their special features in Arabia, invaded Africa from the side of the Red Sea, modifying the type of the Berber, Egyptian, Ethiopian and Negro. The present superiority in physique and intelligence of the Negroes of East Africa is the result of the infiltration of the Caucasian blood. The Negroes least affected by immigration are those of Western Sudan where tribes are found that now approximate closely to the type of the first man.

CHAPTER XXIV

THE NEGROES OF LIBERIA

The Republic of Liberia, comprising in its population mostly Americans and not natives of Africa, was not considered in Volume I of this series in its treatment of the races of West Africa. Before taking leave of Africa, however, the author desires to offer a few remarks upon that republic. Its territory embraces a strip of land lying about 300 miles along the northern Guinea Coast, between the British colony of Sierra Leone and the French colony of the Ivory Coast, and extending inland about 200 miles. It is subject to equatorial rains, and has a luxuriant vegetation and varied fauna, mostly tropical, including a superabundance of reptiles and insects. The country is not favorably situated for agriculture, having only a small coast line of level area, and the hinterland is too hilly and densely forested for the pastoral life. A short distance from the coast the country is very mountainous, some of the peaks rising to a height of 9,000 feet. The population comprising the tangible republic is distributed along the coast region and numbers about 15,000 Americo-Liberians and 40,000 natives.

In the entire area of the republic the population is perhaps as much as 2,000,000.

In 1821 the American Colonization Society began to deport to this country detachments of emancipated Negroes, and a great migration took place during the first half of the nineteenth century. In 1847 the colonists declared their government to be an independent republic, and its status as such was so recognized by most of the powers. Since the Civil War not more than two or three thousand American emigrants have reached this black republic. It has languished, not only from lack of immigrants, but from lack of industrial foundation. It has suffered greatly from wars with the surrounding populations, from encroachments by the French, and from disasters of government financeering. The fiscal conditions of the republic became so serious in 1909 that President Roosevelt appointed a commission to investigate and report what might be done to give relief. Negotiations were set on foot for the adjustment of the Liberian debt, and the placing of United States officials in charge of the customs. An agreement was reached in 1912 whereby the American government, acting in concert with Great Britain, France and Germany, would assume charge of the republic's finances, its military organization, its boundary question, etc.

The Liberian Republic has been severely criticised for its failure to make more substantial progress, and its lack of missionary spirit in reference to the surrounding natives. Within fifty miles of the coast cannibalism is rife and women go naked. Nevinson characterizes the republic as a subject fit only for a comic opera.

Shall we say that this republic has failed because it has been attempted by the Negro race? An affirmative answer would certainly not be justified by the facts. It may be admitted that the Negro race has never shown any aptitude for self-government, and that a few thousand of them just emerged from slavery could not be expected to display very brilliant statesmanship. But even if the republic had been founded and guided by a white race it is doubtful if the outcome would have been very different.

From a sociological point of view it may be laid down as a law that republics in equatorial regions do not flourish, no matter what race may undertake them. Liberia has an equatorial climate. Although much of the hinterland is hilly and even mountainous, it is subject to equatorial rains and has a tropical flora and fauna. Man is overcome by the humidity; and the bounty of nature does not stimulate him to that exercise of muscle and brain which, everywhere in the temperate zones, conduces to the development of reason, foresight and self-control. His passions predominate over his intellectual powers, and he acquires those peculiar characteristics of indolence and instability which everywhere distinguish tropical and sub-tropical races and unfit them for self-government.

BIBLIOGRAPHY

List of the Principal Books referred to in the Text.

Ankermann, B.: "Kulturkreise und Kulturschichten in Afrika." Zeits. für Ethnologie, v. 37.

Avebury, Lord: The Origin of Civilization. New York, 1902.

Bain, Alexander: The Emotions and the Will. New York, 1899.

Bennett, H. L.: Ethnographical Notes on the Fang. Journal Anthropological Institute. N. S., v. 29.

Bordier, A.: Des Idées et des pratiques médicales. Revue Mensuelle de l'École d'Anthropologie, v. 3.

Boshart, August: Zehn Jahre Afrikanischen Lebens. Leipzig, 1898.

Boulger, D. C.: The Congo State. London, 1893.

Bourne, H. R. Fox: Civilization in Congoland. London, 1903.

Brinton, Daniel G.: Religions of Primitive Peoples. New York, 1905.

Bruce, James: Travels into Abyssinia. Boston, 1798.

Buckle, Henry Thos.: History of Civilization. New York, 1910.

Burkhardt, M.: Travels in Egypt and Nubia. London, 1819.

Burton, R. F.: Lake Regions of Central Africa. London, 1860.

Cameron, V. L.: Across Africa, 1877.

Carlile, William W.: "Money from Ornament," Nineteenth Century, v. 58.

Chapman: Travels in the Interior of South Africa. London, 1868.

Closson, C. C.: "Ethnic Stratification and Displacement," Quarterly Jour. Economics, v. 11.

Conder C. R.: "Native Tribes in Bechuanaland," Jour. Anthropological Institute, v. 16.

Combes, Edmond: Voyage en Egypte, en Nubie, etc. Paris, 1846.

Cooley, Charles H.: Social Organization. New York, 1910.

Crawford, John: "Numerals as Evidence of the Progress of Civilization." Transactions of the Ethnological Society. N. S., v. 2.

Crawford, John: "Relation of Domestic Animals to Civilization." Transactions of the Ethnological Society. N. S., v. 2.

Cureau, A.: Essai sur la psychologie des races Nègres de l'Afrique tropicale. Revue générale des sciences, v. 15, pp. 638-652.

Czekanowski, Jan: "Anthropologisch-ethnographische Expeditionsarbeiten in Ostafrika," Zeits. für Ethnographie, v. 41.

Deniker, J.: The Races of Man. New York, 1904.

Dewey, John: "Interpretation of Savage Mind."—Psychological Review.

Dexter, E. Grant: Conduct and the Weather. New York, 1899.

Dowd, J.: The Negro Races. New York, 1907.

Dundas, K. R.: "Tribes of the Baringo District, East Africa." Jour. Anthropological Institute, v. 50.

Dunn, R.: "Civilization and Cerebral Development." Transactions of the Ethnological Society. N. S., v. 4.

Ellwood, Chas. A.: Sociology in its Psychological Aspects. New York, 1912.

Farrar, F. W.: "Aptitudes of Races." Transactions of the Ethnological Society. N. S., v. 5.

Ferree, Barr: "Climatic Influences in Primitive Architecture." American Anthropologist, v. 3.

French-Sheldon (Mrs.): "Customs among the Natives of East Africa." Jour. Anthropological Institute, v. 21.

Fritsch, Gustav: Die Eingeborenen Süd-Afrikas. Breslau, 1872.

Frobenius, L.: "Die Weltanschauung der Naturvölker." Beiträge zur Volks-und Völkerkunde, vols. 6, 7.

Frobenius, L.: "The Origin of African Civilizations." Annual Report Smithsonian Institute, 1898.

Frobenius, L.: "Die bildende Kunst der Afrikaner." Mittheilungen der Anthropologischen Gesellschaft, v. 27.

Galloway, H.: "Divination Among the Natives of Natal." Jour. Anthropological Institute, v. I.

Giddings, F. H.: Inductive Sociology. New York, 1910.

Giddings, F. H.: Principles of Sociology. New York, 1896.

Goodrich, Jos. K.: Africa of To-day. Chicago, 1912.

Grant, James A.: A Walk Across Africa. London, 1864.

Guessfeldt, Paul: "Zur Kenntniss der Loango Neger." Zeits. für Ethnologie, v. 8.

Hahn, Eduard: Die Haustiere und ihre Beziehungen zur Wertschaft des Menchen. Leipzig, 1896.

Hahn, Friedrich: Afrika. Leipzig, 1901.

Halkin, Joseph: Quelques peuplades du district de L'Uelé. Liége, 1907.
Hobhouse, L. T.: Morals in Evolution. London, 1906.
Hobley, C. W.: "Anthropological Studies in Kavirondo and Nandi." Jour. Anthropological Institute, v. 33.
Hollis, A. C.: The Masai, Oxford, 1905.
Huntington, Ellsworth: The Pulse of Asia. New York, 1907.

Irby, Chas. and James M.: Travels in Egypt and Nubia. London, 1823.

Johnston, Sir H. H.: British Central Africa. London, 1897.
Johnston, Sir H. H.: George Grenfell and the Congo. London, 1908.
Johnston, Sir H. H.: The Uganda Protectorate. New York, 1902.
Johnston, Sir H. H.: "On the Races of the Congo and the Portuguese Colonies." Jour. Anthropological Institute, v. 13.
Johnston, Sir H. H., and R. Lydekker, et al.: The Living Races of Mankind. London, 1912.
Junker, Wilhelm: Travels in Africa. London, 1890.

Kallenberg, Freidrich: Auf dem Kriegspfad gegen die Massai. München, 1892.
Keane, A. H.: Man; Past and Present. Cambridge, 1900.
Kidd, Dudley: Savage Childhood. London, 1906.
Kidd, Dudley: Kafir Socialism. London, 1908.
Kingsley, Mary: Travels in West Africa. London, 1900.
Kingsley, Mary: West African Studies. London, 1901.
Koettlitz, R.: "Notes on the Galla of Walega and the Bertat." Jour. Anthropological Institute, v. 30.

Lang, Andrew: Myth, Ritual and Religion. New York, 1901.

Lang, Andrew: Social Origins. New York, 1903.

Lapouge, Georges Vacher de: "Fundamental Laws of Anthropo-sociology." Jour. Political Economy, v. 6.

Letourneau, Chas.: Sociology. London, 1893.

Lippert, Julius: Die Kulturgeschichte in einzelnen Hauptstücken. Leipzig, 1886.

Livingstone, D.: Last Journals. New York, 1875.

Livingstone, D.: Researches in South Africa. New York, 1865.

Long, C. Chaillé: Central Africa. New York, 1877.

Luschan, Felin von: "Eisentechnik in Afrika." Zeitschrift für Ethnologie, v. 41.

Macdonald, J.: "East Central African Customs." Jour. Anthropological Institute, v. 22.

Manouvrier, L.: "Le Tempérament." Revue de l'école d'anthropologie, v. 6.

Marett, R. R.: Anthropology. New York, London, 1912.

McDougall, Wm.: Social Psychology. 1909.

Merker, M.: Die Masai. Berlin, 1904.

Milligan, R. H.: The Jungle Folk of Africa. New York, 1908.

Milligan, R. H. The Fetish Folk of West Africa. New York, 1912.

Mindeleff, Cosmos: "The Influences of Geographic Environment." Jour. American Geographical Society, v. 29.

Montesquieu, Baron de: Spirit of Laws. London, 1302.

Morgan, E. D.: "Remarks on the Lower Congo." Jour. Anthropological Institute, v. 17.

Moffat, Robt.: Missionary Labors in Southern Africa. London, 1842.

Overbergh, Cyr van: Les Bangala. Bruxelles, 1907.

Patten, S. N.: Development of English Thought. New York, 1899.

Paulitschki, Philipp: Ethnographie Nordost-Afrikas. Berlin, 1893.

Peet, Stephen D.: "The Earliest Constructed Dwellings, and the Location in Which Man Made His First Appearance." American Antiquarian, v. 22.

Phillips: Lower Congo.

Préville, A. de: Sociétés Africaines. Paris, 1894.

Ratzel, Friedrich: The History of Mankind. London, 1897.

Reclus, Jean Jacques Elisée: The Earth and Its Inhabitants. New York, 1892.

Ribot, Th.: The Psychology of the Emotions. London, 1900.

Richter, Martin: Kultur und Reich der Marotse. Leipzig, 1903.

Roscoe, J.: "Notes on the Manners and Customs of the Baganda." Jour. Anthropological Institute. N. S., v. 31.

Schrader, Fr.: "Echanges d'activité entre la terre et l'homme." Revue mensuelle de l'école d'anthropologie, v. 6.

Schrader, Fr.: L'impulsion du milieu et la pensée cosmologique." Revue mensuelle de l'école d'anthropologie, v. 16.

Schrader, Fr.: "De l'influence des formes terrestres sur le développment humain." Revue mensuelle de l'école d'anthropologie, v. 3.

Schurtz, Heinrich: "Die geographische Verbreitung der Negertrachten." International Archiv für Ethnologie.

Schweinfurth, George A.: The Heart of Africa. N. Y. 1874.
Schweinitz, H. Hermann Graf von: Deutsch Ost-Afrika. Berlin, 1894.
Semple, Helen: Influences of Geographic Environment. New York, 1911.
Shrubsall, F. C.: "Notes on Crania from the Nile-Welle Watershed." Jour. Anth. Inst. N. S., v. 31.
Shrubsall, F. C.: "A Study of A-Bantu Skulls and Crania." Jour. Anthropological Institute. N. S., v. 1.
Small, Albion W.: General Sociology. Chicago, 1905.
Spitzka, E. A.: A study of the Brain of the Late Maj. J. W. Powell." Am. Anthropologist. N. S., v. 5.
Stanford's Compendium of Geography. Edited by A. H. Keane. London, 1895.
Stanley, H. M.: How I Found Livingstone. London, 1872.
Stanley, H. M.: In Darkest Africa. New York, 1890.
Stanley, H. M.: Through the Dark Continent. New York, 1878.
Steinmitz, S. R.: Ethnologische Studien zur Ersten Entwicklung der Strafe. Leipzig, 1894.
Stückenberg, J. H. W.: Sociology.
Stigand, C. H.: "Natives of Nyassaland and Portuguese Zambesia." Jour. Anthropological Institute, v. 37.
Stuhlmann, Franz: Mit Emin Pasha ins Herz von Afrika. Berlin, 1894.
Stuhlmann, Franz: Deutsch Ost-Afrika. Berlin, 1894.
Sumner, William G.: Folkways. Boston, 1907.
Swann, Alfred J.: Fighting the Slave Trade in Central Africa. Philadelphia, 1910.

Theal, George McCall: South Africa. London, 1902.
Theal, George McCall: History and Ethnography of Africa South of the Zambesi. London, 1907.
Thomas, Wm. I.: Sex and Society. Chicago, 1907.

Thomson, Joseph: Through the Masai Country. 1885.
Tucker, Alfred R.: Uganda and East Africa. London, 1908.
Tylor, E. B.: "Remarks on Totemism." Jour. Anthropological Inst. N. S., v. 1.

Verner, Samuel P.: "The Yellow Men of Central Africa." American Anthropologist, v. 5.

Ward, Herbert: "Congo Tribes." Jour. Anthropological Institute, v. 24.
Ward, Lester F.: Pure Sociology. New York, 1903.
Ward, Robert De C.: "Climate in Its Relations to Man." Popular Science Monthly, v. 76.
Webster, Hutton: Primitive Secret Societies. New York, 1908.
Weiss, M.: Land und Leute von Mpororo." Globus, v. 89.
Welling, Jas. C.: "The Laws of Torture." American Anthropologist, v. 5.
Werne, A.: British Central Africa. London, 1906.
Weule, Karl: Native Life in East Africa. New York, 1909.
Wissmann, Herman von: Meine Zweite Durchquerung Equatorial Afrikas. Frankfurt, 1890.
Wolf, Stabsarzt L.: "Volksstämme Central Afrikas." Zeitschrift für Ethnologie, v. 18.
Woodruff, Chas E.: The Effects of Tropical Light upon the White Men. New York, 1905.
Woodruff, Chas. E.: An Anthropological Study of the Small Brain of Civilized Man and Its Evolution." Am. Jour. Insanity, v. 48.
Wylde, A. B.: Modern Abyssinia. London, 1901.
Williams, Jas. M.: "Outline of a Theory of Social Motives. Am. Jour. Soc., v. XV, No. 6.

INDEX

INDEX

www.ingramcontent.com/pod-product-compliance
Lightning Source LLC
Chambersburg PA
CBHW050804270326
41926CB00025B/4526

9781639237517